Gibson's Fabulous Flat-Top Guitars

An Illustrated History & Guide

Eldon Whitford, David Vinopal & Dan Erlewine

Backbeat Books

An Imprint of Hal Leonard Corporation
New York

Dedication

To David L. Vinopal

Backbeat Books
An Imprint of Hal Leonard Corporation
7777 West Bluemound Road
Milwaukee, WI 53213

Trade Book Division Editorial Offices
19 West 21st Street, New York, NY 10010

Copyright © 1994, 2009 by Eldon Whitford, David Vinopal, and R. Daniel Erlewine

All rights reserved. No part of this book may be reproduced in any form, without written permission, except by a newspaper or magazine reviewer who wishes to quote brief passages in connection with a review.

Second edition published by Backbeat Books (an imprint of Hal Leonard Corporation) in 2009. First edition published by Miller Freeman Books in 1994.

Printed in the United States of America

Text design by Brad Greene

Library of Congress Catalog Card Number (first edition): 93-80494

ISBN: 978-0-87930-962-6

www.backbeatbooks.com

CONTENTS

Foreword v
Acknowledgments vi
Introduction vii

Chapter One **GIBSON AND ITS FLAT-TOPS** 1
Cycles, Trends, Changes: A Gibson Tour over Eight Decades
Color Section: A Gallery of Vintage Gibson Flat-Tops

Chapter Two **THE L-SERIES SMALL-BODY GUITARS** 25
L-0, L-00, L-1
L-2
L-Century
Nick Lucas "Gibson Special"

Chapter Three **THE ROUND-SHOULDER JUMBOS** 38
Jumbo
J-35
Advanced Jumbo
Jumbo Deluxe
J-55
J-45/J-50
Southern Jumbo/SJN/SJ Country-Western
J-25

Chapter Four **THE HAWAIIAN GUITARS** 68
Beginnings: Gibson's Transitional Hawaiian Steel Guitars
HG-24, HG-22, HG-20
Roy Smeck Models
HG-00
HG-Century

Chapter Five **THE NARROW-WAIST JUMBOS** 75
SJ-200
SJ-100
J-185
Everly Brothers/J-180

Chapter Six **LG SERIES** 95
LG-2, B-25
LG-3, B-25N
LG-1
LG-0
F-25
B-15

Chapter Seven   **FLAT-TOPS WITH PICKUPS**   106
CF-100/CF-100E
J-160E
Les Paul Jumbo

Chapter Eight   **THE SQUARE-SHOULDER JUMBOS**   111
Hummingbird
Dove
SJ/SJN/Country-Western
Folk Jumbo FJ-N
Heritage
Blue Ridge
J-45/J-50 Square-Shoulder
J-40
Gospel
J-55
J-35
J-30
JG-0

Chapter Nine   **12-STRINGS**   131
B-45-12/B-45-12N
B-25-12/B-25-12N
Heritage 12
LG-12
Blue Ridge 12
Artist 12

Chapter Ten   **SPECIAL BODY STYLES**   137
Mark Series
Jubilee Series

Chapter Eleven   **MONTANA-BUILT FLAT-TOPS**   143
The Montana Division & Factory Tour
The New Acoustic Models
The Super Jumbos
The Narrow-Waist Jumbos
The Slope-Shoulder Jumbos
The Square-Shoulder Jumbos
Small-Body Guitars
Electric Acoustics
Color Section: Guitars from the Gibson/Montana Custom Shop

Chapter Twelve   **REPAIRING GIBSON'S FABULOUS FLAT-TOPS**   190

Chapter Thirteen   **SERIAL NUMBERS**   196
Gibson's Use of Serial Numbers
Chronology of Gibson Flat-Top Guitars
Gibson Models Produced in Bozeman, Montana

Index   218

FOREWORD

My first guitar was a fourteen-fret, slot-head monstrosity, emblazoned with the name "Suzuki" in flowing golden script. I often wondered (and never found out) whether or not the manufacturer was related to the motorcycle company of the same name, but I wouldn't have been surprised. I didn't care much for their bikes either. Still, I cried like a baby when, sometime during the summer before eighth grade, my brother put his foot through it in retribution for some forgotten transgression of mine. My dad did his best to repair the wreck with some C-clamps and about a gallon of Elmer's Glue-All, but it was no use. The patient died on the operating table.

Over the next couple of years I went through a series of untunable, barely playable castoffs and hand-me-downs, none of which came anywhere near living up to any of the instruments that I lusted after at the local shop. What I really wanted was an electric guitar. I aspired to bending strings and minds like Jimi Hendrix someday, or at least Keith Richards, but my dad wasn't going for it. He was a fan of flamenco guitar, and besides, I was the oldest of five kids and noise levels around the homestead routinely reached MC5 levels as it was. My first new instrument was an inexpensive classical with nylon strings, and it was all I could do to hear myself strumming along to my Beatles, Stones, and Dylan records. But I was determined, and day by day and chord by chord, I persevered.

School, on the other hand, wasn't going so well. Six weeks into the ninth grade, I received my first report card and was only mildly surprised to learn that I had managed to fail every subject in which I was enrolled, except drama. Rather than carry the incriminating document home to my parents, I elected to run away from home.

I slung my Vox Serenader (yes, Vox made acoustics) on my back and headed east. I was only fourteen but fairly fearless, if somewhat gullible. While riding around Houston with a carload of kids who had picked me hitchhiking one night, I was persuaded to get out and ask for directions. As soon as I was out of the vehicle, the door slammed behind me, and I watched in horror as the taillights, along with my guitar, faded into the night.

A few weeks later my parents finally tracked me down, and I landed back in San Antonio guitarless and vowing never to set foot on the campus of Oliver Wendell Holmes High School again, a sentiment that I uncharacteristically shared with the administration. My academic career would have probably ended then and there had it not been for Orville Gibson and my grandmother.

Jewel Earle loved me as much anyone else who ever walked this earth, and when word reached East Texas that her oldest grandson was teetering on the brink of scholastic oblivion, she sprang into action. She walked into the local Western Union office and wired one hundred and fifty dollars to my father with instructions that he purchase the best guitar that one quarter of her life savings would buy, with the proviso that I return to school immediately.

That guitar, a 1970 LG0, was the first of upwards of twenty Gibson flat-tops that I have owned in my life. The next year I dropped out of school (I promised Grandmama that I would return to school—graduating wasn't part of the deal) and began hitchhiking around Texas, playing anywhere anybody would listen. At some point I traded the LG0 for a Martin dreadnought but soon learned the hard way that the nonadjustable steel-rod-reinforced neck didn't like to sleep under bridges. I returned to the Gibson fold and played no other make of acoustic guitar for over thirty years.

—Steve Earle
July 2009

ACKNOWLEDGMENTS

The following individuals have been especially generous with their time, expertise, and encouragement during the researching and writing of this book:

Larry English, Robi Johns, and Ren Ferguson, who hold the key positions of Division President, Senior Product Specialist, and V.P. for Research and Development, respectively, at Gibson/Montana. Without their encouragement and knowledge we could not have covered thoroughly or accurately Gibson's history over the last decade. All three have played essential roles in the Gibson flat-top renaissance.

Gary Burnette, proprietor of Bee Three Vintage in Asheville, N.C., a promoter of vintage-guitar shows and the owner of an impressive collection of Gibson flat-tops, one remarkable for its quality as well as its breadth. Through Gary's hospitality we were able to visit his home on numerous occasions, when we painstakingly catalogued and photographed his unique collection.

Bryan Galloup, owner of the Guitar Hospital in Big Rapids, Mich., which is both a premier repair shop and a repair school. For years Bryan funneled Gibsons to us for cataloguing purposes, collecting the data himself when necessary. By encouraging his former students to watch for specific models and vintages, Bryan helped in gathering information for this book from all over North America.

Stan Werbin, owner of Elderly Instruments in Lansing, Mich. Stan opened his vast vintage-guitar collection to us for inspection on many occasions. His knowledge of classic Gibsons and his encouragement helped greatly in getting this book done.

Mac Yasuda, a world-class collector of vintage guitars. His assistance with the J-200 model especially was of great help. His numerous publications about vintage guitars are excellent reading for all guitar lovers.

The following have helped in numerous ways: Gene Autry, Norman and Nancy Blake, Roy Book Binder, B. Boyck, Walter Carter, Marc Conley, Little Jimmy Dickens, Norm English, Phil and Don Everly, Michael Erlewine, Bill Gonder, Douglas B. Green, George Gruhn, Emmylou Harris, Jim Hutchens, Albert Lee, John Jackson, Steve La Vere, Jim Peat, Doug Rice, Ben Runkle, Richard Schneider, Tim Shaw, Mrs. Roy Smeck, Hank Snow, Stewart-MacDonald Mfg., Akira Tsumura, Mike Voltz, Porter Wagoner, Doc Watson, and Abe Wechter.

Special thanks to the hundreds of Gibson owners trusting enough to let us inspect their guitars from top to bottom, inside and out, over the past decade.

INTRODUCTION

Only during the last decade has a considerable body of literature about stringed musical instruments in general and guitars in particular become available. Although this absence of accurate and thorough information didn't keep players and collectors and lovers of guitars from pursuing their passion, it did make the pursuit trying, if not downright difficult. This void in knowledge has encompassed guitars of all kinds, electric and acoustic and electric/acoustic, from makes long considered as yard-sale specials to the others on the high end, some of which sell for many tens of thousands of dollars. And it is primarily because this void has included Gibson flat-top guitars that the present book has been written.

> *"I just grew up with the Gibson guitar. Dad was a staunch Gibson man. He taught me to play on a Gibson, and they were the only guitars he ever really talked about.*
>
> *You know how some families are raised as a Ford or Chevy family? Well, we were a Gibson family.*
>
> *We Everlys would go to the showrooms and just look at all the Gibsons. And that's all we ever had in our family. Dad liked being able to adjust the neck himself."*
>
> —Don Everly

What has proven in 1993 to be a landslide of literature about vintage instruments developed gradually during the previous decade. In 1982 Tom Wheeler's excellent *American Guitars: An Illustrated History* appeared, the first comprehensive book on the subject. Books published since have ranged far and wide in discussing the versatile guitar, covering the essential as well as the blatantly peripheral. Included among these publications are books about the famous makers (Martin, Gretsch, Gibson electrics, Guild, Fender, National, Rickenbacker) and about the less well-known (Vox, Kay, Burns, Ferrington); about famous models (Gibson Les Paul, Gibson Super 400, Fender Telecaster, Fender Stratocaster); about well-known collections (Roy Acuff, Tsumura, Yasuda); about tubes and amps and electronics companies (Marshall); about the modern guitar, the classic guitar, the old guitar, the fine guitar, the vintage guitar, the complete guitar, the customized guitar, the steel guitar; and, finally, about the guitar. The famine of only a decade ago has become the feast of the 1990s.

Conspicuously absent amid this superabundance of publications, however, has been a thorough and systematic examination of some of the greatest flat-top guitars ever made, by probably the most famous name in the history of guitar-making. *Gibson's Fabulous Flat-Top Guitars* exists, of course, to remedy this situation. This absence is understandable, though, for a number of reasons: the sheer volume of instruments produced by Gibson from 1926 to the present, the occasional inconsistencies and oddities in production, and (speaking charitably) the quirkiness in company records and history. In short, the subject itself proved daunting, enough to frighten off writers and researchers who otherwise might have approached a project that for years had begged to be undertaken.

It is hoped that through its text and photographs this present book manages to give a strong sense of why, in the eyes and ears of many discriminating guitar lovers, Gibson flat-tops are preferred over all others; of why, to borrow an advertising slogan from the War years, "only a Gibson is good enough." Don Everly has phrased the love for Gibsons very simply: "You know how some families are raised as a Ford or Chevy family? Well, we were a Gibson family." The authors of this book will feel at least partially successful if, after paging through this book, the reader understands those unique qualities that make Gibson flat-top guitars *fabulous*.

Eldon Whitford
David Vinopal
Dan Erlewine

HOW THIS BOOK WAS RESEARCHED

No perfect method exists for gathering absolutely accurate and thorough information about Gibson flat-tops. Meticulously cataloguing each and every one ever built would be ideal, but this is an impossibility given the sheer numbers of these instruments produced since the 1920s, the accidents that have permanently removed some instruments from circulation, and the fact that some others have not yet entered circulation, remaining forgotten in attics or closets.

Instead, a judicious sampling of Gibson's output over the past seven decades was undertaken. Because of practical considerations, the number of individual examples of a given model that were catalogued varied widely, from one (the Jumbo Deluxe—only three were made) to over a hundred in the instance of the J-45, a plentiful model. In addition to this systematic examination of all pertinent Gibsons, other methods of collecting data were used:

- consultation with other researchers, collectors, and dealers
- review of books, catalogues, brochures, magazines, old photos, record jackets, and similar sources that could provide information
- inferences and extrapolations (identified as such in the text)
- discussion with many former Gibson employees, from line workers to management
- experiences and observations of the present book's authors on trips to the Kalamazoo factory
- consultation with Gibson/Montana, including trips to the Bozeman factory
- ninety years' collective experience of this book's authors in playing, collecting, and repairing Gibson flat-top guitars

All the resources listed above were both useful and necessary. But at the bottom line is this reality: the guitars themselves had to be the teachers. Model by model and year by year they offered accurate data in a way that no other source could, from Gibson's first flat-top guitar of the 1920s to the most recent from the Bozeman factory.

The present book is by no means the final word. The likelihood exists that inadvertent errors lurk within these pages, and certainly a multitude of questions remain to be answered. For the sake of accuracy in future editions, the authors would greatly appreciate your help. If your guitar differs from what this book says about the model, please send the following information, together with a photo, if possible:

- model
- serial number
- factory order number (printed on neck block)
- scale length
- woods used: back and sides; neck; bridge and fingerboard
- finish
- tuning machines
- original case (please describe)
- unusual features
- how your guitar differs from the book's description of it
- other comments
- your name, address, and phone number

Please send to:
Gibson Data, Box 359-C, Route 1,
Reed City, MI 49677.

Thank you for adding to the knowledge about Gibson flat-top guitars.

Gibson and Its Flat-Tops

Chapter One

CYCLES, TRENDS, CHANGES: A GIBSON TOUR OVER EIGHT DECADES

The L-00 was the perfect guitar for the Depression, delivering excellent quality for little money. The 1934 L-00 featured here was owned by the Three Box Cars, a hillbilly band that in the mid-'30s played on radio station WSAZ in Huntington, West Virginia. Glitter paint was used to put the band's name onto the inexpensive soft case.

Of all the major guitar companies that have made what are now considered vintage guitars, no one has come close to Gibson in creativity, experimentation, and inventiveness. While these three traits are the cause of what may be called occasional quirkiness in Gibson's history, they also go far in explaining the unsurpassed charm, individuality, and uniqueness of the company's guitars over time. If Gibson and its chief competitor in the flat-top market through the years can be compared to automobiles, Martin guitars should be likened to a Mercedes-Benz: undeniable quality predictably reproduced in instrument after instrument and sold to a relatively affluent consumer. The populist Gibsons are like Chevys and Fords, Studebakers and De Sotos, Packards and Cadillacs, pickups and sedans, coupes and convertibles—different sizes and shapes and prices, a model for everyone, rich and poor alike. Since 1926, when the L-0 and L-1 models became the first flat-tops to leave the factory in Kalamazoo, no competitor's guitars have played more easily, looked bolder, sounded better, or exuded more character than these personable Gibson flat-tops.

The great Doc Watson and his wife, Rosa Lee, on the side porch of their home outside Deep Gap, North Carolina. Joining Doc and his Jumbo 35 are Clarence Ashley on banjo and Gaither Carlton on fiddle. Ashley was one of the original Carolina Tar Heels, a famous string band in the 1930s.

Not at all coincidentally, never has Gibson been stodgy, afraid of change, or conservative—except for the period from approximately 1968 through 1984, when the company suffered through self-inflicted hard times. In all other periods Gibson has pursued innovation, purposely placing musicians and luthiers in key decision-making positions. (Current president Henry Juszkiewicz is a former professional guitarist; Julius Bellson, the company historian, and Ted McCarty, Gibson president from 1950 to 1966, also were avid guitarists.) This stacking of the company with musicians paid huge dividends historically. Guitars are, after all, meant to be played, and who can judge instruments better than the players? A partial list of musicians who have worked with Gibson in research and design include Billy Byrd, Hank Garland, Chet Atkins, Ray Whitley, Nick Lucas, the Everly Brothers, Les Paul, Barney Kessel, Johnny Smith, Trini Lopez, and Earl Scruggs.

More so perhaps than other major guitar makers, Gibson has changed with the times to such a degree that the evolution of its instruments, flat-top guitars included, mirrors the social and political history of our country. A person studying these Gibson instruments is in a sense a musical archeologist, one who can understand the nation's past by first uncovering and then studying successive layers of artifacts—in this case Gibson's progression of flat-top guitars. Thus, in looking at the models of any given decade, the Gibson archeologist might learn about that era's society, prosperity (or lack of), politics, topical events, upheavals, fads, and changes—in a word, *culture*.

This mirroring of the changing times was present in the late '20s, when the company's first flat-tops appeared. The Nick Lucas "Gibson Special" was appropriately fancy for the Roaring Twenties. Because our country had shown a fascination for things Hawaiian since World War I, the HG (Hawaiian Gibson) series of flat-tops, introduced in 1929, did its best to transport music lovers to palm tree islands and away from the Great Depression just around the corner. In that same year the stock market crashed, permanently changing our country as well as the guitar industry. By 1932 Gibson had dropped the more exotic and elaborate HG-20, HG-22, and HG-24, replacing them with a "Depression Special," the bargain-basement HG-00 and the non-Hawaiian equivalent, the L-00.

In 1933 Chicago celebrated its centennial with a yearlong Century of Progress Exposition. A couple of hours to the northeast, Gibson joined this celebration, building the ultra-fancy L-C "Century of Progress" model. Peghead and fingerboard were slathered with pearloid, an artificial mother-of-pearl that Gibson had used on elaborate banjos of the period. In stark contrast to the celebratory pearloid was the more sober Michigan curly maple of back and sides, sunburst in an amber that changed to dark brown as it neared the periphery. The L-C was the perfect guitar to honor a small celebration surrounded by a huge depression.

In the early '30s, with the increasing emphasis on singers in country, blues, folk, and cowboy music, the guitar market was moving toward instruments intended to back up vocals. As their largest guitars, Martin had the OM series and Gibson its Nick Lucas model, all relatively small guitars. In 1934 both Gibson and Martin hit the market with large-body, 14-fret flat-top guitars, a combination that has remained the most popular ever since. While Martin called their two models dreadnoughts, after battleships of the period, Gibson named theirs simply Jumbo. At the same time, Gibson introduced two 12-fret Roy Smeck-endorsed versions of the Jumbo for Hawaiian playing, which tells us that the lure of lagoons, hulas, and leis lingered.

Both the Jumbo and the Roy Smeck signature models were relatively expensive. The New Deal and its many programs brought hope but often little else to many, while millions continued to suffer. As often happens in hard times, people turn inward and express themselves musically. Realizing this, Gibson sold instruments and music lessons door to door and established community stringed orchestras. Gibson did what it could to bring the joy of music to people in all economic conditions. An installment plan was made available to those who couldn't manage the full amount up front. Also, specially designed, inexpensive instruments such as the Gibson-owned Kalamazoo line of guitars, banjos, and mandolins became available. Finally, because the $60 Jumbo was a bit too expensive for most buyers, Gibson made changes in the model and created a stripped-down model for $35, the J-35 (J for Jumbo and 35 for its initial price). At the same time, Gibson brought out a fancy rosewood jumbo-body model that sold for $80 (the Advanced Jumbo), showing that at least some people in the music-loving nation had money.

Reacting to the western movie and cowboy crooner craze, in 1937 Gibson went after a different market. In concert with singing cowboy star Ray Whitley, they created the ultimate bunkhouse-roundup-campfire-corral guitar, the SJ-200. Just as the Hawaiian guitar could transport a nation to faraway places, the SJ-200 could hark back to a golden West that never was.

This was the golden age of guitars, for Martin and Gibson both. The two competitors built comparable and equivalent (and, needless to say, superb) guitars in this period. The following list moves from least expensive Gibson and Martin models to costliest:

Gibson	Martin
L-00	00-18
J-35	D-18
Advanced Jumbo	D-28
Nick Lucas	000-28
SJ-200	D-45

Over the years Martin's prices were typically higher than those of their Gibson equivalents.

Gibson's use of rosewood during the period from the late '30s through World War II says a lot about the times. Historically Gibson had built far fewer rosewood guitars than Martin and thus did not have a large stockpile of this wood when the War began. Gibson had always purchased its rosewood from Brazil in that period. Because of war shortages Gibson could not count on a steady supply. Even bananas, which were shipped on the same boat routes as rosewood, were next to impossible to get in the United States at that time.

Meanwhile, two rosewood models, the Advanced Jumbo and the Roy Smeck Radio Grande, had been dropped in 1939, when political tensions already had begun to increase global-

Gibson custom-made this 12-fret SJ-200, as well as a small-body version, for Gene Autry, Hollywood's famous singing cowboy, who introduced the musical western in *Tumbling Tumble Weeds* (1935).

Gibson Factory on Parsons Street in Kalamazoo, c. 1940.

The legendary Woody Guthrie with his 1942 "Banner" Southern Jumbo machine. Woody's L-00 carried the same admonition. No one influenced folk music and the use of the guitar as a political tool more than Woodrow Wilson Guthrie.

Conway Twitty with his late '50s J-50, before he followed his roots back to country music.

Grand Ole Opry star Porter Wagoner and his SJ-200 in the mid-'50s, a period when country music kept flat-tops alive.

ly. Though Gibson did build one batch of rosewood Southern Jumbos in 1942, this apparently exhausted their small supply of the wood. Factory repairs made on rosewood guitars during the War often substituted rosewood-stained mahogany for the real wood.

Even during the War, Gibson began plans for increasing their guitar production, purchasing new equipment and machinery, adding a new mill room, and building a larger, more modern area for storing wood. By late 1945, the War over, new additions and machinery were ready. Apparently buyers were ready, too, for flat-tops and electrics began to sell better than ever, and Gibson was experiencing the fastest growth in their history. The guitar quality was maintained at a high level, while the company closed out their older lineup (the L-00 and the HG-00), replacing them in 1946 or 1947 with other affordable guitars that included the LG-1, the LG-3, and the J-50.

As the 1950s dawned Gibson introduced two excellent models that were 25 years ahead of their time yet failed to achieve commercial success. The CF-100/CF-100E guitars were short-scale cutaways that played beautifully; the E version had onboard electronics, highly innovative at the time. The second model, the maple-body, narrow-waist J-185, is now considered to be one of the finest flat-tops that Gibson ever built; its concept and design are presently imitated by not only private builders but major manufacturers. Its sales figures in the '50s failed to reach expectations, however, probably because of the shadow cast by the larger but similar

Exceptional fingerpicker Rev. Gary Davis and his J-200. The folk revival of the late '50s and '60s "discovered" Rev. Davis and other greats. In the background are Mrs. Anne Davis and Roy Book Binder.

J-200, the "King of the Flat-Tops." After the War, bigger was better.

During the Korean War no model was introduced and no model deleted, for the United States was in a major recession that lasted most of the 1950s. Only two acoustic models appeared in the period from 1952-1959. In 1955 the Country-Western came out, but it was not so much a new model as a relabeled and cosmetically altered Southern Jumbo. The LG-0 was in fact new. Designed to be built and sold cheaply, it was a huge success—for not much money, a person could own a Gibson!

The company did add to their lineup in a big way during this period. In 1957 they bought the rival Epiphone instrument company at a good price. Not only had they eliminated a competitor, they had also acquired a whole new line of guitars and a new network of dealers. All instruments made by Gibson during the '50s, whether acoustic or electric or with the Epiphone label, were characterized by excellent quality control. The electrics especially blossomed in the decade, while the acoustics gathered up strength for the decade ahead. And they would need it.

The '60s: civil rights, Vietnam, the Great Society, love-ins, Woodstock, various advocates, and sundry causes. And guitars. From 1960 to 1963, Gibson introduced seven new models to meet the demand of the times. No longer were their guitars a reflection of 1950s conservatism. The Hummingbird, which was probably intended to appeal to country and western players, found more of a market among the young folk fans. Gibson then created the Dove, the Everly Brothers, the B-45-12, the B-25-12, the F-25, and the FJN.

During this four-year period Gibson nearly doubled in size. More factory space was purchased in 1964, and production almost doubled again in one year. Some guitar models were back-ordered for as long as two years. In Joan Baez, Bob Dylan, and scores of others, folk music and causes had gone mainstream; a generation of American youth wished to emulate their musical heroes, and a guitar was required. Gibson literally couldn't make flat-tops fast enough. This folk boom was to last into the mid-'70s, but not without one important interruption.

In 1969 the nation was in turmoil over Vietnam. At the same time, Gibson had been bought by E. C. L. Industries, Inc. (soon to be renamed Norlin), and 15 years of a different sort of turmoil had begun. Gibson's new president had experience in manufacturing and management but not in the guitar industry. The "strictly business" approach of the new owners was the undoing of Gibson and its reputation. Design suffered, quality control suffered, consumer confidence suffered. A quick profit became more important than investment, reputation, and longer-term return. Further, construction of the Epiphone line moved to Japan, with a resulting product that was markedly inferior to the Kalamazoo-made Epiphones.

Gibson had spent three-quarters of a century building an excellent reputation that under this new ownership quickly sank to a level nearly beyond resuscitation. Profit-driven and wanting nothing to do with warranty work, Norlin redesigned the flat-tops, making them strong and sturdy—and tonally dead. Excellent materials were still used in construction, but the flat-tops were being seriously overbuilt. The Gibson company was lucky to survive this 16-year period of Norlin ownership.

Norlin decided to relocate to a state where labor was less costly. Michigan, where Orville Gibson had planted roots in the 1890s, had been highly industrialized—and unionized. Hourly wages were, across the board, higher in Michigan than in the South. Norlin also stated that for celebrity endorsements and music industry relations Gibson should be in the heart of the music industry, Nashville. The move to Tennessee occurred despite the excellent relations for many years between labor and management at the Kalamazoo factory.

Thus, in 1974 a new plant was built in Nashville expressly for the construction of electrics. The Gibson flat-tops were still made in Kalamazoo, but they had been redesigned. In the opinion of musicians and Gibson dealers, the guitars of this time were without doubt the worst flat-tops ever built by the company. But the profits kept coming in.

There was one shining moment for Gibson during the Norlin period. Bruce Bolen and other Gibson executives became intrigued with the innovative Kasha-style guitars and started putting money and effort into research. Master luthiers Richard Schneider and Abe Wechter were hired to design and build steel-string guitar prototypes that would eventually evolve into a totally new type of flat-top to be named the Mark series, with a total of six models offered.

The extensive scientific research and great effort on this project was remarkable, for Gibson or for any other guitar maker in history. The

Brother and sister duet George and Ethel McCoy, nephew and niece of Memphis Minnie. Custom pickguards grace the J-45.

commitment and the money followed, in both research and marketing. Despite the many merits of the project it never met expectations: the primary problem was the inability to blend master luthier artistry and large manufacturing techniques.

The merger of steel-string guitars with what was basically Kasha-style classical design was only partially successful. After all the impressive research and development, the Mark series was pushed into production prematurely, and the new instruments entered a market unprepared for such a new concept. The project was seen as a failure. Gibson had spent huge amounts of money in an attempt to revive their flat-top reputation, with little to show for it. The results, though not worthy of the great effort, hadn't gone for nought: for example, the parabolic arch on the tops that was designed during that period is still used by Gibson and by many of the best private builders of flat-tops.

As the '80s began, the lineup of flat-tops was selling poorly, and in 1984 the Kalamazoo plant was permanently closed. Gibson sales had fallen precipitously; management had realized, finally, that its reputation had been seriously tarnished. Quick-fix solutions and immediate profits had of course been counterproductive. Norlin, the "fair weather owner," actively tried to divest itself of a great company that had been brought to its knees.

In the early 1980s the Research & Design crew consisting of Bruce Bolen, Chuck Burge, Tim Shaw, and Abe Wechter grew frustrated with how overbuilt and undesirable the Gibson flat-tops had become. They decided, in spite of Norlin, to rededicate Gibson to the pursuit of high-quality guitars—in other words, to restore quality worthy of Gibson's reputation of long standing.

Their first project—reissuing a vintage Les Paul electric—was both safe and successful. Next, they chose to redesign the flat-top line in the vintage vein, with a goal of restoring those construction features that had made Gibsons sound so good for so many years. After studying the older Gibsons of superior tone, they decided to copy four classic flat-tops: the Hummingbird, the Dove, the round-shoulder J-45, and the 1950s J-200. The R&D team reproduced the same general bracing systems of the originals from the 1955-1968 era, dropping the ineffective "double-X system" in use since 1971 and reinstituting small, tapered braces in a "single-X" arrangement.

At the 1984 NAMM show (National Association of Music Merchants), the largest gathering of its type in the world, Gibson proudly displayed the four reissued flat-tops. Although these guitars met the standards of neither the classics nor those now being built by the Montana Division, they were the best thing to happen at Gibson since Norlin became the owner.

In early 1986 the company was purchased for $5,000,000 by partners Dave Berryman, Gary Zebrowski, and Henry Juszkiewicz, who understood and respected quality and tradition. With them arrived a whole new attitude about guitars and guitar building. The Gibson spirit gradually began to return.

The Nashville flat-tops began to look better, sound better, and play better. Although the Tennessee plant had been built primarily for the construction of electrics, the humid climate and inexperienced workers caused problems serious enough to bring production to a grinding halt. It became clear that if Gibson flat-tops were to be restored to their former quality, drastic changes had to be made. A solution appeared in the form of the Flatiron company, an innovative builder of mandolins located in Bozeman, Montana, and owned by Steve Carlson.

Gibson purchased Flatiron, intending to build only mandolins at the facility. Soon plans were made to move flat-top construction from humid Tennessee to Bozeman and its excellent climate. Fortunately for Gibson, master luthier Ren Ferguson was employed by Flatiron and moved to Gibson, bringing with him great talent and extensive experience in the guitar-building business. After putting much of their future in his hands, Gibson then built a new plant in Bozeman in 1989. The company immediately began the difficult climb back to respectability, hiring excellent luthiers and consulting with musicians, a system from which they had profited well since the late '20s.

And climbed back Gibson has. On one front they have carefully designed and built entirely new models, such as the J-2000; at the same time they have gone with winners by reissuing their renowned flat-tops from the 1930s through the 1960s. In the opinion of many, Gibson's flat-top acoustics have never been better—they are destined to become the vintage guitars of tomorrow.

1935 **A**dvanced **J**umbo prototype (left).

1936 **A**dvanced **J**umbo (right).

1992 **A**dvanced **J**umbo reissue (bottom).

1940 Super Jumbo 100 (top left).

An early Everly Brothers model (top right).

1934 Jumbo, the first year of the round-shoulder, wide-waist Gibson flat-tops (center).

Rare pre-War SJ-200 with maple back and sides (left and above).

Pre-War rosewood SJ-200s, like this 1938, are the most highly-sought-after of the model (bottom).

1936 Nick Lucas Special. The Gibson look owes much to the handstained sunburst on Michigan curly maple.

The L-C "Century of Progress" model, c. 1935, with pearloid in reserve (above).

L-Century and SJ-200 (top left).

The oil painting on the Gibson ukulele was done at the factory (left).

Red J-200 (top).

A rare 1936 Nick Lucas Special with ebony finish (bottom left).

1966 Dove with cherry finish on back, sides, and top (bottom right).

A 1968 J-50 in factory red (left).

1936 Roy Smeck Stage DeLuxe (center).

HG-00, Gibson's least expensive Hawaiian guitar, c. 1937 (top left).

1937 **J**-35 with a period sunburst (right).

An ebony finish 1939 L-0 with firestripe pickguard (bottom left).

1939 **J**-35 with natural top (bottom right).

1941 Jumbo 35 (above).

Cherry sunburst on a 1939 J-35, a rare finish on such an early instrument (left).

"Stairstep"
peghead, 1940
Jumbo 55.

Rosewood "Banner" Southern Jumbo made in 1942, the only year of the firestripe teardrop pickguard (top left and right).

"**B**anner" J-45. Because of shortages during the War, maple rather than the standard mahogany was occasionally used for back and sides (bottom left and right).

1943 Skunk-stripe "Banner" Southern Jumbo (top left).

"Tobacco" sunburst, 1949 Southern Jumbo (right and bottom).

Late 1955 J-200 with natural top (top left).

1957 J-185 (top right).

1950 J-45 (center).

1968 J-200 (top left).

A custom built J-200 Citation (top right).

1954 SJ-200 with SJ-200 original construction form used at the Kalamazoo factory (center).

An early 1965 Dove, before the model's neck became narrower (top left).

1966 Faded cherry-burst Hummingbird (top right).

One of the few 1962 maple Hummingbirds (bottom).

The Mark 99, designed and built by Gibson master luthier Richard Schneider. Fewer than a dozen of this expensive model were made.

The L-Series Small-Body Guitars

Chapter Two

Delta blues performer Robert Lockwood, Jr. and his late-'30s L-0, with the great Sonny Boy Williamson.

L-0, L-00, AND L-1: GIBSON'S EARLY FLAT-TOPS

For a span of time during 1933 and 1934, Gibson offered a full half-dozen L-series models: the L-00, L-0, L-1, L-2, L-C (Century), and the "Gibson Special" (Nick Lucas artist model). Because of their unique trim, the latter two have always immediately stood out from other members of the family; likewise, the L-2 presents no real identification problems, although its distinguishing features are not as obvious as those of the L-C and Nick Lucas. It's the other models that cause headaches, for the remaining members of the L-series family are more often mistaken for one another than not.

1939 Ebony L-0.

On the page describing the L-series flat-tops, the 1934 catalogue offers this about "The Perfect Balance of Each Gibson":

> Only an instrument so perfectly balanced can give you absolute satisfaction. Players everywhere are enjoying that smooth, even flow of tone so prevalent in a Gibson and one thing, "perfect balance," is why they do everything you ask of them. Unstinted admiration! Since the first Gibson craftsmen painstakingly developed their early instruments many years ago, artists have freely extended their admiration to Gibson fretted instruments. The nearer an artist and leader arrives to the pinnacle of high achievement, the more they appreciate Gibson quality.

Players over the last 60 years have muttered, "Thank you, Gibson, for the balance and the quality, but which L-series model is my guitar *specifically*?" Throw in the HG-00, a Hawaiian version of the L-00 that almost without exception has been retrofitted in the Spanish style, and you've got a mass of confusion, to such a degree that even vintage-guitar dealers, who are supposed to know about such things, regularly misidentify L-body models.

This task of clarification is not easy. Not only did the company switch around the models almost whimsically, they swapped features and finishes just enough to create wholesale obfuscation. Furthermore, Gibson catalogues from the time tend to mislead rather than elucidate (by using photos of models from previous years, for example), and the fact that catalogues apparently were not produced in some years makes a sense of continuity and of construction evolution impossible. The following points are intended at least to add order to the chaos that has prevailed for over half a century.

The L-series, Gibson's first regular production flat-tops, debuted in 1926, upon the introduction of the L-0 and the L-1. The body was characterized by a very rounded lower half and was shaped much like that of the later SJ-200 but considerably smaller, measuring only 13½" across the lower bout. In 1929 the dimension changed to 14¾", and this represents the more familiar body style, one that is less rounded and more flat on the bottom.

The L-0

With its $35 list price, the L-0 was a less expensive version of the L-1, which cost $50 (1928 prices). As Gibson's 1928 catalogue phrases it, the L-0 is "a true Gibson at a price that will bring a smile to your purse." Maple was used for back and sides of the L-0 during its first two years. The back and top were slightly convex. Its bridge was ebony in the bottom-belly style, though with a pyramid on each wing. (This predates Martin's belly bridge by about four years.) The top and back were bound in white, contrasting with the yellow-brown finish. The ebonized fingerboard had 19 frets; body and neck met at the 12th fret, with pearl dots inlaid at the 5th, 7th, and 9th. "The Gibson" in the old script was silkscreened at approximately a 15-degree angle across the black-lacquered peghead, which in lateral view tapered gradually, the top being thicker. Three-on-a-plate open-gear tuners were common, usually with white buttons but occasionally with black.

By 1928 the L-0 body had become all mahogany, top included. Rosewood was used for its fingerboard and bridge, and ebony for the nut. Double soundhole purfling remained; also, the inside edge of the soundhole was bound. These first L-0s had an extra bridge pin below the six regular pins, centered, acting as a spare tire.

By 1931 Gibson had drastically changed their most inexpensive flat-top. At the lower bout it had become 14¾" wide, taking on the same body shape as the L-2, which had been introduced in 1929. It's likely that Gibson switched all of the L series to this body style before 1931. Also, at this time the bridge was switched to a rectangle of Brazilian rosewood with an angled bone saddle. The fingerboard, too, had become Brazilian rosewood, and was constructed in the short scale. In fact, there were two fingerboard scale lengths used in the L-series guitars, both short. The earliest scale was slightly over 25", while the later scale from around 1931 or 1932 measured 24¾". It's probable that Gibson shortened the scale in about 1932, when they went to the 14-frets-to-the-body neck on all their flat-tops. As an example of how exasperating the research of vintage Gibsons can be, the 1932 catalogue shows pictures of the previous year's 12-fret-neck L-0 but describes a 14-fretter. The company simply didn't go to the bother of keeping their photographs current and accurate.

In 1932 the L-0 was elevated one step on the price hierarchy, vacating the bottom position for the new L-00, which listed at $25. Their differences were minor—the L-00 was without back binding and featured an ebony finish on all wood surfaces, allowing the use of quality but visually flawed material.

The L-0 disappeared by 1933, only to be reintroduced in 1937. This reincarnation was now finished in ebony, like the 1932 L-00. Most L-0s had the striped tortoise pickguards of celluloid, but some 'guards were pure white, which stood out in stunning fashion against the ebony finish.

Meanwhile, the 1937 L-00 had prospered, acquiring a bound back and position markers on the fingerboard edge, in the process relegating the bottom of the price ladder to the L-0, which in 1937 listed for $25, undercutting the L-00 by $5. These prices remained in effect through 1940.

The L-0 was discontinued in 1942.

The L-00

Sometime between late 1929 and early 1931 Gibson introduced their L-00. Because of the absence of catalogues from that period, more accurate dating is difficult. This much is sure: the model first appeared in the 1932 catalogue, but as a fictitious 12-fret model, not as the factual 14-fret instrument of that year. However, an interesting 12-fret L-00 has been examined and catalogued. This guitar has a spruce top single-bound in white celluloid, mahogany back and sides, a solitary pearl dot at the 12th fret, a diagonal "The Gibson" in silver paint silkscreened on the peghead, and multiple bands of wood as soundhole purfling. Much about this instrument points to a date earlier (and maybe much earlier) than 1932. Unfortunately, it had been refinished in the late 1950s, and the owner was unable to recall the top's original color.

L-00 c. 1933 with small sunburst characteristic of that year's model.

The more common examples of the L-00 from this period share these characteristics: black lacquer finish all around, spruce top and mahogany sides and back, white binding on top only, V-shaped neck, rectangular rosewood bridge,

L-00 with maple back and sides instead of the standard mahogany.

L-00 c. 1937 with the sunburst much larger than earlier versions of this model.

14-frets-to-the-body neck with pearl dots in a rosewood fingerboard (twin dots at fret 12), three-on-a-plate open-gear tuners on a tapered peghead, mock-tortoise shell pickguard (a few in white celluloid), and either "The Gibson" or "Gibson" in the old script silkscreened diagonally across the peghead.

By 1934 the finish was sunburst, with an amber area of perhaps only six inches in diameter. By 1937 the L-00 had back binding, and the price was reduced to $30 from its previous price of $37.50, a sign of the lingering Depression. About this time some ¾-size L-00s were produced, selling at the same price as the full-size version.

There were no other changes until 1941, when the model could be bought with either a sunburst or a natural-finish top, the "regular" (sunburst) costing $36.75 and the natural finish $42.00. A couple of other changes were made before the L-00 was discontinued: some 1943 versions are without truss rods; and most L-00s made from 1942 to 1945 have the usual silkscreened logo in white on the peghead, while a few feature the gold "Banner" decal that proclaims "ONLY A GIBSON IS GOOD ENOUGH."

The L-00 was last offered in 1945, having nobly served a generation of guitar players as the poor man's Cadillac.

The L-1

Like the less expensive L-0, the Gibson L-1 was introduced in 1926 and featured the small-body design that was 13½" in maximum width with a narrow waist and a round lower bout. Other construction characteristics are shared by these two similar models, including a 12-frets-to-the-body neck; pearl dots at frets 5, 7, and 9 only; ebony bottom-belly bridge with pyramid wings; and "The Gibson" silkscreened at an angle on the peghead.

The two models differed in their finishes (light amber top/Sheraton brown back and sides on the L-1, amber brown all around on the L-0), their wood for back and sides (mahogany on the L-1, maple on the L-0), and their body binding (white/black/white on the L-1, simple binding on the L-0). Also, the fingerboard of the L-1 was bound.

The L-Series Small-Body Guitars 29

In 1928 changes began. The ebony bridge was changed to a rosewood rectangle with flat wings, the binding ring on the inside of the soundhole was discontinued, the fingerboard was no longer bound, the fretmarker dots extended to the 15th fret, and the top sported a brown mahogany sunburst.

The L-1 body was switched to the larger size (14¾" squarish lower bout), like that of the L-2, and by 1929 the body binding became a simple white on both top and back.

In 1932 the neck was changed to a 14-frets-to-the-body design. The soundhole, bridge, and bracing were also moved upward in compensation.

The following year a pickguard was added to Gibson flat-tops; its shape followed the contour of the body, and the 'guard was made of striped tortoise-style celluloid, with the stripes always running at an angle. In the last couple of years of the L-1, the center of its sunburst increased in size.

After a life of nearly 12 years, the L-1 was discontinued by 1937, the first of the six L-series models to pass into eternal vintagedom.

Because of their high quality, excellent tone and playability, good looks, and low price tag, the L-0, L-00, and L-1 were the right guitars at the right time. Consequently, they sold well, a point that's important now, when vintage guitars are becoming scarce and their prices unreachable to many. Half a century ago, as now, these models offered excellent tone and volume, whether played with a flatpick or in the fingerstyle.

These models owe their exceptional responsiveness to their light construction: they have thin woods, slim braces, and thin finishes. With their L-series models Gibson avoided the syndrome that many

Legendary bluesman Robert Johnson and his L-1.

The small, round-body L-1 and its original case, vintage 1927.

> **K**nown primarily as a flatpicker, Norman Blake also excels at finger-style guitar, using this c. 1930 L-1 for that purpose.
>
> *"I'm so partial to this body size that I have both a 12-fret and a 14-fret to play."*
> —Norman Blake

guitar manufacturers have fallen into—putting durability ahead of tone, thus keeping warranty work to a minimum (and profits higher).

The trade-off to this feather-light construction must be mentioned. Many of these Gibsons have paid the price for being so lightly built. The number-one offender has been the use of heavy strings: a set of Mapes strings on an L-0 could make it sound like a cannon—briefly. As these very thin guitar tops began to bulge and twist under the stress of heavy strings, braces would start to pop loose and other major structural problems develop.

In addition to the very thin body woods (a thin .080" for tops), braces, and tiny maple bridge pads, the braces did not tuck under the kerfing, making them less able to withstand excessive torque from heavy strings. Fortunately, these braces were glued well, and the L-series models perform beautifully with light strings. These potential structural problems should not be blamed on the instruments' design or construction; simply, these models were not built for heavy steel strings.

Because many guitarists are familiar with the small Martin models, such as those with the 0, 00, and 000 body sizes, a comparison might be informative. The following observations can be made about the L-series guitars and the small Martins: the L-body is a cross between a 12-fret 00 and 000 but with deeper sides at the lower end; the Gibson bracing is thinner, lighter, and non-scalloped but tapers toward the outside of the body; Gibson woods are thinnner; Gibson bridges are smaller and lighter; both companies use small bridge plates of maple; Gibson necks feature truss rods, a prominent V-shape, and a more pronounced fingerboard radius; the L-0 and L-00 Gibsons were priced more like the mahogany-top Martin Style-17 guitars.

The dimensions of the L-series are as follows:

Body length	19 ⅜"
Lower sides depth	4 5⁄16"
Upper sides depth	3 ¼"
Soundhole diameter	4"
Upper bout	10 ¼"
Lower bout	14 ¾"
Waist	8 ¼"

The following chart is intended to help in the confusing and often impossible task of identifying the L-0, L-00, and L-1 models.

Finish	Features	Model	Year
BLACK 　black pins 　no pickguard 　"The Gibson" or "Gibson" logo 　unbound back	14 frets to the body	L-00	1932
BLACK 　bound back 　pickguard (tortoise or white)	14 frets to the body	L-0	1937-1942
BLACK 　straight bridge saddle 　heavier braces	12 frets to the body	HG-00	1937-1938
BLACK 　pickguard 　"Gibson" logo 　unbound back	14 frets to the body	L-00	1933
AMBER 　mahogany top	12 frets to the body	L-0	1930-1931
AMBER 　mahogany top	14 frets to the body	L-0	1932
SUNBURST 　20 frets total 　white pins 　no pickguard 　small middle sunburst 　bound back	12 frets to the body	L-1	1930-1931
SUNBURST 　white pins 　no pickguard 　small middle sunburst	14 frets to the body	L-1	1932
SUNBURST 　white pins 　pickguard 　small middle sunburst 　bound back	14 frets to the body	L-1	1933-1936
SUNBURST 　black pins 　pickguard 　small middle sunburst 　unbound back	14 frets to the body	L-00	1933-1935
SUNBURST 　black pins 　pickguard 　medium-size middle sunburst 　unbound back	14 frets to the body	L-00	1936
SUNBURST 　black pins 　pickguard 　large middle sunburst 　bound back	14 frets to the body	L-00	1937-1945

Finish	Features	Model	Year

SUNBURST
    black pins
    straight bridge saddle
    heavier braces
    bound back
	12 frets to the body	HG-00	1937-1945

NATURAL TOP
    black pins
    pickguard
    bound back
	14 frets	L-00	1941-1942

NOTES:
- Some necks were built without truss rods c. 1943
- Some pegheads featured a "Banner" c. 1943-1945
- Some batches of any model may have various and uncharacteristic features in any given year.

A rare 14-fret L-2 with rosewood back and sides c. 1933. Bridge not original.

L-2

This model became the fourth member of the L-series family mid-year in 1929. Of this quartet only the lofty Gibson L-"Special," usually referred to as the Nick Lucas, cost more ($125 in Gibson's 1932 price list), with the L-2 listing at $75, the L-1 at $50, and the L-0 at $35. (The very successful L-00, which was to be introduced in 1932, would list at only $25, a bargain even in the Depression.)

Because the L-2 was only built for a little over four years and in small numbers, not many examples of the model are available for examination purposes. In addition, the company literature is either absent or unreliable during this period. Gibson would often change features gradually and unannounced, instead of waiting for the annual re-tooling and introduction of new models as in the automobile industry. Consequently, total accuracy in placing dates on some of the following feature changes is not always possible with this model. Further complicating the research, the L-2 also offered certain features as options, making difficult the job of defining the "standard model." Thus, some of the following is by necessity educated guesswork.

Upon its introduction the L-2 shared numerous features with the new Nick Lucas model, including body shape and most dimensions, with a lower bout width of 14 ¾" and an overall body length of 19 ¼"; the Lucas had a greater body depth (thickness), however. Both were built with

Brazilian rosewood for backs and sides and northern spruce for tops, which were slightly arched. Befitting their greater cost, the Nick Lucas and the L-2 bodies were triple-bound front and back, their ebony fingerboards double-bound. Also, they often use the same expensive tuners, Grover 98s.

An interesting feature of the L-2 is that its neck meets the body at the 13th fret—again like the Nick Lucas model. Both models featured mahogany necks, the 24¾" scale, and "The Gibson" inlaid in pearl on the peghead. The fingerboard of the L-2 had simple pearl dots, though, unlike the elaborate symmetrical inlays of the Nick Lucas.

The earliest version of the model used a tailpiece and an adjustable rectangular bridge. Despite this tailpiece design, the guitar was "X-braced." This combination has resulted in tops that have sunk in varying degrees over the years: because of string tension a pin bridge is pulled upward, while the tailpiece bridge is pushed downward, creating a depression. Many of the L-2s have been converted to pin bridges for this reason.

Back and sides were switched to mahogany in 1931. Other changes were made about that time: a six-point, flame-like peghead inlay was added; the neck was shortened to a 12-frets-to-the-body design; a gold-sparkle material was inlaid around the edge of the top and soundhole; the sunburst and natural-finish options of the original version changed to what the catalogue refers to as Argentine gray.

Brazilian rosewood was again used for backs and sides in mid- or late 1932. The sparkle trim was dropped at that time, and the top became a natural finish. The pin bridge had become standard, yet the tailpiece adjustable bridge remained an option. Rosewood replaced ebony for the fingerboard. The neck reverted to the original 13-frets-to-the-body neck. The L-2 photo in the 1932 catalogue, however, shows a 12-fret model from 1931, while the text identifies it as a 14-fret model.

By 1933 the peghead logo was shortened to "Gibson," and the tailpiece bridge was no longer available. But an option was added—a glue-on pickguard, which differed from other Gibson pickguards of the era by being smaller at the top and made of an uncommon speckled celluloid. The contoured elevated 'guard of the day, attached like those of the F-model mandolins, was still popular. Also, some L-2s from this era had two identical top braces under the fingerboard extension; the L-0s, L-00s, and L-1s used only one in that area. Finally, around this time the 13-frets-to-the-body neck again disappeared, replaced by a 14-fret design.

The L-2 was discontinued in late 1933 or early 1934.

1934 L-Century with an atypical inlay pattern. The "Century of Progress" model celebrated Chicago's centennial.

L-CENTURY: MOTHER-OF-PEARL(OID)

In 1933 Chicago celebrated its 100th anniversary by hosting the Century of Progress Exhibition. A couple of hours northeast of Chicago, the Gibson Company found this event and its considerable media attention too good to be wasted. So they named a new guitar after it.

In terms of list price, upon its introduction in 1933 the Century held the penultimate position among the four L-body guitars, selling at $55, with only the Nick Lucas Special at $90 costing more, and the L-1 and L-00 less, at $37.50 and $27.50, respectively. All four models shared the L-series body shape (14¾" wide, 19¼" long) and neck dimensions. The curly maple sides and back of the Century quickly distinguish it from all the models listed above, which used mahogany, except for the Nick Lucas guitars that used maple during much of the L-Century era.

1935 L-Century.

At that time Gibson had access to exceptional northern maple, usually red maple and sugar maple species that yielded a very hard and beautifully figured wood. Gibson regularly used slab-sawn or intermediate-sawn curly maple to create the superior sides and backs of numerous period instruments, including the arch-top L-5 guitars and the F-5 mandolins. This choice maple fit the Century perfectly.

1936 L-Century. The sunbursts of this model grew year by year.

The most striking feature of the L-C was its use (and in the eyes of some, overuse) of "pearloid"—artificial pearl, often referred to as "mother of toilet seat" because of a prominent secondary use of this versatile material. Upon a neck of mahogany a strip of pearloid extended from the nut to the very bottom of the fingerboard. Rosewood rectangles were then inlaid into frets 3, 5, 7, 9, 12, and 15; mother-of-pearl in the shape of notched diamonds was in turn inlaid into these rosewood blocks.

This ocean of pearloid swept over the truss rod cover and the peghead, too, which featured a double inlay: first, rosewood was set into the pearloid, and then "Gibson" and a notched diamond were set in mother-of-pearl into the rosewood. Around the peghead edge ran a stripe of black celluloid. Tuning buttons were either black or white, with no correlation between the date of an instrument and the color.

Few changes occurred from 1933 until about 1937. Prior to this the only clearly datable feature involved the changing sunburst, whose yellow center gradually expanded outward up to 1939.

About 1938 Gibson retired the pearloid peghead veneer, replacing it with a rosewood veneer. Two peghead patterns were common. One featured white celluloid around the edge, a pearl "Gibson" in script, a small notched-diamond pearl inlay in the middle, and a pearloid truss rod cover. The second version, pictured in the 1938 catalogue, depicts a peghead free of binding, a black celluloid truss rod cover, and an elongated diamond inlay in pearl.

The L-Century was gradually phased out after 1939, with only three shipped in 1940 and a final one in 1941. Gibson made one ¾-size L-Century, in 1939.

The L-C is to some guitar lovers, even Gibson devotées, an acquired taste. If pearloid is your trim of choice, this model is for you; if it's not, find consolation in the fact that some Gibson banjos of the mid-'30s, especially Style 11s, used this faux-pearl on not only the fingerboard and peghead but the resonator back as well. Pearloid aside, the L-C was the only Gibson of this size with maple back and sides (the Nick Lucas had a deeper body) and was constructed of high-grade woods, including northern curly maple for sides and back, Adirondack red spruce for the top, Honduras mahogany for the neck, and Brazilian rosewood for the fingerboard and bridge. Simply put, it's as nice a small-body guitar as there is on the vintage market.

> 1936 Nick Lucas "Gibson Special." Some guitarists prefer this over all other flat-tops.

THE NICK LUCAS "GIBSON SPECIAL"

When Gibson chose Nick Lucas to lend his name to their special artist's model in the late '20s, they chose well. Although today he is remembered perhaps only for the guitar model named after him, or maybe in notoriety for his hit recording of "Tiptoe Through the Tulips," he played a prominent role in the history of the flat-top guitar. He was among the first few to record guitar solos, in 1922; he was one of the most popular entertainers in both the United States and England, playing command performances for the Prince of Wales and the Queen of Spain; his 1922 recordings of "Pickin' the Guitar" and "Teasin' the Frets" later greatly influenced Merle Travis, who himself influenced the style of Chet Atkins and two generations of country guitar pickers.

Fingerpicker Roy Book Binder with his Nick Lucas, a model famous for its deep sides.

Lucas was a pioneer in using the flat-top guitar as both a rhythm instrument for the big band sound and for accompanying a solo singer. Known as "The Crooning Troubadour," he was the first big radio star to play the guitar, preceding by a few years Jimmie Rodgers, country music's first superstar. Gibson's 1928 catalogue touts its artist, and its new artist's guitar, thus:

> The wizardry of Nick Lucas and his guitar is known to all music lovers. Combining his ideas and knowledge with the skill of Gibson Artist-Craftsmen has given birth to a truly magnificent guitar. Here is an instrument with big, harp-like tone, responsive to the lightest touch, balanced in every register. Crisp, sparkling treble and solid resonant bass that makes your whole being sway to its rhythmic pulsations.

Whatever Gibson was paying Nick Lucas for his name, this ad copy makes it sound as if he were worth more.

Gibson first approached Lucas when he was touring the prestigious Orpheum vaudeville circuit. Frank Campbell, General Sales Manager for Gibson, attempted to persuade Lucas to get rid of his usual guitar and play a Gibson instead. Lucas replied that he would, if Gibson would design and build an instrument to his specifications. The result was not only the first artist-endorsed model for Gibson, it was in some minds one of the best acoustic guitars ever made.

Costing $125 in 1928, the year of its introduction, the Nick Lucas was easily Gibson's most expensive flat-top, compared to $35 for the L-0 and $50 for the L-1. This high price not only kept the production relatively small but resulted in a large number of customized Nick Lucas guitars, two facts that make a thorough and accurate description of this guitar difficult. Furthermore, the model was often treated as a custom-built Gibson, allowing many special features and personalized touches that did not conform to catalogue text or illustrations. In this context, although it may be impossible to describe annual feature variations, the following information should give a relatively accurate sequence of the changes in the Nick Lucas model over its 11-year life.

The new "Gibson Special" body was rounded, much like a mini version of the SJ-200, but much smaller at 13½" wide (lower bout). The greater depth of the Nick Lucas distinguishes it from other flat-tops of the time: front to back, this model measured 4¼" at the neck and 4⅝" at the endpin. In contrast, the popular mid-'30s L-00, with external body measurements seemingly equivalent to the Nick Lucas, was much shallower, measuring a slim 3½" at the neck and 4⅜" at the tail. This 1928 Nick Lucas had mahogany back and sides and a spruce top, with its back and top slightly arched. The pyramid-style rosewood bridge displayed a slight bottom belly and white pins, with a solitary seventh pin stored beneath the in-line six. Top and back were triple-bound, as was the rosewood fingerboard inlaid in pearl with intricate symmetrical design; no two inlays were of the same pattern. Angling across the peghead was "The Gibson" in pearl, balanced by Grover G-98 tuners with metal buttons. Soundhole purfling consisted of two multi-ply groupings. A French heel graced the neck, which met the sunburst body at the 12th fret. Affixed to the inside of the back was a round beige label announcing "Nick Lucas Special," stating the maker's name, and featuring a picture of Nick himself, holding of course his namesake guitar.

In the next year the body width was increased to 14¾", and the lower bout lost its circular appearance, becoming more flat-bottomed. Gone, too, was the mahogany of sides and back, replaced by rosewood. The redesigned bridge became a simple rosewood rectangle, while typically the fingerboard inlays became bolder and more elaborate. Many guitars from late 1929 or early 1930 had 13-frets-to-the-body necks, fleurs-de-lis as peghead inlays, and logos that had been shortened to only "Gibson," still in the old-style script.

It's likely that most if not all Nick Lucas guitars had become 14-frets-to-the-body construction by 1932, even though the Gibson catalogue for that year uses a 12-fret model from early 1929 in illustration. A trapeze tailpiece with an adjustable bridge was offered as an option in '32. (It is also quite possible that these tailpieces were used on many of the 13-fret rosewood-version Nick Lucas Specials.) Most guitars that year came with elevated pickguards, while other 'guards were glued onto the tops. The 1932 catalogue listed this model as having mahogany back and sides and an ebony fingerboard.

Gibson's literature of 1933 specifies the Lucas as a rosewood instrument. With all of the changes in design, material, options, custom orders, and prototype batches, it's no wonder that in the period from 1929 through 1933 the Nick Lucas "Gibson Special" is difficult to pin down as exhibiting specific characteristics at a specific time.

Numerous changes occurred by or in 1934: curly maple was used for the back and sides, although some instruments were still made with mahogany; the arch-top-style elevated pickguard had been replaced by glued-on 'guards; all Lucases had become 14-fret construction; top, back, and sides were sunburst; and, as a sign of continuing hard times nationwide, the price was reduced to $90.

The model stabilized from the mid-'30s until it was deleted from the lineup in 1938. One noticeable difference involved an evolution in the sunburst finish. The 'burst itself (the amber area), which had remained small from 1928 through 1936, covering only the bridge area, radiated during the model's last three years until it covered most of the lower bout.

Although it's not known how many of the Nick Lucas model were made before 1937, long-time Gibson employee and company historian

1936 Nick Lucas "Gibson Special" with ebony finish.

Julius Bellson has supplied a list of shipping totals covering the five years after that:

Year	Number Shipped
1937	35
1938	15
1939	3
1940	2
1941	2

The Nick Lucas "Gibson Special" is an outstanding vintage guitar, one of the all-time great designs. Materials and workmanship are exceptional, the equal of any vintage flat-top. But let the Gibson catalogue of the day have the last word:

> To play it is to know a measure of the same inspiration that has carried Nick Lucas to great heights. You love the feel as it comes to life with the touch of your fingers. Your regard grows like a rare flower watered by the crystal drops of purest melody. It is indeed an instrument by an artist, for an artist. This is the guitar used by many famous professionals exclusively for radio broadcasting, recording, and stage. Conducive to amazing progress in the hands of the student or amateur because of its fast easy action.

The Round-Shoulder Jumbos

Chapter Three

1934 Jumbo, the first year Gibson made this large-body guitar.

THE JUMBO: GIBSON'S FIRST LARGE-BODY FLAT-TOP

At the beginning of 1934 Gibson's largest flat-top guitar was the Nick Lucas model, an instrument closely based on the L-series bodies but with deeper sides. According to the 1932 catalogue the company apparently hoped that this increased dimension would satisfy a buying public growing tired of the smaller parlor guitar: "The extra depth of body—a deeper tone chamber producing unusual depth and roundness of tone . . . . [the Nick Lucas model] is an exceptional guitar for vocal accompaniment on the stage, radio, and records." Though the Nick Lucas model was an improvement, it fell far short of offering the tone and volume possible only in a much larger guitar; and when Martin brought out their large-body D (Dreadnought) series in 1932, Gibson was left temporarily uncompetitive, the Nick Lucas failing to fill the void.

But in 1934 Gibson created a formidable opponent in its new Jumbo, which, at 1¼" wider, 1" longer and ½" deeper than the L-series flat-tops, was well named. That year's catalogue, despite the company's reputation for hyperbole in its promotional material, described the Jumbo only with unvarnished truth: "This greater body size produces a heavy, booming tone so popular with many players who do vocal or small combination accompaniment for both personal and radio appearances. The bass of this model will amaze you, and of course the clear, brilliant treble is in perfect balance." Listening to one of these exceptional guitars proves the accuracy of this description.

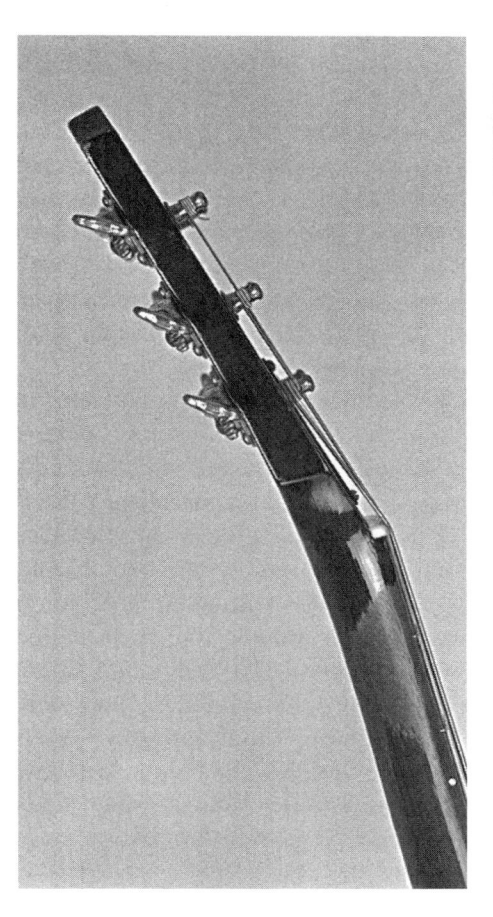

1934 Jumbo peghead.

The Jumbos are scarce because of a short production run (two years) and because they cost $60, without a case, in the heart of the Great Depression, a time when music lovers, against their wishes, put food before guitars. So little has been written about these rare instruments that even when they do surface, they are often misidentified, usually in the generic as "old Gibson flat-tops." This is like calling a sapphire an old blue stone.

The Jumbo quickly became a much-sought-after guitar. Just as many singing cowboy stars are associated with their "identity" guitars—such as the J-200s of Roy Rogers, Ray Whitley, Tex Ritter, Jimmy Wakely, and Gene Autry—the Jumbo had its stars, though of a lesser magnitude than the aforementioned. Bob Baker, for example, who emerged from the National Barn Dance (a 50,000-watt country music program broadcast by Chicago's WLS) to become a popular singing cowboy movie star in the mid-1930s, always appeared with his trusty and beautiful companion, a 1934 Gibson Jumbo. Also, pre-bluegrass greats Wiley Morris (of the Morris Brothers hillbilly band) and Charlie Monroe (Bill's brother and a major talent in his own right) both played 1934 Jumbos.

It's no wonder that these and other stars of the Depression era, who could afford to purchase any guitar on the market, made the Jumbo their instrument of preference. Exceptional, incredible tone (and words are poor substitutes here for sound) convinced many buyers. The quality of workmanship and materials—much easier to write about—was another essential attribute. The Jumbo presents itself as a marriage of proper proportions and woods, with mahogany back and sides and a top of spruce, each instrument individually finished in a muted sunburst that in the mid-'30s moved from a black-brown at the periphery into an amber at the characteristically small center that covered about one-quarter of the top. (The 1935 version expanded the amber center to nearly one-third of the total area.) The overall impression: an exceedingly fine guitar that is visually striking, harmonious, and in a sense relaxing, as though its main function—to make music—is an afterthought to its artistic statement.

The body dimensions that led to the "Jumbo" designation are 16" wide, 10¼" long, and on average 4½" deep, with white ivoroid accentuating the subtle sunbursts on the body's back and top. Though not obviously so, the sides taper gently from bottom to top, 4½" deep at the bottom and 4⅜" at the top. The soundhole diameter measures 3¾", narrower than the 4" of the L-Series predecessors, perhaps an attempt to enhance the bass response. The pickguard, in the standard Gibson shape of the era, was formed of beautiful "striped" or "flamed" celluloid, with colors ranging from yellow-brown to a vivid orange-red.

Internally, the Jumbo has mahogany kerfing and end blocks. The serial number is inked upon a neck block whose vertical edge is sawed at a 45-degree taper. The small maple bridge plate is glued under a bridge kept in place without bolts—only later would Gibson mix metal with wood and glue in an attempt to make the small bridges stay put. Some of the thin and tall top braces are scalloped, others not. (Why the variation? Gibson probably experimented with brace design in searching for the perfect compromise of tonal response and strength.) A "single-X" pattern, formed by braces that measure 9/16" high by ¼" wide, begins about 1⅛" from the soundhole and is angled at about 100 degrees. The Jumbo and some of the earlier J-35s have three of the transverse "tone bar" braces that support the top between the braces forming the "X," as opposed to the usual two used on Martins and other Gibson models. Further, in most Jumbos the three tone bars and rear of the "X-braces" have a long scallop pattern. It's obvious that these braces needed this design, to support and help resonance in the red spruce tops that were thin, roughly .115"; and like the backs, the tops were slightly arched, for power and strength.

> By 1935 the Jumbos had acquired bound fingerboards and slightly larger sunbursts.

At the bottom of the V-shaped mahogany neck is a pointed French heel, while the headstock maintains the symmetrical hill-ravine-hill profile. The nut for the 1¾" neck is bone, as is the bridge saddle, the white standing out against the rosewood of both the unbound fingerboard of the 1934 models (fingerboard binding was most likely not added until the 1935 Jumbo) and the small, rectangular bridge. A pearl "Gibson" in script contrasts with the wood of the peghead, which remained without binding through the two-year run of the model. Tuning keys are nickel-plated individual Grover G-98s.

Jumbos have a short scale of roughly 24¾". Featuring the standard Gibson truss-rod system, the Jumbos have excellent neck sets and most have remained eminently playable over the years. The distance between the soundhole and the fingerboard end seems to be greater on the Jumbo than on the Advanced Jumbo. This perception deceives, though, for two reasons: the soundhole is smaller on the Jumbo, and the scale length is shorter. These two factors considered together equal the difference in measurement between the two models. Significant changes in soundhole size were just around the corner, however, in the J-35 model.

It is notoriously difficult to describe tone verbally, especially in a way understandable to others. This notwithstanding, in the opinion of many vintage-guitar authorities the Jumbo is as good-

Crazed finish on a 1937 Jumbo 35.

sounding as any mahogany guitar ever built—loud, rich, warm, and balanced, with an exceptionally big, clear bass response. Ironically, the magnificent Jumbo has been kept from becoming a "Holy Grail" guitar only by its rarity; so few arrive on the market that only the cognoscenti know of the Jumbo's existence. It's too bad that such a fine guitar made its debut in the throes of the Great Depression, that it had such a short production run (1934, 1935, and probably part of 1936), and that it cost more than most musicians who at the time were struggling to keep body and soul together could afford—$60 for a 1934 Jumbo, an extra $15 for a hard case.

JUMBO 35 : MUCH FOR LITTLE IN THE DEPRESSION ERA

Hard times in the country, hard times in town. By the mid-'30s the Great Depression showed little sign of abating, despite make-work and back-to-work programs begun by the government in Washington. Although the N.R.A. (National Recovery Act), the C.C.C. (Civilian Conservation Corps Reforestation Relief Act), and other federal initiatives made the difference between food and hunger in thousands of American families, commercial country music popular in the mid-'30s shows us how tenaciously the Depression still gripped the nation. Country music, then as now, was facts-of-life music, reflecting the joys and sorrows of common folk in their daily lives. Many songs from the time show us a nation depressed and desperate: "All I Got's Gone" (E. V. Stoneman), "Breadline Blues" (Slim Smith), "Old Age Pension Check" (Roy Acuff), "How Can a Poor Man Stand Such Times and Live" (Blind Alfred Reed), "No Depression in Heaven" (Carter Family). The music said it all.

With this grim reality as an economic backdrop, Gibson realized that to remain profitable it needed new models, affordable models. Their only jumbo (or at least their only non-Hawaiian jumbo) was, at $60.00, simply beyond the economic means of many music lovers at that time. In 1936, with two givens in mind—that the public wanted large-body guitars, and wanted an *affordable* model—Gibson brought two new guitars to market, one at each end of the price range. The Advanced Jumbo, of rosewood and with fancy trim, sold for $80 and was intended to challenge Martin's D-28; the other new model, a less expensive version of the Jumbo, retailed for only $35 and competed with Martin's cheaper large-body, the D-18.

Gibson's new large-body was designated "Jumbo 35," the model's name having been created by combining "Jumbo," a word that fairly describes the body's size and shape, with the guitar's original retail price, $35. The J-35 apparently was produced from 1936 to mid-year 1942, though there is disagreement about both ends of the production run. Some dealers, for example, allege that the J-35 was built until the end of WW II, but this is unlikely; to the contrary, research indicates that in mid- to late-1942 Gibson switched from the J-35 to the J-45, after which no more J-35s were produced. Similarly, records are unclear regarding the precise time in 1936 that the J-35 came to market.

Admittedly, it's possible that a few "composite" guitars exist, such as a J-45 with a J-35 neck, yet this is doubtful, for any leftover J-35 necks could have been used for the L-00, which was still in production. There are tales of "Banner J-35s," but without any evidence they remain only tales. And the situation gets more murky: Because so much confusion has existed about the difference between a J-35 and the later "Banner" J-45, misinformation has resulted. For example, a catalogue picture from a prominent vintage-guitar dealer shows a 1940s J-45 that is mislabeled as a 1935 J-35, in spite of the fact that J-35s were not produced in 1935.

While Gibson knew that a jumbo-size guitar at a low price was needed to fill a niche, the company could not simply make more Jumbos and sell them for $35 each, at least not and stay in business. To reduce the price from the $60 Jumbo to the J-35, the following changes were made:

- Neck, back, and sides, which on the Jumbo were sunburst, became a dark red mahogany.
- Neck binding was dropped.
- Individual Grover G-98 tuners were replaced with less expensive, three-on-a-plate plastic-button tuners (often Kluson).
- Pearl-inlaid "Gibson" script was replaced with a white silkscreen.
- Some early J-35s were made without back binding (binding was soon added).
- Many though not necessarily all early J-35s were constructed without scalloped braces.

Other changes, in addition to those for lowering cost, were made to further distinguish the J-35 from the Jumbo. For example, bridge screws were added, and the soundhole aperture was increased from 3¾" to 4" in diameter. The most significant structural change, though, was in the depth of the sides. The following chart shows the evolution in side depth, from the Jumbo to the J-35 to the J-45 (in inches):

	1934 Jumbo	1937 J-35	1943 J-45	1958 J-45
Depth of sides at rear	4 ⅝	4 13/16	4 ⅞	4 29/32
Depth of sides at front	4 ¼	3 13/16	3 13/16	3 ⅞
Average depth of sides	4.44	4.31	4.34	4.39

1937 J-35.

was haphazardly, not chronologically. Each red spruce top and its individual strength—or weakness—was perhaps the determinant, as was the tonal response of each after bracing had been glued and had dried enough for sound-testing. In a sense, then, the scalloping of some braces but not others was a rough way of tuning the characteristically thin tops on early J-35s.

By 1939 Gibson had dropped the three-tone-bar system designed for the Jumbos and had reverted to using two bars, as on their other models. Again, some were scalloped and some were not. The two-bar system's design was additionally significant. Instead of the widely spread "X-brace" of the previous Gibson Jumbos, it featured a brace angle of about 95 degrees, with the brace itself moved further from the soundhole, similar to the Martins of the period.

All sounded excellent, but many musicians feel that the three tone bars with scalloped braces were, in general, superior. It should be quickly added that flat-top players covet J-35s from each and all of the four configurations: three-tone-bar scalloped, three-tone-bar unscalloped, two-tone-bar scalloped, and two-tone-bar unscalloped.

Another of the numerous changes in the J-35 that occurred from 1936 to 1942, the production run of this model, is perhaps the most visible yet the most overlooked, and that's the guitar's finish. In the first three years of the production run (up through 1938), the sunburst was in fact the only finish available, but a beautiful sight it was, with the 'burst on the instrument's top a near-black at the outside, moving to a rich amber middle, with a yellow at the very center. In Gibson's description, this was their "chocolate brown sunburst." And the 'burst gradually grew, from a yellow-orange barely covering the bridge-to-soundhole area (1936) to within 3" of the lower bout's edges within a few years.

In 1939 the J-35 was offered only in a natural-finish top, according to the company catalogue. However, here's another example of Gibson's notorious inconsistency, for at least two original cherry sunburst J-35s were made. This may be the earliest that Gibson experimented with their now-famous cherry sunburst; it's also possible that these rare sunbursts were custom orders. In any case, by 1941 the J-35 could be purchased either in sunburst or with a natural top, and this choice remained until 1942, the last year that J-35s were made.

These changes in dimensions, though slight, created a somewhat smoother tonal response in the J-35, in contrast to the big, raw, quick response of the Jumbo.

As the J-35 itself evolved in numerous ways from 1936 to 1942, common ground between it and the Jumbo lessened at each turn. Early J-35s, for example, came onto the market with the same bracing system as the Jumbo, yet with a difference—the Jumbo had scalloped braces, while the J-35, for an indeterminable period, did not; and when scallop-braced J-35s did begin to appear, it

44   *Gibson's Fabulous Flat-Top Guitars*

1939 J-35, the first year a natural top was offered on this model.

1941 Sunburst J-35.

kept by longtime Gibson employee and company historian Julius Bellson:

1937	385
1938	335
1939	497
1940	435
1941	825
TOTAL	2,477

During that same period Martin built 2,162 D-18s, this model being the primary competitor of the Gibson J-35. Following is a brief comparison of these two wonderful guitars.

The J-35 neck shape also evolved. The V-neck was a carryover from the Jumbo and is found in the early versions of the J-35. Gradually the neck became rounded, and by 1939 almost all examples of the model featured these round necks. A similar transition took place on the heel. Early J-35s featured the more pointy French heel, which itself became rounded. Apparently these four steps in the neck metamorphosis were made over several years. In contrast to these changes are the J-35 pegheads, which, as on all vintage Gibsons, were angled at 17 degrees and in profile were tapered, the top being thinner than the part joining the neck. Similarly, the J-35 retained the 24¾" scale and the Brazilian rosewood fingerboard. This combination of a short scale, pronounced fingerboard radius, and substantial neck is in demand with serious guitarists, who find J-35s of this construction extremely comfortable to play.

It's uncertain how many J-35s were produced in the first and last years of production; however, for the in-between years there are personal records

1941 Sunburst J-35 peghead.

the longer-scale D-18 offers a tighter-feeling string and the potential for more amplification but with diminished tonal richness and harmonics. The fingerboard radius, truss rod system, and neck sets offer a superior-playing guitar. The Martin tends to have a tonal energy focused around a note's fundamental, whereas the Gibson emphasizes more of the harmonics, resulting in a warmer, sweeter presence. Increased harmonics are particularly more audible in the higher octaves. This accounts for the reputation the Gibsons have for higher-frequency tone color.

> "My J-35 is one of my all-time favorite guitars. I play my Martin D-18 when I want an unadorned, biting, harsh, clear sound, but when I want a big, warm, sweet tone, I reach for my J-35."
> —Norman Blake

Randell Hilton, who makes his living performing as a solo act at bluegrass festivals, sums up why he uses Gibsons: "If I played bluegrass only in parking-lot settings, I might consider a Martin. In a solo act, I need a guitar to be many instruments with a wide variety of sounds. Therefore, I play Gibsons."

The $64 question, one guaranteed to result in an animated discussion between guitar players who otherwise are normal and rational: Which is better, a pre-War Martin D-18 or a Gibson J-35? That's like asking parents which one of their two children is better. Neither. Both. A musician in the market for a quality guitar should follow personal preference. Both guitars have strengths. Either the J-35 or the D-18 would, after all, be a great choice.

Forgetting about this friendly competition between two great guitars from rival companies, it can be stated with certainty that the J-35s are exceptional guitars, and with around 3,000 produced, there should still be some out there looking for a home. No other large Gibson flat-top of the day comes close to the J-35's total production. And J-35s have been revered for decades. A perusal of old country-music books quickly shows that many stars used the J-35, including the great Doc Watson and Hank Williams. Gibson produced enough of this model to make pursuing one a realistic goal for a determined collector or musician.

The D-18 was built more consistently, with few variations. The J-35s, on the other hand, varied widely—three tone bars/two tone bars, scalloped braces/non-scalloped braces, small back braces/large back braces, round necks/V-necks, and minor variations in soundhole placement. This seems to say something about the two companies, one extremely conservative and the other more experimental and flexible. And with good reason it might be said that Martin was the more organized of the two companies, at least in some time periods, and that the more haphazard organization of the Gibson company was conducive to variation. This wide range of J-35 options adds considerable personality to the model line, while offering some combination of construction, appearance, tone, and playability that serious musicians and collectors welcome.

While the 24¾" scale of the J-35 provides a feel and tonal response so popular with blues artists,

Doc Watson playing a J-35 on the front porch of his home near Deep Gap, North Carolina, c. 1960. Doc was in his late thirties and as yet "undiscovered." Left to right, Doc, Clarence Ashley (of the original Carolina Tar Heels string band), and Gaither Carlton.

"I just can't say enough good things about those old Gibson jumbos.

The old Gibson J-35 that I played was as good a guitar as I have ever played. It truly was. It was a good old well-used guitar, with scratches and scuff marks on it—it had some "prestige," in other words. It was a borrowed guitar, loaned to me by a very good friend, Ray Hamby, who I played with when I was much younger. Merle learned on that guitar. In fact, Merle played that same guitar on the Doc Watson and Son album, even if the guitar's not in the picture they used on the record cover. I played that J-35 from about 1960 to around '64.

I experimented with a lot of different strings on that old J-35 jumbo, and just about any strings you put on it made it sound great. There was a semi-flatwound medium-gauge Gretsch string that was supposed to be for an electric guitar. In the '50s I played a Les Paul and I used the Gretsch strings on it. So I had extra sets, and when I started playing acoustic guitar again—the J-35—I used the Gretsch strings on it, too. And God, they sounded good on that thing."

—Doc Watson

In an eat-your-heart-out conclusion, let's follow the price transition of the J-35, those same instruments that as of this writing are getting up to a couple thousand dollars on the market:

1936	$35.00
1937	$37.50
1938	$37.50
1939	$37.50
1941 (Sept.)	$40.00 Sunburst Finish
	$45.00 Natural Finish
1941 (Oct.)	$42.00 Sunburst Finish
	$47.25 Natural Finish
1942	$42.00 Sunburst Finish
	$47.25 Natural Finish

While we fantasize about going to Gibson's Kalamazoo factory in 1936 (but with today's dollars) and ordering 100 J-35s for $3,500, we must remember that in the Great Depression, $35 was for millions of families much more than a weekly salary. But why face reality now? Let's remain in our fantasy mode, in Kalamazoo, and in 1942—then we can pick up an additional dozen or so J-45s, of course at an inflated $45 each. Excluding case.

ADVANCED JUMBO: TO MANY, THE ULTIMATE FLAT-TOP GUITAR

The Gibson catalogue of 1937 says it best:

Do you like a deep, throaty guitar—one that has a bass so deep, rich and full that it can be "felt" as well as heard—and a treble that responds to the bass with harmonious singing brilliancy? The new Advanced Jumbo is that guitar!

Gibson was telling the truth, for when their craftsmen designed the Advanced Jumbo in 1935, they set as their goal the best-sounding, most powerful flat-top to date. And in the opinion of many, they were successful, absolutely and totally. The resulting Advanced Jumbo was an amazing guitar with no compromises, unsurpassed in pure firepower.

Hard times faced the country in the mid-'30s, including makers of stringed musical instruments. Like its competitors, Gibson constantly looked for ways to remain fiscally solvent. Its new models catalogue of October 1, 1935, shows that Gibson hoped prosperity would result from a new line of "advanced" guitars. This catalogue featured the new Super 400, as well as a whole fleet of other "advanced" (meaning a body of larger dimensions) arch-top models, including the L-5, L-7, L-10, and L-12, all with enlarged bodies. By repeating this new buzzword, the company hoped to increase or at least maintain sales figures. In fact, Gibson created arch-top guitars of such high quality that more than a half-century later they number among the most sought-after in the world. "Advanced" apparently worked.

This new product line of large-body guitars extended beyond the arch-tops. In 1935 the Kalamazoo luthiers built prototypes of two soon-to-appear flat-top models, the Advanced Jumbo and the Jumbo 35 (J-35), both of which arrived on the market in 1936. These two were to replace the Jumbo, which at $60 retailed at $25 more than the J-35 but $20 less than the more fancy AJ.

At $80 (in 1936 Depression dollars) the Advanced Jumbo was an exceptional guitar, though beyond the means of many musicians at the time. As a result only 300 were made from 1936 through the end of its run three years later. (The final two actually left the Kalamazoo plant in 1940.) Because of its rarity, this model would have remained relatively unknown to players, had it not been for the excellent reissues that Gibson made in 1990. Vintage-

Prototype of the original Advanced Jumbo and the model for the Montana AJ reissues.

Two 1936 AJs with period decals.

instrument collectors and dealers, as you might expect, have long valued these instruments. George Gruhn, for example, says that "The Advanced Jumbo was probably the best flat-top in Gibson's entire history. . . . A wonderful guitar." North Carolinian Gary Burnette, who owns a flotilla of pre-War Gibsons and Martins, refers to his Advanced Jumbos as "bone crushers." If you're lucky enough to play one of these pre-War creations, be prepared for attitude readjustment and brain alteration; the Advanced Jumbo becomes the frame of reference for every other flattop you will ever play.

Gibson did well in choosing Burnette's 1935 AJ prototype as a model in developing their new reissue. In comparison with other pre-War Martins and Gibsons, the AJ model was at least the equal of the very best ever made, in terms of tone, volume, and playability.

Upon its introduction in late 1936 the Advanced Jumbo shared the same round-shoulder shape with the Jumbo, its predecessor. There were differences, though, some subtle and others more obvious. A few examples of the first group: a larger soundhole; a longer, 25½" scale of the AJ, giving it sheer power not found in the Jumbo; slightly narrower waists (10 11/32") in the AJ, creating a slightly more focused and balanced response.

An obvious difference is the use of rosewood in the AJ, in contrast to the mahogany of the Jumbo, and herein lies a debate of long standing: whether the rosewood used by Gibson on the Advanced Jumbos and SJ-200 models was Brazilian. For years collectors and vintage dealers have recognized that the hue and cut of the Gibson rosewood differs from the Brazilian rosewood found in Martins of that era, and from this difference they have inferred that the Gibson wood must have come from some country other than Brazil. In fact, both the Gibson literature and many of its employees during that time have said that their *only* source of rosewood in the 1930s was Brazil. It's probable that Gibson and Martin used different suppliers in procuring their stock, and it's certainly true that each company had its own way of finishing the rosewood once it arrived from Brazil. Gibson, for example, used quartersawn rosewood that was graded for straightness of grain. The filler, staining, and finishing also differed considerably.

The rosewood backs of AJs are two-piece and book-matched, as are the sides. The tops, described in the catalogue as "select mountain spruce," were of the best available Adirondack red spruce—with

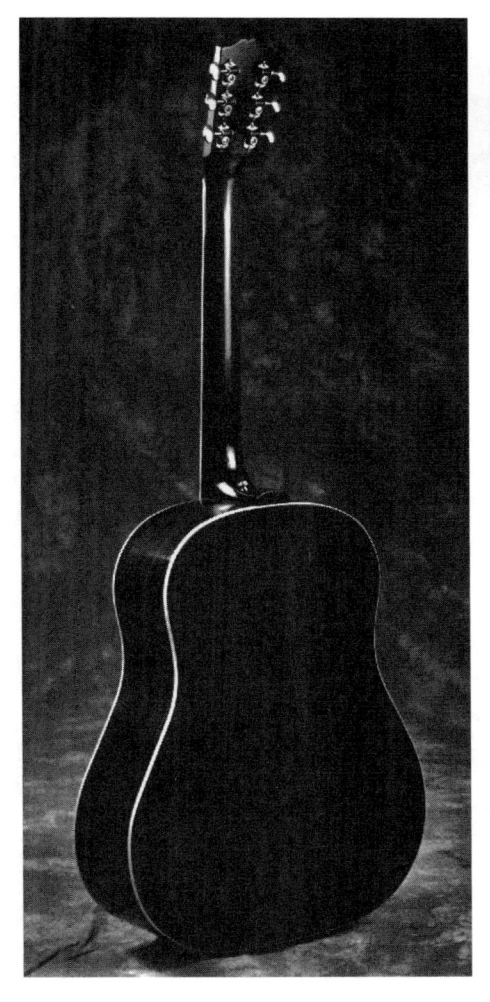

Rare 1938 AJ with peghead back painted black.

close and evenly spaced grain, perfectly quartered and book-matched. Amazingly, on numerous examples of pre-War AJs the "X-braces" and tone bars had tiny plane marks, indicating a slow and tedious hand tuning of the braces. Because the interior of each Advanced Jumbo is identical, including the characteristics of the plane marks, it's probable that the same luthier hand-tuned each and every AJ top that left the factory. Ren Ferguson, Gibson's master craftsman at their Montana factory and the developer of the new AJ reissue, agrees that the tops of pre-War Advanced Jumbos were tuned in this manner.

The design, construction, and materials were perfectly wed in the Advanced Jumbo body, producing maximum tonal response with minimal restriction or dampening. The dimensions of the large sound box explain some of this: 16 1/16" wide at the lower bout and 20 1/2" long, with sides 4 13/16" deep at the rear and 3 7/8" at the front.

The thin red spruce top is tapered at its edges and finished with a particularly striking sunburst, under which are top braces measuring approximately 1/2" high and 1/4" thick. The two tone bars (one fewer than the early J-35s of the time) run parallel, with a distance of 1 3/16" between them, angling off the treble "X-brace" at just over 60 degrees.

Located 1" below the 4" soundhole is the "X-brace" itself, whose 102-degree angle accounts for some of the wide-open, expansive tone the instrument is noted for. At 1 1/8" wide, the maple bridge pad is relatively small. The large back braces, roughly 5/16" thick and 1/2" high on the front two and 3/4" thick and 3/8" high on the pair at the rear, are typical of the era. The sides' supports are made of quartersawn spruce.

Against such a large body, the Brazilian rosewood bridge seems very small, in fact measuring .910" wide and 6.1" long, and requiring two tiny bolts to help hold it down. The bridge tapers on the treble side and features a bone saddle. Musicians and builders who have experimented widely with tone feel that the size and design of this bridge is near perfect.

And the Advanced Jumbo plays very well, too, with the one-piece mahogany V-neck, truss rod, and 12"-radius Brazilian rosewood fingerboard. The heel is always rounded and sunburst. The AJ

Of the three made, this is the only Jumbo Deluxe known to exist. The original "moustache" bridge with the individual adjusters has been replaced.

came with a bone nut and nickel-plated individual Grover G-98 tuning machines. Neck sets were typically excellent, with plenty of saddle. Like most quality guitars, over the decades the Advanced Jumbos will most likely require a neck set, after everything stops moving and stretching.

The top and back are bound in white, as is the fingerboard, whose pearl inlays are cut into a distinctive diamonds-and-arrowheads symmetry. The peghead features the same pattern, though vertically; at the top is the company logo, in script and on a line parallel to the nut, in the same layout as its predecessor, the Jumbo. The pickguard is the same as the other Gibsons of the day, flame celluloid. During its life, few changes interfered with the near perfection of the AJs. One obvious change involved the sunburst, which on the 1936 AJ has a smaller middle, typical of all Gibson 'bursts of the day. By 1938 and 1939 the amber area had been expanded considerably.

If these words have failed to convince you of the pure magic that characterizes the Advanced Jumbo, play one. If you can't find an old specimen (and this is becoming increasingly likely), carefully take an AJ reissue off the rack and compare it with all you have played before. Tastes, of course, differ, but many professionals feel that the Gibson pre-War Advanced Jumbo is the best guitar ever designed for pure power, tone, clarity, and balance.

JUMBO DELUXE

It's primarily for the sake of thoroughness that the Jumbo Deluxe is mentioned, for this is a guitar that few are likely to see, ever, because only three are known to have been made, probably in 1938. It's likely that Gibson intended this guitar to fill a void between the J-35 and the J-55; probably all were built as prototypes, and certainly this model never entered production, for unknown reasons.

Although it could be honestly stated that fully one-third the total production run of the Jumbo Deluxe has been carefully examined, a more sober interpretation might be that the following remarks are based on a single instrument, one in the collection of Gibson authority Gary Burnette. Perhaps because this instrument served as a Gibson prototype, there are irregularities in construction, two of which are especially noticeable: its sides are hand-bent and non-symmetrical, and the round shoulders are not smoothly contoured.

Like other Jumbo models, the Deluxe has single-layer binding on the body, front and back. Other similarities include the all-over sunbursts (top, back, sides, neck), a mahogany V-shaped neck, a mahogany body with a spruce top, a 19-fret fingerboard with pearl dots, and a pearl "Gibson" in script on the peghead. Differences include a 4" soundhole, a more rounded lower bout, bracing identical to that of the J-55, and a see-through "moustache" bridge with individual adjusters like those found on SJ-200s of the day.

THE PRE-WAR JUMBO 55 (J-55): A SHORT BUT HAPPY LIFE

The J-55 was the last of four jumbo-body flat-tops offered by Gibson in the 1930s. (Not included are the two Roy Smeck autograph J-size Hawaiians and the Jumbo Deluxe, only three of which were produced.) The decade's genealogy is as follows: the Jumbo was introduced in 1934 and was replaced by the J-35 in 1936; the fancy Advanced Jumbo (with rosewood instead of mahogany) was offered from 1936 through 1939, when it was dropped; enter the Jumbo 55, which was to live from 1939 through 1942.

In its fifth year of existence, the jumbo body thus appeared in its fourth configuration, in the form of the J-55. When the fancy Advanced Jumbo with its rosewood back and sides was phased out, possibly because of increasing difficulty in getting Brazilian wood just before the outbreak of WW II, Gibson needed some flash in its lineup. The J-55, at only $55, was still fancier than the J-35, at $37.50. For comparison's sake, at that time the Martin D-18 and D-28 large-bodies sold for $65.00 and $100.00, respectively. Today, the D-18 and J-55 of similar vintage sell for about the same price.

The 1939 catalogue copy showed great expectations for the J-55: "You can feel as well as hear the deep, rich, full throatiness of the new Jumbo '55.' It will be used by many future artists of stage, radio, and screen and is ideal for voice accompaniment." The short production run kept the model from those many future artists, but it has indeed become a much-sought-after guitar more than a half-century later. The catalogue photo, in spite of heavy retouching, shows a typical beautiful round-shoulder jumbo of these well-chosen dimensions: 16" wide at the lower bout, 10 5/8" wide at the waist, 20 1/4" long, and 4 3/16" thick. The back, sides, and neck are of mahogany; the top is spruce, finished with what the advertising calls a "golden sunburst," which moves from dark

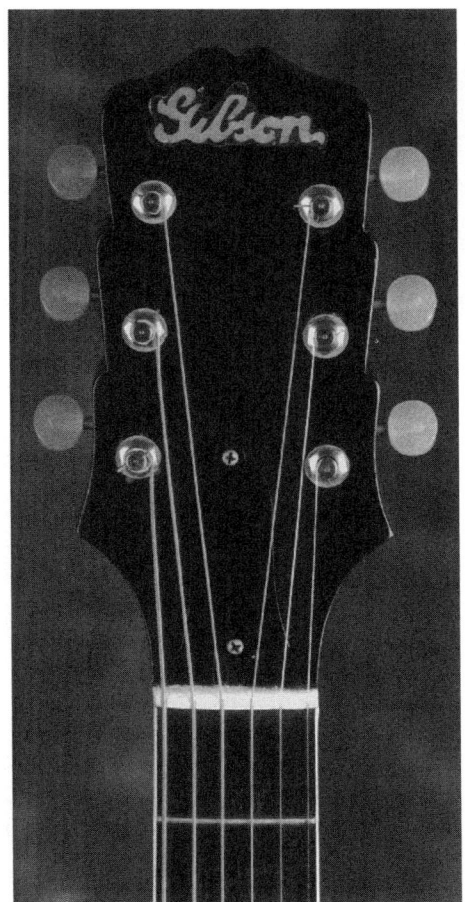

1940 Jumbo 55 with its "stairstep" peghead.

1940 J-55 with "moustache" bridge.

Extremely rare J-55, possibly the only one with rosewood back and sides. Note the smaller script on the peghead.

1940 J-55 with a non-"stair-step" peghead.

brown at the outside to an amber middle, all bound in white ivoroid, as were the back and fingerboard. The J-55 sunburst is less black than that on the J-35s of the day.

From the 1939 catalogue the prospective guitar owner could recognize a trio of changes from previous jumbos. In that year Gibson introduced three design features, innovations that the J-55 in fact shared with the SJ-100, a stripped-down version of the SJ-200. The first shared feature is the stair-step peghead (scallops on the peghead sides, increasing in width from top to bottom). This is a feature unique to Gibson and seen only on these two models, and for only a couple of years.

The second shared feature is an elongated "terraced" pickguard that stretches from just above the bridge top to within 2" or so of the body's top. The same "striped" or "flamed" celluloid typical of 1930s Gibsons is used on this 'guard.

The last of these features is an "open-moustache" bridge, similar to the famous style used on the SJ-200, though the one found on the J-55 and SJ-100 is shorter and narrower, with the bridge pins arranged in a semicircular pattern behind a bone saddle and the two pearl dots covering the bridge bolts. The J-55 bridge was, like the fingerboard, of "genuine polished coffeewood," which at a glance looks remarkably like ebony.

The company name is prominent on the peghead, pearl inlaid in the "fat" script, parallel to the nut, in the style of the SJ-200 and SJ-100. The '39 catalogue depicts the logo at an angle, a discrepancy attributable to photos that had been altered for emphasis and effect. Indeed, most catalogue pictures show this style of script, as well as oversized fingerboard dots and wider white binding. The tuners were originally individual Kluson tuners with amber buttons.

The one-piece mahogany neck on the J-55 has the baseball-bat shape and a round heel that decreased in size over the model's life. The 1939 J-55 was introduced with a bound coffeewood fingerboard. Another of the anomalies that make the Gibson history so colorful and interesting: there is at least one rosewood J-55 in existence from 1939. It might have been a prototype, but maybe a full batch of rosewood J-55s was made.

Changes in the J-55 came not long after its introduction. The first variation on the original J-55 design was to discontinue the stair-step peghead because of the difficulty and expense in making it. By 1941 the coffeewood "moustache" bridge was also dropped, in favor of a three-pointed, or bat-wing, design of Brazilian rosewood, whose three pearl dots covered bridge bolts, and whose bridge pins are in a straight line, not in an arc. Following suit, the SJ-100 switched to this bridge in 1941. (This bridge had been previously used on some of the Ray Whitley Recording King guitars, made by Gibson for Montgomery Ward—good instruments, but less expensive than the regular Gibson line.) Regarding bridges, apparently all or most 1939 and 1940 J-55s with the "moustache" bridges were constructed with the long scale, while the three-dot bridges went with the shorter version. It's possible that when Gibson switched to the less expensive bridge, they also substituted the J-35 neck and fingerboard.

Also changed in 1941 was the coffeewood fingerboard, to Brazilian rosewood. Some of the fingerboards in that year were from stock ordered by and fabricated for Cromwell guitars, a Gibson-made inexpensive line for another marketer. This fingerboard has a white strip running down the center and larger-than-usual pearl dots. This stripe is not commonly found on the J-35; probably Gibson underpriced this model and needed to find ways to manufacture it less expensively without raising the price too much. Using a previously-made neck would have helped. Gibson also started putting less expensive machine heads on their later J-55s.

Internally the J-55 is unique for a late-1930s Gibson. Its maple bridge pads are wider than in any other jumbos, no doubt because the bridges themselves became wider. Different also are the top braces of the shoulder area—they are slightly heavier and closer together, some scalloped and others not, like the other Jumbo models of the '30s. Originally the back braces were large, as on other earlier Jumbo models, but toward the end of the model's run these braces became tall and thin, which is consistent with the later J-35s, the J-45s, and the Southern Jumbos. The early J-55s have wood rib-reinforcement strips, and the later ones, fabric. All these variations followed the structural changes that Gibson made in that era.

The J-55 retailed for $68.25 in its last year of production. Its typical hardshell case from that era has a black, arched outside with an orange stripe around the lid, and a rich purple interior.

Though some reports allege that the J-55 was made as late as 1943, or even until the end of WW II, it's more likely that the J-35s and J-55s were discontinued in order to introduce the J-45 and Southern Jumbo, in 1942.

Gibson built this J-55 with Cromwell-style fingerboard and a bridge like those on Ray Whitley Recording King models.

Blues/ragtime fingerpicker Roy Book Binder with his Jumbo 55.

Records show the following numbers of J-55s were produced:

1939	55
1940	111
1941	145
1942	unknown

Apparently fewer than 400 J-55s were constructed, making it a rare and highly desired vintage model.

J-45 & ITS NATURAL TWIN, THE J-50

Surviving the 1930s hadn't been easy, but Gibson somehow managed, maintaining high quality throughout the decade and in fact introducing such models as the J-200, the J-35, and the Advanced Jumbo, exceptional instruments that bring very high prices on the vintage market more than half a century later. The '40s (or so

> "*I*'ll be frank with you—I sure do love my Gibson.
>
> I bought my Gibson used in October, 1964. It was a J-50 and I paid $50 for it. It's made somewhere between 1950 and 1955.
>
> I had quit playin' in 1946 and didn't pick up a guitar no more 'til '64. This rock 'n' roll and all that come up and there wasn't no demand for old folk music and the blues. 'Til I got discovered.
>
> What's special about the J-50 for me? It has better bass than a Martin. And the fretboard seems slimmer—you can go up and down the fretboard so much faster than on most other guitars."
>
> —John Jackson

Country blues artist John Jackson with his favorite guitar, an early 1950s J-50.

people thought) were sure to bring prosperity to Kalamazoo, for all those musicians who deferred their guitar purchases during the previous decade doubtless would spend their money once they got back to steady work. Dependable jobs came, all right, but only on the coattails of the War; the Great Depression had ended, but the cure was worse than the disease. And while numerous middle-aged men and women entered (or re-entered, in the case of the army of unemployed) the work force, millions of people in their twenties and thirties—people who in peacetime would have bought stringed instruments—were in the Armed Forces, home and abroad, in neither the mood nor the position to buy guitars or other non-necessities of life.

This loss of potential customers wasn't the only problem facing Gibson. The government in Washington looked at the company and saw what it sorely needed for the war effort—a trained work force with proven expertise in woodworking and electronics. Thus, 90% of Gibson's craftsmen were taken off instrument work and appropriated for military projects. There was, though, a silver lining: the 10% assigned to work on stringed instruments were the most experienced. At no other time in Gibson's history did they have such a select, experienced crew of builders. Guitars from that era prove this.

Although Gibson overcame these first two shortages caused by the War—customers and then employees—one that they had little control over remained. The shortage of quality raw materials, which even before World War II had been a nagging irritation, by 1942 had become a serious problem. Among the materials in short supply were rosewood for backs and sides, metal for truss rods and tuners, large mahogany planks for necks and end blocks, and red spruce in widths great enough for two-piece tops. As best it could, Gibson had to rely on stockpiled parts. The availability of these supplies dictated which instrument models would be deleted and which would be introduced, as well as the design, appearance, and construction of those additions. As the War progressed, Gibson stopped producing most electrics, banjos, mandolins, and Kalamazoo (their "budget" line) instruments. Their flat-tops suffered from these wartime conditions, too, as witnessed by the discontinuation of the SJ-100, the J-35, and the J-55 in 1942, and the ultra-fancy SJ-200 a year later.

In a letter to their retailers in 1943, Gibson announced that because of severe reductions in skilled workers and materials, changes had to be made. Truss rods would be eliminated, replaced by hardwood reinforcers; the brand and quality of tuners could not be guaranteed, and all would be of the "three-on-a-plate" design; and all guitars would be sunburst.

But these changes weren't all. Gibson was forced to reduce their guitar offerings to only six models, including two arch-tops and the following four flat-tops: the L-00, LG-2, Southern Jumbo, and J-45. In fact, already in 1942 the Southern Jumbo had supplanted the J-55, after its

"Banner" peghead of a 1942 J-45. The "Banner" was used from 1942 through 1946.

The 1942 J-45s had firestripe pickguards, multiple body-binding, and "Banner" pegheads. Some later 1942 J-45s were built without truss rods.

life of four years, while the J-35, after a seven-year run, had been replaced by the J-45.

The J-45 differed from the J-35 in minor ways only. The teardrop pickguard was one obvious change. Another was the lack of options in top finish—sunburst and only sunburst. Additionally, the peghead of the J-45 contrasted with its predecessor's in three ways: gone were the straight sides of the J-35 peghead, replaced by slight inward radiuses; gone too was the white silkscreened "Gibson" of the J-35, for the J-45 featured a fancier Gibson logo in gold silkscreened script; finally, the J-45, like all other flat-tops made from 1942 to 1946, was a "banner" model, proclaiming "ONLY A GIBSON IS GOOD ENOUGH."

These and other small differences notwithstanding, the J-45 was a collected progression of changes that Gibson would have used to modify the J-35, even if the new J-45 model hadn't been introduced. Some aspects of the J-45 were not changes per se but instead a solidification of design evolution. Baseball-bat necks replacing the "V-shape" of the 1930s, rounded heels, tall and thin back braces, and scalloped top braces are examples of modifications that the company would have incorporated in its flat-top, new model or not. The top bracing was strengthened slightly on the J-45, with an "X-brace" set 1" behind the soundhole at about a 102-degree angle. The excellent string action and bridge saddle height results from this forward and wide-spread "X-brace" in combination with a short scale and small bridge/bridge plate. Compare the J-45's characteristic rounded top bulge and substantial top area behind the bridge to long-scale guitars with "X-braces" set deeper back in order to begin understanding the rich, deep, warm sound of the J-45; and because sides and back are mahogany, the J-45 is well balanced, with a fat high-frequency response.

The body dimensions are as follows:

Lower bout	16 1/8"
Waist	10 9/16"
Front bout	11 5/8"
Rear side depth	4 7/8"
Front side depth	3 27/32"
Nut width	1 3/4"

The first J-45s, made in late 1942, feature pickguards in the new teardrop shape but of the flamed celluloid that had long before become a Gibson trademark. Within a year mock-tortoise shell had replaced the flame material. These first J-45s also had multiple binding on both top and back. Late in that year, because of War shortages, Gibson began constructing necks without truss rods. In a given batch some J-45s would have truss rods (no doubt from stockpiles), while others contained the ebony bar running the length of the neck.

By 1943 the situation apparently had worsened: from the factory came J-45s with maple necks, no doubt made from neck blanks set aside for electrics. Also, poplar was being substituted for mahogany neck blocks.

Problems Gibson faced in securing high-quality spruce are obvious in instruments of this era, for some tops are not book-matched, while others have four-piece tops rather than the usual two. The company decided that rather than use wide but mediocre spruce, two pieces per top, they would glue up four pieces of narrower but select spruce. This was a good decision and, judging from the beautiful tone of these instruments, one that dispels some of the myths about top construction

Doc Watson and neighbors, c. 1960. Left to right, Fiddling Fred Price, Jack Johnson, Tommy Moore (with ventriloquist's dummy), Doc playing a J-45, and Clint Howard with an LG-2.

Blues singer Rev. Robert Wilkins with his J-45, 1971.

1943 "Banner" J-45 with a factory "skunk stripe" painted in black lacquer.

Flame maple J-45, c. 1945. Gibson used this guitar to recreate the reissue "Banner" peghead.

and tonal response. The obvious drawback of a four-piece top—its appearance—was dealt with by Gibson's decision to offer only sunbursts during that period.

Also in 1943, Gibson began painting a narrow black stripe down the middle of some tops, either to draw attention away from the pieced edges of spruce or simply as decoration. These Gibsons are commonly referred to as "skunk stripe" guitars.

By 1944 Gibson necks again featured truss rods. The company's decision of two years earlier to save metal for the War effort had been mostly symbolic, in any case. The Gibson quality had suffered: incapable of being adjusted, these no-truss-rod necks often didn't have the proper neck straightness or relief needed for the best possible playability—a Gibson trademark.

From the mid-'40s into the early '50s mahogany tops were occasionally put on J-45s, resulting in guitars that sounded very good but of course very different from those with the standard spruce. By no means was this new to American guitars—for decades Martin had built guitars with tops of either Honduras or koa (Hawaiian) mahogany. It's likely that Gibson, due to a shortage of quality spruce, used exceptional mahogany backs, but as tops.

About 1945 Gibson started putting laminated maple backs and sides on J-45s. Toward the War's end, they also resorted to five-piece necks constructed of what appears to be maple sandwiching glued-up walnut strips. Whatever large planks they had stockpiled before the War doubtless had been consumed by this time, probably on their defense contracts, and they had been unable to get new wood supplies, especially Honduras mahogany and Brazilian rosewood. Some of these maple J-45s have beautiful curly grain, and all are finished in a dark walnut stain. Gibson probably diverted these backs and sides from their original destinations as arch-top guitars. As you would expect from the maple, these J-45s have a big and punchy sound.

The necks gradually became thinner from 1943 until 1945 or 1946. By 1945, as materials again became available, most necks reverted to mahogany, but some retain the poplar neck blocks. Sometime in 1946 the banner was dropped from the peghead, but the same gold silkscreened script was retained. A couple of years later the modern block script was introduced.

All these aforementioned changes may seem minor, but because of Gibson's failure to use serial

The Round-Shoulder Jumbos 59

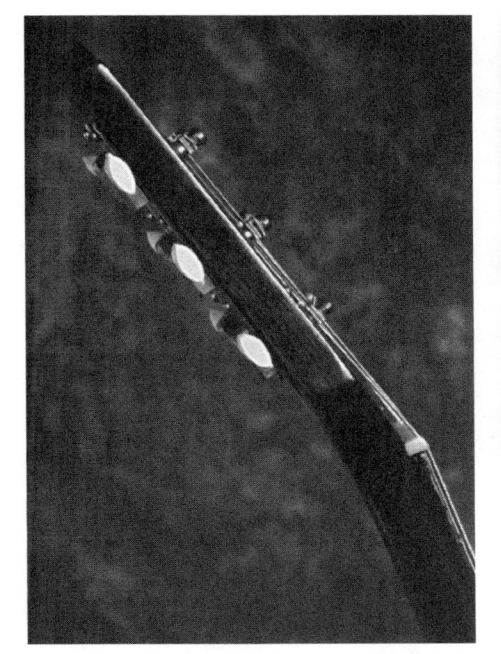

1948 J-50.

Tapered peghead of a 1950 J-45. The taper had disappeared on J-45s by c. 1953.

Early 1950s J-45, with three-on-a-plate enclosed Kluson Deluxe tuners.

numbers during the war they are crucial in attempting to date a J-45 of this period.

At War's end Gibson regrouped. In 1946 the fancy J-200 reappeared, in the company of a new model, the LG-3. Then in late 1947 came the introduction of the J-50, which was basically identical to the J-45 except for its natural finish and black/white purfling around the top. A few post-War J-45s with this purfling exist—in all probability they were intended as J-50s, but for whatever reasons the factory finishers decided to sunburst them.

In general, though, consistency marks the workmanship and specifications on all the 1940s J-45s, so much so that an instrument from 1942 was remarkably similar to one from the end of the decade. Significant changes didn't come until the early 1950s. Soon the top-belly bridge design replaced the tried-and-true rectangle. The new

1953 J-50 with teardrop pickguard and a 19-fret neck.

Singer/guitarist John Hiatt with his early '50s J-45.

bridge construction offered a little more resistance to the top bellying, without interfering with any vibration behind the bridge, a guitar top's most crucial area. A second change found in the early-'50s instruments is the absence of fabric side-supports. Perhaps it was at this time that Gibson began experimenting with laminated sides, or maybe the builders felt that the well-known stability of mahogany obviated any further strengthening. One certainty is that the spruce side-supports were used briefly.

In 1955 Gibson lengthened the fingerboard by adding a 20th fret. About that time, they also dropped the teardrop pickguard, replacing it with the style found on their J-185 model—with the point in the upper bout. Another change during this time was even more significant. The tall, scalloped top braces were phased out in favor of shorter, unscalloped braces that tapered slightly at the ends, resulting in a very light system. This alteration in braces was not unique to the J-45/J-50 models; rather, it was common to most company flat-tops of the time.

Before the 1950s ended, Gibson made three more changes on the J-45. Taking a page from its arch-tops, in 1956 Gibson offered an adjustable bridge saddle as an option, a move that proved popular with the consumers but that had the demerit of increasing the potential for adjustment abuse. And more to the point, the tone and volume suffered. In a less drastic change, beginning in 1959 the J-45/50 and all other flat-tops were offered only with the wide-crown frets that since have be-

> *"The second Gibson acoustic I owned was an early '50s J-45, with the bone saddle and a gorgeous sunburst. What a sound that mahogany guitar made!*
> *Now I own two Montana J-45s, great guitars that serve me beautifully and that compare favorably to the vintage models."*
> —*John Hiatt*

come a Gibson trademark. Finally, during the late 1950s Gibsons had an unusual three-tone sunburst top—from the outside, graduations of cremona brown, moving to reddish brown, and centered in amber. This sunburst was used until the cherry sunburst and the natural-top J-50s replaced it in about 1962. On the whole, J-45s of the 1950s were very well built and consistently of high quality, much like those of the previous decade.

As an omen of the many bad decisions that were to plague Gibson throughout this next decade, in the early 1960s the traditional bridge pads of solid maple were dropped on most models in favor of maple laminates. The earlier solid pads were .125" thick and 1 7/16" wide, while the oversized three-piece plywood pad measured .140" thick and 2¼" wide. The increase in dimensions was an attempt to stabilize the top around the bridge so that lightweight tops and braces could continue in use.

This jettisoning of a proven design—the solid maple pads—seems foolish now, but it should be kept in mind that good repair shops and qualified luthiers were in short supply in those days, and Gibson was looking for a bridge pad that wouldn't need replacement. These good intentions led to problems, though, for these plywood pads didn't have the tensile strength, the "give," that solid wood, and especially flat-sawn maple, has. Ironically enough, these new laminated pads turned out to be less durable than those they replaced, because of the glue lines breaking down from inflexibility.

Another problem involved the J-45 finish, in particular the popular cherry sunburst, which in 1962 replaced the more traditional brown 'burst. From mid-1964 through 1966 or so, many of these cherry sunbursts faded because of some natural instability in the red tint.

Numerous other changes made to the J-45s in the '60s should be mentioned:

1956 J-50, with large pickguard and a 20-fret neck.

Blues great Lightnin' Hopkins and his J-50.

- By the early 1960s: J-45s had a double soundhole purfling.
- By 1965: the pickguard had become thicker; J-45s (like other Gibson flat-tops) had switched to a 14-degree from a 17-degree peghead angle; the necks had become narrow and featured chrome-plated tuners.
- By 1966: a Gibson logo had been added to pickguards.
- 1968: the last year for the round-shoulder J-45, though, with much larger braces, a huge solid wood bridge pad and a bottom-belly bridge, this version differed greatly from that of 1967. (The 1969 square-shoulder J-45 is covered in a separate section.)

Gibson offered solid-color J-50s with white pick guards in 1968.

Jorma Kaukonen of Jefferson Airplane and Hot Tuna with his J-50.

> *"My first good guitar was a J-50, which I bought when I was still in high school. They were the best guitars for the money. Still are. I wish I still had that guitar. I just spent all day in the studio, and that's the model the lead guitarist was using. The J-50 is a wonderful studio guitar."*
> *—Emmylou Harris*

Some highly unusual J-45 hybrids were made during this period, but they are almost impossible to date more specifically. Because Michigan has such a preponderance of these one-of-a-kind instruments, it's possible that apprentices at the Gibson factory built guitars for themselves, mixing parts from then-current models with leftover parts from previous years—for example, long-scale necks with short-scale fingerboards, with the neck then meeting the body between the 13th and 14th frets. These numerous oddballs are interesting but impossible to classify neatly.

In 1984 the popular slope-shoulder J-45 was reinstated to coincide with Gibson's "90th Anniversary Acoustic series." These Nashville-built guitars had reverted to a "single-X" bracing system, using tall, thin top braces that were not scalloped but that tapered as they went toward the guitar sides. These lightly built flat-tops are quite good, but many suffered from problems resulting from too much humidity at the factory in Tennessee. (Part of the factory was climate controlled, but not all. The craftsmen found it nearly impossible to control guitar building with such quick changes in the area's climate.)

In a limited run, Gibson in 1985 produced exactly 90 J-45 "Celebrities," elaborate special issues

> *"When I was sixteen, two important events occurred: I got my driver's license and I got my first Gibson.*
> *The discovery of cars, girls, and Gibson flat-tops were so intertwined in my teen-age years that it is hard to say which is the more important."*
> *—Jorma Kaukonen*

that featured small but fancy mock-tortoise shell pickguards and rosewood backs and sides. Gibson took great pains in creating exceptional abalone decoration, with intricate inlays on the fingerboard and an extraordinarily fancy peghead of the company logo riding a fern inlay, reminiscent of the 1920s and 1930s F-5 mandolins.

In sum, the renowned J-45/J-50 slope-shoulder guitars occupy a prominent position in American music history. This famous model has been so widely used by famous folk and blues artists that few *haven't* played one at some point in their careers. Over the years, the J-45/J-50 flat-tops have surpassed the competition in offering excellence, quality, and affordability in a widely available guitar. And because so many of them were made (an average of 1,400 J-45s annually from 1948 to 1958, a conservative period for Gibson), an average musician can aspire to quality at a fair price.

In *Frets* magazine Leo Kottke gives the sort of free endorsement that a guitar company can only dream of: "The piece [guitar] I'm happiest with is that pre-War Gibson J-45. I love Gibsons, they're my favorite guitars. . . . Those old Gibsons have such a nice fat sound anyhow, it works real well. They cut through the microphone better, they cut through the pickup better, and I'm really happy with it."

THE SOUTHERN JUMBO (SJN, SJ COUNTRY-WESTERN)

According to Gibson legend, their sales representative for the states below the Mason-Dixon Line requested that the company build a flat-top just for the South; he felt that Gibson flat-tops were especially appreciated in that area and that a guitar specifically dedicated to the sweet old sunny South would be Gibson's tribute to Dixie, especially its great music and its greater musicians.

It was under these perhaps apocryphal circumstances that Gibson designed a fancy new model that it brought to market in 1942, along with another newcomer, the J-45, to replace the J-35 and J-55, which were being phased out. Of these two new guitars, Gibson gave this fancier one a name that evokes warmth, tradition, romance, and wistfulness—the Southerner Jumbo. Because it was the most expensive of Gibson's flat-top line of the day, the Southern Jumbo—its original name was quickly shortened to this affectionate form—received the best materials available, in spite of shortages of supplies due to the War. Further, though nearly 90% of Gibson's work force was taken from guitar production and put to work on war contracts, the 10% remaining were the company's seasoned, experienced craftsmen. The SJs built during the War are especially remarkable creations, given the inevitable difficulties and upheavals stemming from the conflict and from the changes in personnel.

Rare Southern Jumbo with back and sides of Brazilian rosewood.

Non-truss rod 1943 Southern Jumbo.

The Southern Jumbo and its fellow newcomer, the J-45, show signs of improvisation in their construction, as Gibson dealt with changes forced upon them by the War: necks of maple rather than the usual mahogany (many without truss rods), maple backs and sides (rather than mahogany), and poplar neck blocks.

In its detailing and personality, the original SJ stands apart from Gibson's preceding jumbo-body guitars, as well as its contemporary J-45. On the top is multiple binding (also used on the J-45, but only in 1942), while down the middle of the two-piece back runs a dark wooden stripe; the heel is capped with a white laminate; the rosewood bridge is characteristically of the bottom-belly design (with two pearl dots), though some are rectangular; a multiple-ring soundhole purfling is standard, as is the tiger-stripe celluloid pickguard in a teardrop shape; neck, sides, and back are of mahogany, with choice spruce on top; lastly, and perhaps most distinctively, twin parallelograms of inlaid pearl grace the unbound rosewood fingerboard. The "ONLY A GIBSON IS GOOD ENOUGH" banner on the peghead is not unique to the Southern Jumbo—instead, it is characteristically found on nearly all Gibson flat-tops built from 1942 to 1946. (It is said that Gibson dropped the peghead's banner logo because of a clever advertisement by Epiphone, a rival guitar company eventually bought out by Gibson, that turned the tables by stating in their ads, "When good enough isn't good enough.")

In addition to the standard mahogany versions, Gibson made an undetermined but small number of Brazilian rosewood SJs in 1942. All were from batch 910, probably the first Southern Jumbo group to be built. It's possible that these were a prototype grouping, though it's also possible that the guitar builders, unsure of future rosewood supplies, decided to use up the stores that they had on this beautiful new model. It's likely that the 900-series Factory Order Numbers (FON) were the 1942 prototypes for the Southern Jumbo, J-45, and LG-2. Probably when these guitars went into regular production, Gibson jumped to the 2000-series FON. This uncertainty arises because serial numbers were not used in the War years, when Gibson dramatically downsized its instrument production.

All these rosewoods feature the older, striped celluloid pickguard material but in the teardrop shape. This batch of guitars is gorgeous, and individual instruments command a handsome price on the vintage market.

Like the J-45, the Southern Jumbos by 1943 had begun using poplar neck blocks. Some still were without truss rods, and the mock-tortoise shell celluloid had replaced the tiger-stripe material in the pickguards. The bottom-belly bridges, exceptionally well sculptured in this period, predominated, but rectangular ones existed, too.

Variations in the SJ abound during the War years. Many during this time, and particularly in 1943, have a black "skunk stripe" lacquered down the center of the two-piece top. Numerous neck styles can be found from SJs of this era, too.

Although most have mahogany necks, some of laminated maple exist from the period. Like those of the J-45s, the necks on the SJs gradually grew thinner during this time, the trend continuing into the early 1950s. In sum, the "Banner" Southern Jumbos were constructed precisely and consistently well. They are superb vintage guitars, highly valued by country musicians and blues musicians alike.

In or around 1947 the next series of feature changes occurred. First was the addition of fingerboard binding. Following that change, the pearl twin-parallelogram fingerboard inlays were dropped for pearloid inlays of the same shape. "Pearloid" was a Gibson coinage for a synthetic, pearl-like material. In vintage-guitar circles, this synthetic concoction is referred to as "mother-of-toilet-seat," because of its similarity to a particular deluxe composition found in vintage bathrooms from the 1940s and 1950s. These man-made twin-parallelogram inlays first appeared just before the addition of fingerboard binding on the SJs.

By 1949, the Southern Jumbo had the new block script logo, in gold, on the peghead. Its bridge had also taken on the top-belly design.

> Non-truss rod 1943 Skunkstripe "Banner" Southern Jumbo. Gibson painted the stripe apparently for decoration only.
>
> By 1949 the Southern Jumbo had acquired a bound fingerboard and pearloid (artificial pearl) inlays.

In the early '50s the peghead that in lateral view tapered slightly from top to bottom became a uniform thickness. Apparently no other significant changes appeared until the mid-1950s. All SJs featured sunburst finishes until 1954, when a natural spruce top was offered. In about 1956, this natural Southern Jumbo was named the SJN as an option to the standard Southerner Jumbo. Also at this time the teardrop pickguard was dropped in favor of the longer style used on the J-185. In about 1955, the 19-fret fingerboard was changed to a 20-fret version.

In this same general time period Gibson dropped the top-bracing system that had been used since the introduction of this model, switching to the lower, non-scalloped bracing construction that became standard on most Gibson flat-tops of the mid-'50s. By 1956 or so the gold silkscreened "Gibson" was replaced by pearl, and the pearl "crown" logo was inlaid below it.

Before the original round-shoulder Southern Jumbo evolved into the square-shoulder shape, a couple of changes occurred. For example, in 1962 the natural-finish guitars were renamed, to the

> "*Dad bought my Southern Jumbo brand-new for me in 1953 at a music shop in Knoxville, Tennessee. I vividly remember that day. It was my first brand-new guitar. It's still one of the best-sounding guitars you'll find. "Wake Up, Little Suzie," "Bye Bye, Love" and many other songs were recorded with that guitar. I've still got it.*
>
> *I still like the Southern Jumbo to write with or just to play a little music around the house.*"
>
> —Don Everly

"SJN Country-Western." Appropriately enough, these latter guitars feature a rope edge around their beige ovoid label. Additionally, there are some late-1961 cherry sunburst Country-Westerns, but how rare they are is unclear.

Apparently, in late 1962 Gibson switched to the square-shoulder Southern Jumbo with the three-point pickguard. Most other construction issues and changes of that time parallel the similar alterations in the J-45 and J-50 models. The SJ in this new body shape was built through 1977, when production ceased.

The round-shoulder Southern Jumbo did not reappear until 1991, in the form of a Montana reissue of the revered "Banner" SJ. (The first few of these "Banner reissues," ironically enough, were bannerless, because the silkscreen was not ready

1953 Southern Jumbo. The original Kluson tuners with white buttons have been replaced.

> "*I'm still looking for a Southern Jumbo like the one Don Everly has. Most people assume it was a J-200 on the early Everly Brothers hits, but it was the SJ, usually tuned to open-G, and capoed at the 7th fret in the case of "Wake Up, Little Suzie." The Southern Jumbos have a wonderfully woody and percussive sound, one that's almost boxy in the best sense of the word.*"
>
> —Albert Lee

by the time the guitars were produced.) This reissue is discussed elsewhere in this book.

The original "Banner" Southern Jumbo was the most expensive Gibson flat-top of its day. Its warm and mellow tone are legendary.

J-25: GIBSON'S ANSWER TO OVATION

By early 1980 two serious and related problems faced the Gibson company: quality control and competition. The first problem wasn't really solved until the high-quality Gibson guitars started to come out of the Bozeman, Montana, factory in 1989; the second assault on the company name, though, was met head-on in the form of the J-25, a new, space-age guitar.

In addition to the usual competition from the Martin Guitar Company, Gibson had to confront a serious challenge from Guild, a well-run organization that had been around for less than two decades but whose quality instruments had cut into Gibson sales. Yet a third challenger was Ovation, like Guild a fledgling company, having been founded in 1967. While Guild became a competitive threat through exceptional quality control exhibited in its guitars of traditional design and construction, Ovation set off to explore new planets rather than new worlds. Its founder, who had designed for the aerospace industry, brought a new way of thinking to the guitar industry. The striking result was a unique guitar consisting of a parabola constructed of synthetic resins, with the body shape a shallower version of the old Neapolitan mandolin—the round-backed "potato bug." The sound of this innovative instrument was no more traditional than its design, and the Ovations appealed to a whole different group of players, for many and various reasons. When country-pop star Glen Campbell began to endorse Ovations in 1969, the company received considerable good press, and the sales figures climbed quickly.

Gibson paid attention, noting the existence of a new breed of guitar players who would not only tolerate but welcome synthetic instruments, ones that could be manufactured inexpensively, for the new guitars needed considerably less woodworking and no exotic woods. The new design had numerous attributes that Gibson would hope to imitate. The Ovations, for example, responded beautifully to a microphone: because of their lack of overtones, sustain, and bass response, they were excellent guitars to amplify loudly. Many stars of the stage used these guitars specifically because of this ease in miking. These round-backs also played well, looked attractively contemporary, and were low-maintenance instruments that traveled well on the road.

Thus, Gibson decided to build a guitar to garner its share of this same audience. The J-25 was introduced in 1984, as part of the Gibson "90th Anniversary Series," and was their least expensive guitar. From the front, the body looks like the traditional round-shoulder jumbo guitar with a radiused, laminated spruce top finished in a sunburst and featuring "single-X" bracing. The top binding is multiple, unusual in that it is the front, visible edge of the molded back, the top fitting down inside the concavity. Beneath this conventional-looking outward appearance lurk the innovations: specifically, a molded synthetic back, asymmetrical and made of ³⁄₁₆"-thick vacuum-formed ABS plastic.

"Gibson" in gold block script angles across the black peghead face, balanced by individual nickel tuners with pearloid keystone-style buttons (referred to by Gibson as "emerald-escent"). Typical of all 1984 Gibson flat-tops is a truss rod cover in black, bordered with white. On the mahogany neck measuring 1¹¹⁄₁₆" in width at the nut rests an Indian rosewood fingerboard of 20 frets, pearl position dots, and a 24¾" scale. Multiple purfling rings the soundhole, and translucent tortoise shell in the traditional teardrop shape forms the pickguard. Among all the 1984 flat-top models, only the J-25 uses the bottom-belly bridge like those Gibson favored throughout the 1970s and early 1980s. Because this was the first year of the return to the top-belly bridge, Gibson may very well have had lots of unused bottom bellies waiting to be employed on some model. The 1984 J-25 has a specially labeled "Gibson 90th Anniversary" insignia.

One-man-band Dr. Isiah Ross with his Southern Jumbo of 1960 vintage.

Considering its goals, Gibson succeeded well enough in the J-25—literally a bottom-of-the-line, synthetic-backed guitar with laminated spruce on top. The model was dropped in 1987, though, as Gibson continued to upgrade its whole line of guitars.

The Hawaiian Guitars

Chapter Four

The great Roy Smeck, "Wizard of the Strings," playing one of his numerous namesake models, late 1930s.

After WW I, when doughboys returned from faraway places with strange-sounding names, America (including rural America) was ready to accept a new, exotic sound in its music. Hawaiian bands took the country by storm, in the process popularizing Islands music and two instruments in particular, the ukulele and the Hawaiian steel guitar. While the ukulele long ago faded in popularity (Arthur Godfrey in the 1950s was its last well-known supporter), the unamplified steel guitar has retained its popularity in country music, in its original form as well as in its more famous successors—dobros, lap steels, and pedal steels. These latter three have played an essential part in creating the country sound, and each is clearly a variant of the Hawaiian steel guitar.

The steel slide guitar apparently was developed in the Islands at the latter part of the 19th century, often differing from the standard "Spanish" guitar only in having a raised nut that elevated the strings above the fingerboard a half-inch or so, thus allowing the slide to be moved smoothly up and down the strings. In the 1920s a number of bands featured this new Hawaiian style, including Darby and Tarleton, the Dixon Brothers, and Cliff Carlisle. This exposure, combined with numerous Hawaiian music studios that opened in the U. S., and especially on the West Coast, created a national craving for this exotic music and its new guitar sound. And Gibson certainly fostered this craving. Its 1928 catalogue contains this unattributed quotation of otherworldly connotations: "The music of the Hawaiians . . . weird and fascinating . . . is still in my ears. It haunts me waking and sleeping." The clincher came in the form of Jimmie Rodgers—country music's first superstar—who in 1928 began to feature Ellsworth T. Cozzens and other musicians playing what was then known as the Hawaiian steel guitar on numerous songs, including his "Blue Yodels" and his famous "Waiting for a Train." The nation had quickly acquired a yen for this novel musical genre.

Some guitar makers quickly brought out models to help feed this new national passion. The well-named Oahu Company in the 1920s cashed in by producing a guitar that was the standard Spanish style, except for images of palm trees and lagoons stenciled on sides and top. Gibson aided and abetted this fad by appealing, Madison Avenue-style, to that generation's hidden desires. "By organizing a group of acquaintances for ensemble playing in the Hawaiian style," the 1928 catalogue states, "you can have unlimited fun and quickly become the center of popularity in your locality. You will receive many more invitations than you will be able to accept." No truth-in-advertising in those days, apparently, or every lonely American would have bought Gibson Hawaiians, millions and millions of them. All such advertising hyperbole aside, the fact remains that Americans couldn't get enough of this Hawaiian dream, or the music. In those days, if you said you played guitar, the quick question would be, "Spanish or Hawaiian?" Not since then have the two styles been such equal rivals in popularity. Give a listen to *Hula Blues* (Rounder Records 1012) to get a good sense of this music's alluring qualities, or simply if the fantasy of grass skirts and the sound of breakers reaching the shore appeal to you, as they did to all America in the '20s.

BEGINNINGS: TRANSITIONAL HAWAIIAN STEEL GUITARS

Thus the major players entered the market, including Martin and of course Gibson, which jumped in around 1928. Gibson initially suggested that the best of both worlds—Spanish and Hawaiian—was available in a single, easily converted guitar:

> Formerly a great objection was that guitars made for steel playing could not be used for American or Spanish style. However, all Gibson guitars are so built that they can be quickly equipped for steel playing and as quickly changed back again, thus providing virtually two instruments in one.
>
> (1928 Gibson catalogue)

But as the company soon discovered, this two-in-one promise was more easily said than done. To cash in on the Hawaiian music craze while tooling up for "pure" Hawaiian guitars (those made specifically for that kind of music), in 1928 Gibson suggested that some of its flat-top Spanish guitars, three in particular, could be played effectively as steel guitars: "Gibson Guitars style L-0, L-1, and Nick Lucas Special are especially good for Hawaiian or steel playing. The name Gibson guarantees the quality." However, neither the catalogue illustration nor the description for each of the three varied from the parallel non-Hawaiian version, and the 1928 catalogue describes the "Hawaiian Special Style L-1" no differently from the standard L-1, making no mention of high nut or straight (non-offset) saddle. At that time, though, the company did offer hardware for converting Spanish guitars to the Hawaiian set-up, including finger picks, slide steels (bars), high nuts, and raised saddles. This jury-rigging of guitars was to be short-lived: fortunately, musicians had to wait only until the next year for the slide steel purebreds, in the form of the HG Series, to be offered to the public.

THE HG (HAWAIIAN GIBSON) SERIES: HG-24, HG-22, HG-20

Depending on which open-chord tuning the guitar players used, they ran the risk of damaging neck, bridge, and bracing when tuning up to Hawaiian pitch. Gibson's 1934 catalogue suggests both the regular A tuning (*E C# A E A E*) as well as the *E7th* (*E B G# E D E*). The string tension created by these no doubt damaged numerous instruments, especially those left in the high pitch for extended periods. Furthermore, the company in 1928 was redesigning their flat-tops, moving to larger, more lightly constructed guitars, ones especially susceptible to this sort of accidental damage. Fortunately for present-day lovers of Gibsons, the company in 1929 came out with three stronger Hawaiian guitars designed specifically to tolerate the extra tension resulting from those tunings that were pitched considerably higher than the standard Spanish *E A D G B E*. The three new Hawaiians advertised in the 1932 catalogue (in fact the only catalogue to mention them) were the HG-24, HG-22, and HG-20. The latter two models were built according to these dimensions: 14½" at the lower bout, 10 ⅜" at the upper, 9 ⅝" at the waist; a scale of 24 ¾"; a body depth of 4 ¼" at the rear and 3 ½" at the front. The larger model, the HG-24, ushered in Gibson's new "jumbo" shape.

All three models, referred to as "double-rimmed" guitars, contained an inner-rim baffle that not only offered extra top support but was designed to eliminate an overpowering bass response. Large and booming, they produced an unexpectedly powerful sound, in ways similar to that created by the National and the Dobro, fellow resonator guitars, but with decided overtones of wood rather than metal. The HG series never reached sales expectations, due primarily to the expense in construction stemming from the baffle and the four extra soundholes. More importantly, even after conversion for Spanish-style playing, the HGs couldn't produce a sound favorable to the buying public's ear.

The HG-24

This was Gibson's top-of-the-line Hawaiian, selling for $160 in 1932 ($35 more than the Nick Lucas model, the most expensive Spanish guitar) and offering a considerable increase in volume because of its new "jumbo" shape. Differences between the HG-24 and the contemporary Spanish guitars, except for the soundholes, were not readily apparent from the outside. The back and sides were Brazilian rosewood; the top, either sunburst or natural finish, was spruce; and the neck was crafted from Honduras mahogany, with an inner truss rod, dot or large pearl block inlays (some poorly done), and an elevated fingerboard extension that began at the twelfth fret. The rosewood bridge was a narrow rectangle with a flat-topped saddle parallel to the nut—a good set-up for playing with a slide. The peghead was inlaid with a mother-of-pearl fleur-de-lis, with "The Gibson" above it. The exterior was thus attractive but unremarkable. The considerable differences between the Hawaiian guitars and their Spanish counterparts lurked beneath the surface.

The novel construction that Gibson introduced on all of its HG models was the special inner baffle. This design, though often described as an inner-wall system, was in fact a true baffle: of mahogany, it followed the same shape as the sides and was glued to the top about 2" from them, from the top descending to about 1" from the back,

An HG-20, with internal baffles. HG stands for "Hawaiian Gibson."

leaving only that small area for the sound to pass through. The baffle system served two functions: it added rigidity to the top, for higher-tension tuning; and it broke up the low-end frequencies—a common problem in large-bodied acoustics that are played slide-steel style. Gibson diagnosed this problem well, for modern-day builders of resophonic guitars also feel that a sound-well inhibits the tone, while if nothing is used, unpleasant overtones result. Baffles solve the problem.

The guitar top's apertures consisted of a small round soundhole in the normal position, joined by four *f*-holes between the sides and baffle. The *f*-holes in the upper bout were relatively small, compared to those in the lower end. The round hole was inlaid black-and-white purfling, with the inside edge of the soundhole also bound.

The majority of players who complain about the HG's tone refer only to those guitars that have been converted to the Spanish style. When played in the Hawaiian style, these are among the best-sounding all-wood slide guitars ever made, especially the HG-20 and the HG-22.

The HG-22

Unlike its Spanish counterparts that used rosewood, the HG-22 featured "northern air-seasoned maple" for its back, sides, and internal chamber. The choice of woods for the HG makes sense, for Gibson purchased their maple locally, knowing that the colder Michigan climate and unlimited selection allowed for ample supplies of wood that produced excellent tone. The company did, however, occasionally substitute beech for maple on their lower-end instruments. In the first part of the 20th century a huge beech forest, spreading for hundreds of square miles, grew just north of Gibson's factory in Kalamazoo. Gibson no doubt put away huge amounts of beech during this period, when their buyers could pick and choose from such a selection.

Spruce finished in brown, with a small sunburst at the bridge, was used for the top, which featured the same soundholes configuration as the HG-24. Both the top and back were bound in white ivoroid. The Honduras mahogany neck, meeting the body at the fourteenth fret, contained a truss rod and a bound rosewood fingerboard with dot inlays. This guitar sold for $80 in 1932, a little more than the small-body L-2.

The HG-20

As an inexpensive version of the HG-22, the HG-20 lacked the sunburst finish, having instead a solid deep brown that approached black. Selling for $45.50 in 1932, nearly double the price of the L-00, it retained the soundholes arrangement of the other two models. Most if not all HG-20s have top binding and a white celluloid pickguard.

The rarity of the HG-24, HG-22, and HG-20 makes definitive statements about feature changes difficult. It is generally agreed that these three should be played in the style for which they were designed to be played—Hawaiian. Although most have been converted to Spanish over the years, the tonal results often have been disappointing.

Although these three HGs were absent in the 1933 Gibson catalogue, they may have been produced until the Roy Smeck Hawaiian models appeared in 1934. It wasn't until 1937 that Gibson reintroduced the small-bodied Hawaiian guitars, in the form of the HG-00 and the HG-Century models.

THE ROY SMECK HAWAIIAN GUITARS

In 1934 Gibson introduced the Jumbo, with sides the same shape as the earlier HG-24 Hawaiians, only deeper. The Jumbo was the company's first large-body flat-top meant for playing upright (in the Spanish style, as opposed to laptop or tabletop position) and had a 14-fret neck. This development of a large-body replacement to the HG series by using the same body as the Jumbo was a logical step on Gibson's part. Structurally, this new Hawaiian guitar that was marketed as the Roy Smeck series shared body dimensions with the Jumbo but used a 12-frets-to-the-body neck that was 2 ¼" wide at the nut, changes necessary to facilitate the use of a slide. Also, because of two fewer frets on the neck, the bridge and bracing were moved back on the body, and the angled bridge saddle paralleled the nut. This new Hawaiian was a well-balanced amalgam of the old and the new: while retaining the new Spanish-style Jumbo features, including the small, rectangular lacquered bridge, the V-shaped neck, and the Jumbo's body

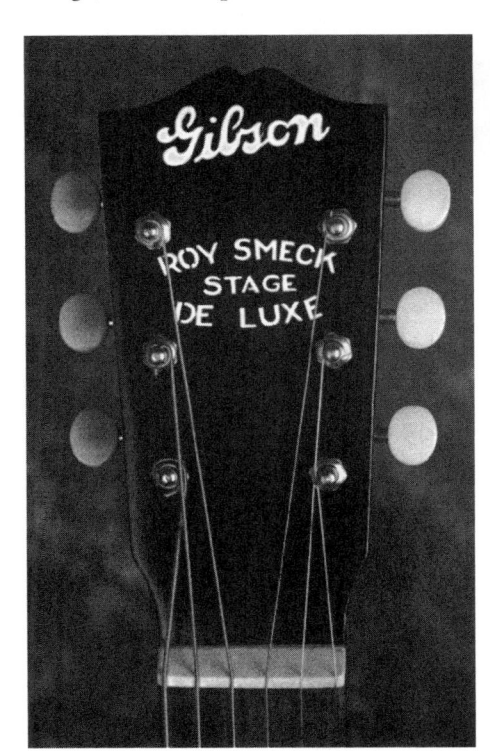

Peghead, 1936 Roy Smeck Stage DeLuxe.

trim, it underwent a minimum of changes—only those necessary for playing with a slide.

As part of their advertising campaign, for years Gibson had used endorsements by famous musicians. With Nick Lucas and Eddie Lang singing Gibson's praises in catalogues from as far back as the '20s, it was only natural that Roy Smeck had two models named after him. Why Roy Smeck? Gibson's 1934 catalogue says it best:

> Known the world over as "The Wizard of the Strings,"—an excellent description, for when Roy Smeck goes on the stage with his guitars, banjo, and ukulele he receives applause such as few acts merit—his recording and radio work receive equal enthusiasm. It is natural that in maintaining his reputation Mr. Smeck must have the finest guitar possible to produce—the Roy Smeck Hawaiian guitars are really duplicates of instruments made for Mr. Smeck to use personally in all his professional work.

Thus, what logically could be called an HG-Jumbo became known as either the Roy Smeck Stage DeLuxe or the Roy Smeck Radio Grande, depending on the woods and trim used in construction.

Stage DeLuxe

Selling for $50, $10 less than the Jumbo, the Stage DeLuxe had much in common with its Spanish cousin: Honduras mahogany back, sides, and neck; a spruce top; a rosewood fingerboard; identical instrument dimensions except, of course, for 12 frets to the body on the Stage DeLuxe and a raised nut and high bone saddle; a brown finish with a sunburst at the bridge; and white ivoroid purfling around the sides of the top, back, and soundhole. The Smeck models needed slightly more rugged bracing than the Jumbos and used only two tone bars, because of the bridge location. The pegheads clearly distinguish the two. The Jumbo features a solitary "Gibson," in pearl, while the Hawaiian adds a silkscreened "Roy Smeck Stage DeLuxe" under the company logo. Another distinction is that both Roy Smeck Hawaiians feature inlaid strips of ivoroid flush with the fingerboard instead of protruding frets. Further, the company catalogue refers to the "special construction and bracing" of its Roy Smeck models, though none is specified.

The Stage DeLuxe was produced at least through 1942. In the years between its introduction and demise, minor variations on the standard

Norman Blake's 1935 Roy Smeck Stage DeLuxe. A narrower, 12-frets-to-the-body neck replaces the original wide version intended for Hawaiian playing.

model came from Kalamazoo. For example, the neck inlay patterns were inconsistent (in 1935 the fingerboard was bound and fancier pearl inlays, similar to those on the Nick Lucas model, were used), some Stage DeLuxes had Radio Grande fittings, and at least one was made with the pearloid Century decor. During its time the Stage DeLuxe was not a big seller, perhaps only matching the sales figures of the Advanced Jumbos.

Radio Grande

Selling at $100 in 1934, the Radio Grande was exactly twice as expensive as the Stage DeLuxe and featured rosewood back and sides as well as a natural-finish spruce top. Its shaded neck presented a fingerboard bound with ivoroid and intricate pearl inlays, Nick Lucas-style. Under a script "Gibson" was "Radio Grande" silkscreened on the peghead. The Roy Smeck Radio Grande disappeared from

"My Roy Smeck has a wider, more developed tone than say a J-35, especially in the trebles. It's a great guitar."

— Norman Blake

1936 Roy Smeck Stage DeLuxe with original high nut.

Crazed finish of Norman Blake's Roy Smeck conversion.

the literature by 1937, but records indicate 24 were shipped that year, 1 in 1938, and 26 in 1939.

Over the years many of these wonderful, full-sounding Roy Smeck Hawaiian guitars were converted to regular-style (Spanish) guitar use. The conversion was relatively simple: the nuts and saddles were lowered, and the inlaid fret markers were replaced by true frets. Because the original saddles were straight, for slide playing, bass-side intonation became slightly off due to this conversion, but the result was a unique and big-sounding 12-fret Jumbo. If a player appreciates the dobro sound with the honeyed sound of wood rather than metal, a re-conversion to the original Hawaiian set-up is equally simple.

THE HG-00

Gibson's least expensive Hawaiian guitar at the time, the HG-00 was introduced in 1937 and shared all major features with its Spanish counterpart, the L-00; in fact, both cost $30 that year. Differences are only what should be expected in a slide guitar set-up: the HG-00 has a 12-frets-to-the-body neck, with the soundhole, bridge, and bracing set back, as on the early 12-fret versions of the L-0 and L-1. Bracing is also heavier on the HG-00 because of the extra tension that results from strings tuned to standard Hawaiian pitch. Also, the HG came with a high bone nut and a straight bone bridge saddle.

The guitar was mahogany finished deep red, except for a sunburst spruce top. Pearl fret markers, soundhole purfling, an ivoroid binding around the top and bottom edges of the binding, and an inlaid brown celluloid pickguard were the trim package. Kalamazoo produced at least a few of this model with a maple back and sides instead of mahogany. According to Gibson historian Julius Bellson, approximately 300 HG-00s were built.

A late 1930s HG-00. The original high nut for Hawaiian-style playing has been lowered.

THE HG-CENTURY

As with the HG-00, the Hawaiian Century entered the market in 1937, for a three-year run, and was Gibson's top-of-the-line model, selling for $60.00, compared to $50.00 for the Roy Smeck model and $30.00 for the HG-00. The HG-Century differed from the Spanish L-Century model predictably: it came with a 12-frets-to-the-body neck, a bridge and heavier bracing located further to the rear of the guitar, and the bridge saddle slotted straight in the bridge rather than offset. Other features paralleled those of the contemporary L-Century. Only 32 HG-Centuries were produced in 1937 and 1938. Any examples of this model with a 12-fret neck are Hawaiian originals that have undergone conversion.

In 1939 one ¾-size HG-Century was built, no doubt a custom order for some young musician whose mother and father envisioned the next Roy Smeck in their family.

Narrow-Waist Jumbos

Chapter Five

Super Jumbo 200 (J-200): Gibson's King of the Flat-Tops

SUPER JUMBO 200 (J-200): GIBSON'S KING OF THE FLAT-TOPS

It's doubtful that any guitar, flat-top or archtop, acoustic or electric, or any combination of same, can surpass the Super Jumbo 200 in distinctiveness of appearance. To those who grew up watching double features of singing cowboys at the thousands of neighborhood Bijou theaters nationwide, this striking guitar was a close third place among things-you-remember from the Saturday matinee, right after the white-hatted handsome hero and his college-graduate horse (of course); this guitar, at least to little boys, finished sunsets ahead of the cowboy's sweetheart (a distant fourth place), no matter how wholesome or beautiful the town's schoolmistress might have been. And to those lucky little buckaroos who loved music, the Ray Whitleys, the Johnny Mack Browns, the Rex Allens, and the Jimmy Wakelys—all cowboy crooners who shared the Silver Screen with barnyards of cowpokes named Slim or Tex or Kid—were held in even greater awe by dint of their unmistakable guitars. No Hollywood cowboy hero would be caught dead (figuratively speaking) at round-up time without his Super Jumbo 200. Accompanying the authentic voice of a Gene Autry or another horse opera heartthrob, this Gibson helped create romantic music of a Golden West that never was, warming the campfire and bunkhouse with tales of tumbleweed and songs of sagebrush. Of course, not all cowboys played the Super Jumbo 200. But they should have. It was this model that stood out among the herds of others. Simply put, this unique guitar was and is a giant among jumbos. The SJ-200 was destined to become more than a guitar—it became a cowboy icon.

Now, after the two-horse chase scene, cut to the present. Emmylou Harris, a sometime cowgirl and a full-time superstar in at least three genres of music—country, folk, and rock—speaks about this guitar:

> The J-200 has a unique place in musical history, bridging the gap in all different kinds of music, from western to blues to folk to rock to country. It's sturdy and yet so very musical, a guitar tonally unique, big, and absolutely beautiful. To me, this guitar represents the best of American art, and in some ways the J-200 transcends art, although in a sense it's only a tool. The J-200 is my guitar of choice. It has such a distinctive sound, feel, and look. It is simply a thing of beauty—an American original with its shape and appearance. Nothing else even comes close.

Emmylou is by no means alone among well-known performers who have chosen the Super

Emmylou Harris performing at the Ryman Auditorium in Nashville. Her 1960s J-200 belonged to Gram Parsons.

> "*My main road guitar is a 1960s J-200 that belonged to Gram Parsons. Sentimentally speaking, it is the most valuable thing that I own, and it is also my best stage guitar. I bought it in pieces from Nancy Parsons and had it rebuilt. I really wanted it because it was Gram's guitar. It has the real narrow neck that works so well for me that I had Gibson copy it for the custom J-200 I ordered from them.*"
> —*Emmylou Harris*

Jumbo 200 (a.k.a. the Super Jumbo, the SJ-200, or the J-200, depending on which step of the model's evolution over the last half-century you're referring to). The following constitutes only a partial list of stars who have played or currently play J-200s: Eric Andersen, Eddy Arnold, Gene Autry, Clint Black, Elton Britt, Garth Brooks, Johnny Cash, Mark Collie, Ray Corrigan, David Crosby, Rev. Gary Davis, Neil Diamond, Little Jimmy Dickens, Bob Dylan, Dave Dudley, Ike Everly, The Everly Brothers, Lefty Frizzell, Vince Gill, "Ranger Doug," Hawkshaw Hawkins, Bobby Hill, Chris Hillman, Buddy Holly, Pee Wee King, Willy Lamothe, Albert Lee, Melba Montgomery, Ricky Nelson, Gram Parsons, Elvis Presley, John Prine, Jim Reeves, Tex Ritter, Roy Rogers, Bob Seger, Red Sovine, Cat Stevens, Stephen Stills, Pam Tillis, Dave Van Ronk, Townes Van Zandt, Porter Wagoner, Jimmy Wakely, Slim Whitman, The Wilburn Brothers, Ray Whitley, and the York Brothers. The allure of the Super Jumbo 200 indeed ranges far and wide, touching rock, pop, blues, gospel, country, folk, hillbilly, and of course cowboy (as in country-*western*).

Ray Whitley, the penultimate on the above list, was the prime mover behind the creation of this famous model. One of the first singing cowboy movie stars, Ray in the mid-'30s first gained fame by co-hosting the WHN Barn Dance (with Tex Ritter) in The Big Apple, moving from New York to Hollywood and RKO Studios, where he made a score of musical shorts under his own name, as well as acting as sidekick to the better-known Tim Holt. In 1937, when Ray was appearing as a rhinestone cowboy at the annual rodeo in New York City's Madison Square Garden, he related his ideas for a fancy flat-top to Guy Hart of the Gibson Company. Ray suggested something ultra-fancy and, of course, ultra-country, given his profession and interests. Hart followed up on the idea, eventually bringing Whitley to the Gibson headquarters in Kalamazoo, where he and company designers planned the guitar that was to become not so much a fancy flat-top as *the* fancy flat-top. Ray recommended that Gibson build a better-looking, deeper-sounding guitar than anything on the market. Gibson responded that they would build Ray the guitar of his dreams. And they did.

The results were a landmark in the evolution of the acoustic flat-top. In December 1937 Gibson presented him with the world's first Super Jumbo, honoring the musician who had guided its construction step by step.

1938 SJ-200 "moustache" bridge.

Ray Whitley's dream guitar and prototype of a long line of Jumbo 200s was a sunburst rosewood flat-top shaped much like a Gibson L-5, one of the company's fanciest, most expensive arch-tops of the day, though ⅛" narrower in the lower bout than the 17"-wide L-5. Soon the Jumbos shared dimensions with the L-5 and borrowed the narrow neck of that model. A pearl inlay on the peghead proclaimed "CUSTOM MADE FOR RAY WHITLEY," while his engraved initials highlighted the truss rod cover. The large pearl rectangles inlaid in the fingerboard feature engraved western scenes. The huge pickguard of mottled and multiple-bound celluloid had been borrowed from the Super 400, Gibson's fanciest arch-top that had been introduced only three years earlier.

The remarkable, one-of-a-kind bridge, forever after known as the "moustache" design, had four ribbons of pearl inlaid behind the bone saddle kept in the straight-through (exposed at both ends) slot. Befitting its rank at the top of the flat-tops, the SJ-200 was bound with nine layers of alternating white/black celluloid on the body, both front and back; likewise, the peghead and fingerboard were fancily bound.

A certificate presented to Whitley by Gibson attested that his new guitar was the finest ever built by the company. Two other custom-built SJ-200s soon were produced for Ray, both 12-frets-to-the-body versions rather than the 14 of the prototype. According to guitar expert Ranger Doug of Opry stars Riders in the Sky, one of these 12-fret SJ-200s was stolen, and the other burned in an automobile fire. Whitley fortunately and generously donated the lone survivor to the Country Music Hall of Fame and Museum in Nashville in 1974. Although this beautiful and

Cowboy crooner Jimmy Wakely with his custom pre-War SJ-200.

Singing and yodeling cowboy Ranger Doug, of Grand Ole Opry performers Riders in the Sky, with his 1938 SJ-200.

historic guitar alone is worth the price of admission, complementing it is the famous rose-inlaid, black J-200 of Emmylou Harris; as a replacement, Gibson presented Emmylou with a near duplicate.

Through the influence of Ray Whitley, many stars of the singing-cowboy mold either bought the standard SJ-200s or placed custom orders for modified versions of the model. Gene Autry, for example, in the minds of many the best musical cowboy of them all, ordered a 12-fret version that took the western motif to the limit: a simulated lariat binding looped around the top's periphery, while horse-and-rider pearl inlays westernized both the peghead and fingerboard, where his name was spelled out—also in pearl, of course.

Country Music Hall of Famer Tex Ritter ordered two fancy 12-fret models, one sunburst and the other natural; Roy Rogers, who vied with Gene Autry for the "King of The Cowboys" title, also played his custom SJ-200 (called the "King of the Flat-Tops" in Gibson's advertising); Jimmy Wakely, graced with the best natural voice of all the cowboy crooners, played an uncommonly standard J-200 made for him, though with his name engraved in the pickguard. Other guitar models, whether made by a rival company or by Gibson itself, soon seemed tediously ordinary to any self-respecting Hollywood cowboy. The symbols of the motion-picture Old West had become the Stetson, the Colts, and the Super Jumbo 200.

For years a story of the granddaddy of all J-200s—one that predates Ray Whitley's—has circulated among vintage-guitar lovers. According to this piece of apocrypha, prior to 1935 a prototype was built for Joe Wolverton, a highly accomplished professional musician of the '30s and '40s. While there's no doubt that Wolverton owned and regularly played an early Super Jumbo 200 (numerous photographs, as well as the word of Joe himself, prove this), the date of this instrument is the matter in question. Ray Whitley's guitar, on the other hand, is solidly documented. Wolverton's in fact seems to be only a very early production model, possibly from early 1938, but definitely postdating Whitley's.

In the same vein, some vintage dealers have advertised SJ-200s of a 1937 vintage (and some even a 1936 provenance). The fact: after the Ray

Whitley original, delivered to him in December of 1937, none was shipped until 1938.

These regular-production SJ-200s that began leaving the Kalamazoo factory in 1938, though differing from Whitley's in particulars, were things of beauty. Let the 1938 Gibson catalogue supply the salients:

Super Jumbo

SIZE: Super Jumbo—16 7/8" wide, 21" long, and 4 1/2" deep.

WOODS: Finest eastern spruce top; beautifully figured rosewood back and rim; curly maple neck; ebony fingerboard.

FINISH: Rich Cremona brown top with golden sunburst; back and rims in natural rosewood, highly polished to bring out figure of wood; neck finished in chocolate brown.

FITTINGS: Gold-plated, individual machine heads, new design ebony bridge with individual adjustable bearing for each string; large inlaid brown celluloid fingerrest; white bone nut; side position marks; white end pin; gold plated brackets for holding neck cord to end pin and peghead.

Price $200.00

In a footnote the catalogue adds, probably for the benefit of aspiring cowboys and cowgirls, that a "personal guitar—[with] your own name and special decorations etched on pearl inlays in fingerboard" was available for an additional $50.00.

Some additional information should supplement the catalogue copy: the huge pickguard, with an outward point on the upper bout, featured a flowers-and-vines decoration in relief and was Gibson's first foray into pickguard engraving, an art the company maintained right through the Dove and Hummingbird models; the large and elaborate fingerboard inlays, in pearl, were of the "cloud" design (sometimes called "crest") and are unique to the SJ-200 family; most of these early rosewood models have a bottom-pointed fingerboard, though not all.

The 1938 catalogue was the first to mention this new model, referring to it only as the Super Jumbo. By 1939 Gibson had renamed it the Super

> In 1954 the SJ-200 still featured a stripe around the pickguard edge.
>
> 1938 SJ-200 with rosewood back and sides.
>
> "The J-200 is really a classic, sounding like no other guitar. It must be a great design because I've not heard a bad one made in recent years."
> —Albert Lee

> **C**ountry blues singer "Hacksaw" Harney playing a J-200 at the 1971 National Folk Festival in Vienna, Virginia.
>
> 1954 J-200 with tapered peghead. Other models had lost their taper by that time.

Jumbo 200, the number added to reflect the guitar's list price, had widened the lower bout to 17", and had included a marquetry strip, a "zipper," down the center of the back. The 1940s version offered a one-piece bone saddle instead of the previous six-piece design.

In 1941 Gibson switched to rosewood fingerboards and bridges. The last year for the "pre-War" SJ-200s was probably 1942, though there are claims that some were made after that, right through the war years. If indeed any were made during that period, they were strictly special-order. Best indications are that approximately 100 pre-War SJ-200s were built.

The top-bracing pattern of the earliest rosewood SJ-200s was a wide-angled "double-X," a system with twin tone bars glued transversely. The main "X," in the lower bout, forms a radical 128-degree angle and approaches to within ⅞" of the soundhole. The "X-brace" of the upper bout, approximately the same angle, crosses under the fingerboard tongue ¾" from the soundhole's front. This particular bracing pattern offers excellent potential for tonal balance and a richness of sound. Such a large body might otherwise be too bottom-end-heavy and rumbly. The bracing design was superseded by a fairly standard "single-X," either in 1942 or immediately after the War. However, by 1952 the "double-X" pattern with transverse tone bars was reinstituted, to remain for many years.

After WW II, when supplies and expert personnel were no longer so scarce, Gibson resumed full production of the SJ-200. The 1947 catalogue for the first time referred to this model as the J-200, although their labels continued to read "SJ-200" into the early '50s, after which the simple "J-200" ruled. Thus, in less than ten years of life this model had already been given three names: Super Jumbo (1938), Super Jumbo 200 (1939), and the SJ-200/J-200 combination (from 1947 to the present, though with an additional N designator for natural finish).

The first post-War models (1946), like all standard versions since, substituted maple for back and sides, in place of the original rosewood (though at least two pre-War maple versions were made). In 1948 two obvious changes were made: a natural finish was offered (the J-200N), and the pegheads became single-bound.

By the late 1940s, in one step of a gradual trend, the body depth was increased from 4½" to

4¾". By 1952, this dimension was again changed, to 4⅞", and some built in the mid-1960s measure a full 5".

About mid-1955, Gibson changed the famous pickguard on the J-200, though slightly—the etched stripe around the edge of the 'guard was removed and the pickguard material was changed to a more transparent, swirly celluloid.

The J-200 rested relatively unchanged until 1959, when the model featured Grover tuning machines and the large, crown-head frets currently in use. Throughout the '50s the "King of the Flat-Tops" was housed in a hardshell case with a lining of either plush pink or brown flannel.

By 1960 the J-200 had changed to an adjustable bridge, which underwent further alteration in the early '60s, when it was changed to the "closed moustache" type with a "Tune-O-Matic" saddle. (The "cutout" effect was simulated with pearl inlays to represent the voids.) The four pearl-inlaid ribbons that had been used since Ray Whitley's original were dropped, and the pins were repositioned, imitating the bottom cutaway of the bridge. Pearl inlays appeared in the handlebars of the closed bridge, replacing the four ribbons. Additional changes included a much larger one-piece neck block that wrapped around under the fingerboard extension and a larger maple bridge pad.

The most unusual change was the addition of a large, suspended wooden brace located under the top, between the bridge and the soundhole, fastened into a special side bracket. In the middle of the brace is a threaded rod with a large, flat metal end screwed to the top, presumably to keep the front of the bridge from sinking.

There were actually two versions of this brace: the one described above was designed by Walter Fuller, a Gibson manager and guitar demonstrator, while the other pushed up behind the bridge via a threaded anchor. This one was referred to as the Snyder version, named after Hartford Snyder, who worked in the plant in Kalamazoo. Both versions did their job—too well, in fact, killing tone and volume in the process. Many of these braces by now have been removed: their owners simply needed to cut them in two with a small saw and then remove them by hand.

Late 1955 natural finish J-200. Note pickguard changes from the 1954 model.

Versatile guitar-stylist Mance Lipscomb with his late 1960s J-200. Lipscomb didn't record until he was 65.

Country Music Hall of Fame member Little Jimmy Dickens with his 1956 J-200. This guitar was chosen at the Kalamazoo factory by country star Billy Grammer, who gave it to Dickens in 1957.

Unique 1956 J-200 with Super 400 neck and rosewood back and sides.

Two more design changes made in the 1960s should be mentioned. First, in 1963 Gibson switched to tuning machines with triangular metal buttons (though by 1968 they had returned to the standard gold-plated Grover Rotomatics). Also, at about the same time the neck that in the '50s had been a three-piece laminate—two pieces of maple sandwiching a rosewood center strip—was changed to a five-piece and narrowed in the process, following the lead of the other Gibson necks of that era. By the mid-'60s, the necks had become even more slim, like an electric's neck, offering greater freedom in making tight chords. The J-200 of this period came in a black hardshell case with yellow plush lining.

In the 1970s Gibson made numerous alterations to the J-200. Probably the most noticeable involved the bridge, which no longer bore any resemblance to the beautiful "moustache" design that had prevailed since 1937. This new, sculpted bridge looked more like a bat/butterfly hybrid in flight, with two pearl inlaid curlicues looking like cat whiskers. This "improved" bridge was identical to that used on the Dove model at the time, though with different inlays and made of rosewood rather than ebony.

This was a very different bridge. Being so much thinner and lighter than its "moustache" predecessor, it was prone to splitting, particularly at the front treble side of the saddle. Metal screws, notorious for causing splits, were not used on this bridge. Instead, a fiber insert to avoid splitting at the pins was incorporated into some of them.

In yet another change in the bracing pattern, Gibson in 1971 reverted to a "double-X" system, employing bulky braces on the tops of many models including the J-200. In place of the usual tone bars is another "X" with a large maple plywood bridge pad fitting tightly in the diamond-shaped area between the bottom of the upper "X" and the top of the one beneath. Not only does this "double-X" pattern restrict the top's acoustics, it results in structural unsoundness: the bridge pad, because of its length, narrowness, and inflexibility, has an unfortunate tendency to loosen up. When it does, the problem is compounded, because the four braces surrounding the bridge pad make its extrication difficult.

Two other models, both offshoots of the basic J-200, came out of the Kalamazoo factory in that decade. The J-250R, produced from about 1970 to 1978, was a standard-issue J-200, but with rosewood back and sides.

1968 J-200 with closed (non-cutout) "moustache" bridge typical of that era.

Rear view of 1956 J-200 custom.

The second model, the J-300 Artist, proved a more interesting variation, although it lasted only a year after its introduction in 1970. This striking guitar, also with rosewood sides and back, differs visually with its delicate, pearl fleurs-de-lis gracing each side of the bridge, the lower bout of the pickguard, and the peghead. Sadly, this J-200 upgrade sold too poorly to justify its existence.

In sum, Gibson went to different construction methods in the 1970s, some sounder than others, due primarily to the need for producing larger numbers of guitars. The folk boom had hit full force, causing the demand for flat-tops to reach an all-time high. In retrospect, the Gibson company itself acknowledges that not all innovations and other changes of that decade were necessarily conducive to good guitars nor subject to quality control.

The 1980s signified a return to the basics and to the construction techniques that had produced such fine guitars in the late '40s and '50s. In 1984, to celebrate their 90th anniversary, Gibson redesigned the J-200, returning to the basic design of the highly successful 1950s J-200.

In preparation for production Gibson's Abe Wechter and Tim Shaw visited Elderly Instruments in Lansing, Michigan, to study a vintage J-200 that would serve as their model. Gibson's having to consult a privately owned J-200 says a lot about the difficult times that the company had gone through. It's surprising that a "Gibson Collection" consisting of one of each model and of each option, owned by the company, didn't exist.

The bracing on these Nashville-made J-200s was different from that of any previous J-200. The tall and thin top bracing, tapered towards each end, overall was refreshingly light compared to the hulking versions of the 1970s. The 100-degree "X-brace" was positioned slightly more than 1" from the soundhole. To compensate for such a huge belly area on a guitar this size, the designers borrowed a concept from the first Gibson Jumbos, adding a third tone bar to keep the belly relatively stable. A J-200 with much-improved tone was born.

Blues and ragtime star Rev. Gary Davis with his J-200.

> "I originally started playing J-200s for their tone and playability, but I soon fell in love with their unique look.
>
> I own quite a few J-200s. I'm a rhythm player, and I think that they are the best rhythm guitar available. But they're really good for playing lead, too.
>
> My first J-200 had belonged to Joe Walsh of the Eagles. It was a 1950s sunburst with a factory pickup. I wasn't even looking for a guitar, but I played one chord on it and bought it. A great guitar—I used it on a lot of recording sessions.
>
> All great guitars are fragile, but the J-200 is sturdy enough to be taken on the road. I won't travel with anything else. I tried taking a lesser guitar on the road with me, but I felt like I was shortchanging my audience and myself. The feel and sound of my guitar on stage is essential to my performance. I sing off my guitar, and it is part of my song and me.
>
> My guitars all have different personalities that change as I use them. They become family to me."
>
> —Emmylou Harris

The "open moustache" bridge reappeared, with minor changes: it was not as skillfully cut as the earlier ones and was missing the top pair of ribbons, presumably to allow the saddle to be moved back further, for intonation purposes, and to relocate the bridge pins closer to the saddle. Another visual change involved the sunburst finish, which had more of a hand-rubbed look than did the 1970s sprayed 'bursts.

All in all these 90th Anniversary instruments were clear signs that Gibson had solved the serious problems of the previous 15 years or so and were again living up to their famous name. Many of these J-200s are very fine guitars.

In another clear sign of progress, Abe Wechter of Gibson's custom shop built a J-200 Elite in 1984 for well-known folksinger John Denver. This was to become the prototype for the J-200 Celebrity, which was introduced in 1985 with rosewood back and sides. This new variation also featured a smaller yet fancy pickguard, intricate fingerboard inlays, and on the peghead a fern inlay like those on the 1920s F-5 mandolins. In 1986 the traditional large pickguard had been restored. However, by 1987 the J-200 Celebrity had been deleted from the Gibson line with few having been built, due to a combination of low sales and production slowed by excessive humidity in the Nashville factory.

Today's J-200s are made at the Gibson plant in Bozeman, Montana, and are the same high quality as the best ever built. The J-200's dramatic beauty, booming resonance, and penetrating carrying power have again made this famous model a much-in-demand guitar, especially among those performers who require the ultimate in a stage guitar. Over the decades Gibson catalogues have accurately referred to the Super Jumbo/SJ 200/J-200 model as "King of the Flat-Tops."

> The SJ-100 was traditionally thought of as a country guitar, but Lonnie Johnson used his for playing the blues. Johnson influenced everyone from Robert Johnson to B. B. King.
>
> 1940 SJ-100 with "moustache" bridge.

SUPER JUMBO 100: AN ECONOMICAL SJ-200

In 1939 Gibson introduced two large guitars in great demand on the vintage market. They shared numerous features, including mahogany backs and sides, "moustache" bridges, bound fingerboards with pearl dot inlays, unusual stair-step pegheads, and pickguards of a new shape. One of these newcomers was the J-55, a $55 fancy version of the J-35; the Super Jumbo 100, constructed with the same dimensions as the Super Jumbo 200 but at $100 costing half as much, was the second.

The 1939 catalogue states that the SJ-100 "is an instrument that never fails to bring forth superlative praise from those desiring a deep, brilliant tone guitar at a price considerably below the top." By top, Gibson means the SJ-200, whose body dimensions were identical to those of its half-price relative: a lower bout 17" wide, a body length of 21", and a body depth of 4 ½". Although only with great difficulty could someone confuse these two models, it's as if Gibson took pains in adding individualistic details to the SJ-100 to give it a separate personality and to distance it from the SJ-200.

The stair-step peghead is the model's most distinctive feature, one that was shared only with the J-55 among production-line guitars in Gibson's history. The shoulder-shape pickguard of mock-tortoise shell celluloid was another distinguishing feature, though it, too, was shared with the J-55 of the day. The "moustache" bridge differed from that of the SJ-200 only in having less trim (two dots of inlaid pearl covering the bridge bolts, as opposed to an additional four ribbons of pearl on the more expensive model); characteristics in common include white bridge pins in an arc and a saddle of individually adjustable "bearings."

For a model intended as a stripped-down version of the SJ-200, the SJ-100 was an attractive, high-quality instrument. In woods it featured a select spruce top, a mahogany back and sides, a marquetry backseam, a curly maple neck, and ebony for the bridge and fingerboard, which had a pointed end, simple inlays, and a long scale of almost 26". The "single-X" system with angled tone bars formed the bracing. A dark-brown mahogany sunburst was the only finish available.

A pearl "Gibson" in the old script was inlaid straight across the unbound peghead that featured individual tuners—the nickel-plated Kluson "seal-fast" design with butterfly buttons. The three-ply top binding consisted of white/black/white strips, while the back and fingerboard were simple white celluloid; seven-ply binding alternated black and white as elaborate soundhole purfling.

Of its three most distinctive features, by 1941 only the shoulder-shape pickguard remained. The stair-step peghead had been replaced by the less expensive, traditional Gibson shape, and the butterfly tuners were supplanted by round buttons. The "moustache" bridge, which had been costly to produce because of its cutouts, was dropped in favor of a rosewood "flying bat" shape found on the J-55s and some contemporary Ray Whitley Recording Kings, Gibson-made budget guitars produced for Montgomery Ward; this bridge incorporated a one-piece, non-adjustable saddle. The fingerboard was changed to rosewood from ebony at this time. The price had increased from $100 to $125 by September 1941; a month later the list was $131.25.

The cases for the SJ-100 of the time were both hardshell. The more expensive one, at $28, was covered with heavy waterproof "aeroplane cloth," with sturdier luggage catches and plush silk lining. The other, a three-ply hardshell with a heavy imitation black leather cover and purple flannel lining, sold for $18. A zippered protective cover of tan canvas, with leather binding and metal bumpers, listed at $15.

The last of the SJ-100s were made in 1942 and shipped in 1943. According to Gibson historian and longtime employee Julius Bellson, 138 guitars were made through 1941 and an undetermined number built in 1942. Included in the total are some with variations made on the stock SJ-100, such as one with pearl block fingerboard inlays and another with an SJ-200 neck. The model was not re-established after WW II.

In 1972 Gibson reintroduced the model, calling it the J-100 and listing it at $495. This newer J-100 shared body dimensions with the J-200: 17" wide at the lower bout, 21" long, and 4⅞" deep (⅜" deeper than the original SJ-100). Like the original, it was constructed with mahogany back

John Hiatt with his J-100.

"Gibsons rule. I've never understood the Martin sound —it's not as open and full as the Gibsons."
—John Hiatt

The Nitty Gritty Dirt Band playing black J-100s, a popular Nashville stage guitar.

and sides, but the new neck was mahogany, not curly maple, and some tops were cedar. The Gibson crown and modern script, in pearl, graced the peghead. While the rosewood fingerboar retained the dot inlays, its binding was dropped and the scale shortened somewhat, to 25½". The rosewood bridge was a simple bottom-belly design. Body binding was white, both top and back. The simple pickguard was a teardrop of black celluloid.

The model sold relatively well in 1972, when 236 instruments were shipped; 51 left the factory the next year, none in 1974, and a final four departed in 1975. These final few were no doubt stragglers, for this model was no longer listed in the catalogue as of June 1973.

In 1985 the J-100 again returned, in the same body shape but with a maple back and sides, a top-belly rosewood pin bridge, a teardrop pickguard in mock-tortoise shell, and individual tuners with pearloid keystone buttons. The scale length of 25 ½" was retained. Two finishes were available, sunburst and natural.

These were Nashville-produced flat-tops. Even though they were built better than those from the '70s and early '80s, they still had problems. The new Nashville plant had many inexperienced workers, different equipment, a different and far more humid climate, and unfamiliar designs. Too many changes at once without experienced leadership conspired to postpone Gibson's return to their glory days of the mid-'60s and before.

The J-100 resurfaced in 1991 as part of the Gibson/Montana "Limited Editions" series and differed from the J-200 in ornamentation only—just as the SJ-100 differed from the expensive SJ-200 in 1939. A handful were custom-ordered with the original stair-step pegheads, the "moustache" bridges, and the original shoulder-shape pickguard.

As of 1993 this venerable model with so many lives is still available, in a production model known as the J-100 Xtra, which is the 1939 body with a "moustache" bridge and the "ONLY A GIBSON IS GOOD ENOUGH" banner on the peghead. The J-200 Junior model may have usurped the customary role of the J-100 as understudy to the J-200, "King of the Flat-Tops."

J-185: A COMPACT AND AFFORDABLE J-200

The J-185 is one of the nicest Gibson flat-tops ever built. Many guitar devotées have fallen in love with this relatively rare model, but to the general public it has remained a well-kept secret ever since its discontinuation in 1959. To those who know their Gibson flat-tops, though, this is a highly coveted model. Jeff Hanna of The Nitty Gritty Dirt Band, for example, prefers his original J-185 over the many competitors.

Delta bluesman Skip James with his J-185.

Sunburst J-185, 1957 vintage.

For whatever reason, Gibson underpromoted the J-185 right from its debut in 1951, a disappointing marketing decision given the model's quality and the fact that it filled a void perfectly. The model from which it was derived—the J-200—had for decades sold well due to its big, boomy sound, its quality construction, and its image of fanciness. Gibson correctly identified a niche for its new guitar: the J-185 was to be a slightly smaller and less expensive version of the famous J-200 and was to appeal to the same sort of guitarist who wanted but perhaps couldn't afford the J-200. The major use of guitars in the '50s was for rhythm playing, and big instruments with cutting power and volume were favored for the music popular at the time. The J-185 filled the bill, and, with its smaller price tag and "masculine" image, seemed to be the right guitar at the right time.

The J-185 listed for about two-thirds the price of the top-of-the-line J-200 and yielded a similar big sound despite its slightly smaller dimensions: the J-185 body was 20¼" long (versus 21" in the J-200) and at 16" wide at its lower bout was 1" narrower than its famous predecessor; the sides of both were 4⅞" deep at the endpins. Thus, the J-185 was small only in comparison to the J-200 and was equal in size (though not in shape) to the round-shoulder jumbos of the day.

The body shape created by the sides of the J-185 was new among Gibson flat-tops, though numerous arch-tops shared this outline, including the ES-125, ES-150, L-48, and L-50; the sides of the J-185 were higher than those of the electrics, however. The Everly Brothers flat-top model that appeared in 1962 copied the side shape of the J-185 but the depth of the electrics.

The back and sides were constructed of figured maple, an excellent tonewood and a natural for Gibson, which had ample supplies in its back yard. Three types of figured maple are native to the Kalamazoo area. Silver maple offers more frequent and often bolder curl but is the softest of the three; red maple flourishes in southern Michigan around the original Gibson factory but is not very hard; the sugar maple is not only the hardest but also the most desirable tonewood. Though certain select pieces of maple can give the musician the best of both worlds—both tone and attractive figure, usually there's a trade-off, for the harder the wood, the less pronounced the figure is apt to be. As a rule, Gibson preferred the hardest maple for their instruments, most of it slab-sawn, though occasionally beauty would win out in the case of a hand-picked, exceptional piece of "bubble" or curly wood of softer maple.

Rosewood was used for both the fingerboard and the bridge, which was a top-belly design typical of the time, except for the two Maltese crosses inlaid in pearl, one on each wing.

On the peghead's face are pearl inlays of the standard crown and "Gibson" in script. Gold-plated Kluson tuners with individual machine heads and keystone pearloid buttons are featured. On the mahogany neck is a single-bound rosewood fingerboard with twin-parallelogram inlays, Southern Jumbo-style.

The top is constructed of Sitka spruce, triple-bound in white/black/white strips, as is the back. The standard finish of the J-185 is sunburst, on the top, sides, back, and neck; the J-185N designation referred to the natural-finish option.

The pickguard imitates the shape of the J-200 'guard, generally following the contour of the body but with a point in the guitar's upper bout; instead of the intricately engraved vine-and-blossoms pattern of the J-200 pickguard, though, the J-185's is made of a subtle tortoise shell finish. The J-185 was the first Gibson to use this 'guard style; it became standard on the slope-shoulder jumbos and LG-series guitars in 1955.

The following shipping totals indicate yearly production of the J-185, sunburst and natural finish:

Year	Natural Finish	Sunburst Finish	Annual Total
1951	11	66	77
1952	24	137	161
1953	32	119	151
1954	31	97	128
1955	17	59	76
1956	59	65	124
1957	33	71	104
1958	35	34	69
1959	28	0	28

The Ken Curtis house band for *Song Story*, an early-'50s television show. Curtis joined the Sons of the Pioneers in 1949. His guitarist, Rex Dennis, plays a J-185.

Hank Snow's hybrid, custom-built for him by Gibson in 1961. The body size is that of a J-185, but this fancy guitar combines features from many models.

Phil and Don Everly with their namesake guitars, c. 1964. Gibson based the Everly Brothers model on the J-185 body.

The only major change in the J-185 occurred about 1955. Prior to that, its braces were tall and scalloped (as in the Southern Jumbos). When Gibson in the mid-'50s changed to the shorter, non-scalloped braces on most of their flat-tops, the J-185 followed suit. Both bracing versions very well suited the J-185 and no doubt helped create its reputation as a guitar of excellent tone and volume.

Gibson discontinued this lovely guitar after only eight years, to the disappointment of guitar lovers then and now. True, it wasn't an outstanding seller, but considering that it was relatively expensive and certainly undermarketed, the J-185 sold consistently over the course of its brief life. A likely reason was economic pressure. In 1958 the inexpensive LG-0 was introduced and was a major success. A year later, and at the tail end of a recession, Gibson dropped the J-185, which was, after the J-200, the Company's most expensive flat-top. Because fewer than 1,000 J-185s were produced, they are highly desirable on the vintage market.

A footnote: Gibson made at least one more guitar of this body size after the J-185 had been officially phased out. In 1961 their craftsmen constructed an elaborate custom guitar for "The Singing Ranger," Hank Snow, one of country music's true superstars. This guitar is a fascinating combination of features characteristic of many other models: back and sides are rosewood; the bridge is in the "open moustache" style of the J-200; the saddle is a Tune-O-Matic (adjustable); the binding is as fancy as anyone would want; the pickguard is borrowed from the Hummingbird; an abalone flowerpot graces the peghead; and of course Hank's name is inlaid in the fingerboard. If a model has to die, this is the way to do it—in an out-of-this-world custom order.

THE EVERLY BROTHERS SIGNATURE GUITAR: J-180

Phil and Don Everly, unsurpassed close-harmony singers and hillbilly-pop heartthrobs to a generation of Americans, were raised in a rock-solid country family. Their father, Ike, was a highly influential guitar player, having taught the great Merle Travis a thing or two about the style that became known as Travis picking. Ike's two sons were brought up on Gibsons, flat- and arch-top alike, and before Gibson created this famous signature guitar, the brothers played the company's fanciest and most expensive guitar, the J-200, as well as a 1953 Southern Jumbo. A special guitar, capable of creating a strong rhythm, needed to be designed, though, for these singers of the sweetest country duets since Ira and Charlie Louvin.

Thus, in collaboration with Phil and Don, Gibson set out to create a new model—"an unusual concept in jumbo flat-top guitars, designed and

> "Up in Kentucky there was the thumb-picking music from Muhlenberg County, players like Merle Travis, Ike Everly, Mose Rager, Kennedy Jones, and Arnold Shultz. Those coalminers . . . that whole sound . . . they all had Gibsons. This was back in the '40s. Mose Rager was one of the finest blues guitar pickers I've ever heard—country blues.
>
> My father, Ike Everly, that's all he ever played is a Gibson.
>
> Virtually everybody I knew in Kentucky played the guitar—and they mostly played Gibsons.
>
> If it hadn't have been for my father's thumb-pick guitar style and the friendship that developed between Dad and Chet Atkins, the Everly Brothers would never have been. When we came to Nashville we were an oddity, bordering on rock 'n' roll even then. Chet liked our music when a lot of people wouldn't have cared for it. If it weren't for him, I don't think I'd have had the courage to stick it out. He's still the king to me.
>
> Chet wasn't from Muhlenberg County, he was from East Tennessee. But he was the one that took that thumbpick style and made it world-famous—as well-known as Segovia in the guitar world.
>
> Chet was playing Knoxville. We had just lost our job on radio. Chet and Dad were talking, and Chet said he'd listen to us. He gave us his home number, which we used within a couple of months. He told us to come on over, so we went to Nashville. Chet's was the first real encouragement, outside of the family, we ever had. Through Chet, we got a song I wrote, 'Thou Shalt Not Steal,' recorded by Kitty Wells."
>
> —Don Everly

developed in close cooperation with the Everly Brothers" (Gibson catalogue, 1963). On a piece of brown paper Don cut out the pickguard shape he desired and sent it to Kalamazoo, requesting that pickguards in this form be used on the new guitars Gibson was building for them. These new guitars were to be black J-200s with large and white double pickguards, in mirror image, one on each side of the soundhole. (British guitar virtuoso Albert Lee has Don Everly's prototype J-200.)

Don and Phil Everly's black J-200s with custom pickguards.

According to Gibson historian Julius Bellson, Gibson finally decided to go with the slightly smaller J-185 size primarily because that model had been discontinued (1958) and this "artist's model" would resurrect a fine guitar; secondarily, the J-200 size would have competed directly with the J-200, which had sold well since 1937 except for a gap during the war years.

White J-200s with oversize pickguards designed by Don Everly.

This was a smart decision on Gibson's part for another reason. The J-185 body style simply made a great guitar. These proportions and dimensions produced a lot of power without the boominess of a J-200 or a wide-waist jumbo. To further enhance the quick projection needed, Gibson made the sides shallower, yielding these body dimensions: 20¼" long, 16¼" wide, and 4⅜" deep (½" shallower than the sides of the J-185).

Gibson kept the maple back and sides and spruce top, a combination that emphasized the punchy sound while lessening overall sustain. The 24¾" scale on a slim, one-piece mahogany neck ensured excellent playability. To a degree further diminishing the sustain, Don's two huge pickguards of celluloid were added, as well as a special, oversize adjustable bridge. The result? One of the best rhythm guitars ever.

The Everly Brothers model is a guitar of stars, for stars. Most noticeable are the ten pearl stars inlaid on the rosewood fingerboard, with an eleventh on the peghead, under the Gibson script. To these add a duet of huge, mock-tortoise shell pickguards, white binding on the top, back, and fingerboard; and you have an unmistakable-looking guitar, uniquely suited to the talents of the two brothers whose name graces the model—a great stage guitar.

The following list gives total annual production and finishes, from 1962 to 1971 (information courtesy of Julius Bellson via the Gibson Everly Brothers Owners Club):

1962	2 cherry sunburst
1963	102 cherry sunburst
	46 natural top/cherry sunburst-finish back and sides
1964	69 jet black (a few in 1964 may have been cherry sunburst)
1965	41 jet black
1966	22 jet black
1967	8 jet black
1968	48 assume jet black (literature did not indicate finish)
1969	51 natural top/walnut stain back and sides
1970	60 natural top/walnut stain back and sides
1971	39 natural top/walnut stain back and sides

TOTAL: 488

One small point of disagreement with Mr. Bellson: it's almost certain that the guitars built in 1962, 1963, and 1964 were available in a black finish only, and that many, if not most, built in 1968 had natural tops.

Guitar-great Ike Everly fingerpicking his J-200 as his son Don looks on.

"Guitars are one of those products that don't pollute —they make the world go 'round."
—Don Everly

1963 **Everly Brothers model.**

Of course, it's difficult to be absolute about these things, for there were special-order guitars, seconds, employee guitars, and other non-standard instruments with unusual finishes, pickguards, or other features. These anomalies in fact make Gibson's history sometimes exasperating but always fascinating. As an example, one of the most beautiful oddballs was an Everly/Dove hybrid: to a beautiful black-finish Everly body was incorporated a trim package found on the standard Dove models, including a sculpted bridge, a single pickguard (with inlaid dove), and twin-parallelogram fingerboard inlays.

When the top finish moved from jet black to natural in 1968, Gibson at the same time changed the pickguard for the sake of visual contrast. The large, tortoise 'guard became a smaller black laminate that stood out vividly against the light spruce top. This was the only other major change made in this model before its demise in 1972.

In 1984 Gibson examined its total lineup of flat-tops, trying to choose models for which there was an anticipated desire. It was thus that the Everly Brothers model returned to the lineup in 1986, renamed the J-180.

The new ones looked much like the old version, but many improvements made this an all-around better guitar. Gibson advertising stated that this reconstituted guitar was "inspired" by the earlier Everly Brothers model.

Only two changes bordered on major: the sides were deepened, like those of the original J-185, and a simple top-belly bridge replaced that old and

"I always dreamed of owning a guitar like the Everlys played. Eventually I worked with Don Everly in the late '70s, playing guitar and singing Phil's part. Knowing how much I loved his J-200, Don simply gave it to me. As you can imagine, this guitar, along with the '58 Les Paul Custom that Eric Clapton gave to me, is my pride and joy."

—Albert Lee

stout pin-free bridge. On a minor note, the tuners are individual units with pearloid keystone buttons instead of the metal keystone buttons of the originals. Internally, these Nashville-built guitars differ from the preceding Everly Brothers model by being lightly constructed, with thin tops, slim and tapered braces, and small maple bridge plates. Sadly, few of these guitars were made.

In 1980, the Gibson Everly Brothers Owners Club was established (ownership of an EB model guitar is required for membership). Headquartered in The Netherlands, the elite club has two major goals: to share their passion for this model and also to ascertain the number of these beautiful guitars still left. Albert Lee, who has a number of Everly Brothers guitars, was the club's first member. What this group of guitar lovers has done with the classic Everly Brothers guitar should happen to all the great models: they first collect a membership and then send questionnaires to these lucky few in order to gather data. Members get to share information about their beloved guitars and receive stickers bearing the club logo and other paraphernalia. (For more information about this club, write to Mr. B. Poyck, Kallenlaan 3, 6132 BH Sittard, The Netherlands.)

Thirty years after its introduction, the Everly Brothers model has increased approximately twenty times in value, showing an abiding interest in this excellent model named after two country boys who took their great talent, and their beautiful Gibsons, to the top.

British guitar wizard Albert Lee with a J-200 given to him by Don Everly.

Nashville-built J-180 body and neck and J-200 body, showing the dovetail assembly used during that time. Jim Triggs was a custom builder for Gibson.

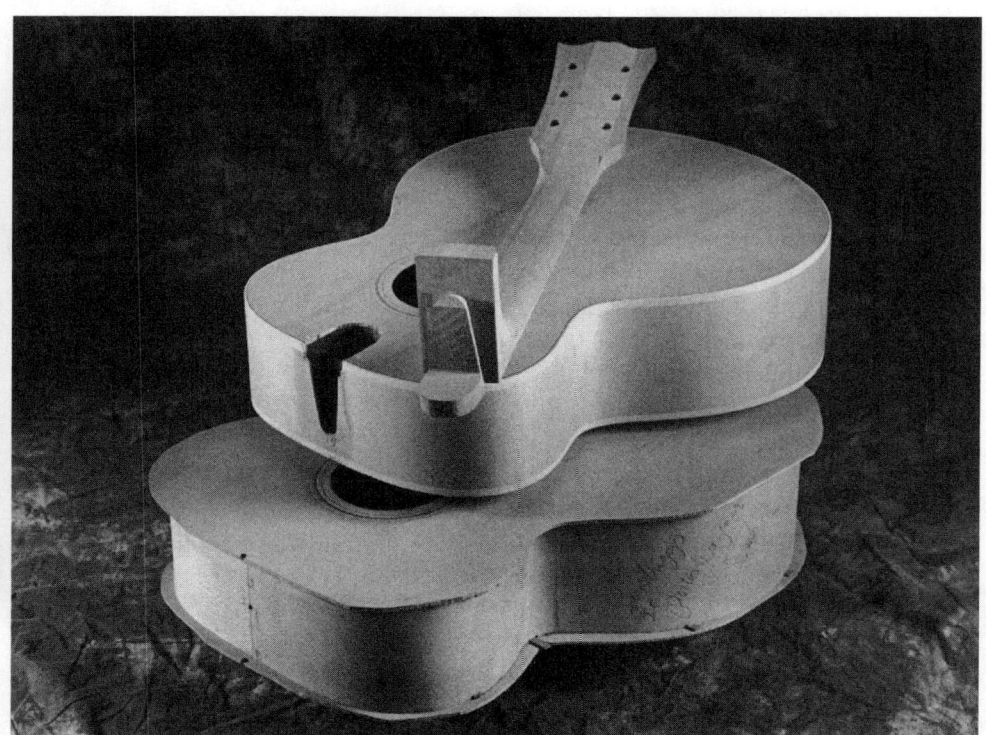

LG Series

Chapter Six

THE LG-2 AND ITS SUCCESSOR, THE B-25

Introduced in late 1942, the LG-2 was the first of the LG series that was eventually to include the LG-0, LG-1, LG-3, and the LG-2 ¾. The Gibson catalogue of 1956 shows what little difference there was between the LG-3 and the LG-2: "The LG-2 is of precisely the same specifications as the LG-3 but is finished in a warm brown shade with golden sunburst." On the lower end of the price scale, the LG-1 ". . . has the same general specifications as the LG-2 except that the materials do not quite measure up to the requirements of the higher priced models. . . . The finish is somewhat darker than the LG-2 and the sunburst is smaller."

At the time there were two compelling reasons for Gibson to create the LG series. First, because wide spruce was in short supply, a guitar with a narrower top was needed. The LG-2 is a full 2" narrower than the J-45 and the Southern Jumbo, two of its contemporaries. It was even ½" narrower than the L-00, a highly popular small-body model produced from 1932 through 1945. Also, Gibson wished to convert all their guitars to the "new style" neck and peghead, like those of the J-45 and Southern Jumbo, which featured a rounded neck, rounded heel, and radiused sides to the peghead. Finally, perhaps Gibson intended to phase out the L-00 immediately upon the introduction of the LG-2; if so, they must have discovered that because of the shortage of materials and the consequent need to build guitars from existing parts and materials, they would have to keep the L-00 in production longer than originally planned.

One of the all-time great blues singers, Johnny Shines, with his 1960s B-25. Shines was a sidekick of Robert Johnson.

"Banner" LG-2 with maple back and sides, c. 1945.

A 1942 LG-2 "Banner." The pickguard's fire-stripe pattern and the multiple binding are shared by the J-45s and the Southern Jumbos of that period.

The dimensions of this new body style were 14 1/8" wide, 19 1/4" long, and 4 1/2" deep. With its relatively wide waist, the LG-2 was close to the size and shape of classical guitars and offered a very balanced response. (In about 1958, in fact, Gibson started using the LG-series molds for their classical guitars, even though the classicals had shallower sides.)

The neck used the 24 3/4" scale and was of a 14-frets-to-the-body design, with 19 frets total. Unlike that of the L-series Gibson, which was V-shaped, the neck of the early LG-2 was rounded and substantial, particularly in 1942 and 1943. It was during this period that many Gibsons used no truss rods; consequently, necks were built stronger to compensate. Numerous guitarists prefer the playability of these heftier "baseball bat" necks. Most of these early "Banner" ("ONLY A GIBSON IS GOOD ENOUGH") necks were mahogany, until about 1944, when maple was used. During the War many of the flat-tops were built with poplar neck blocks and end blocks, particularly around 1943 and 1944. From this period, LG-2s, J-45s, and Southern Jumbos with hefty necks are likely to have the poplar blocks and not mahogany.

In wartime especially, Gibson used whatever materials were available; this explains the existence of some LG-2 batches with maple backs and sides instead of the usual mahogany. By 1945 maple LG-2s were common, because the mahogany supply had been nearly depleted. These maple versions have excellent sound, with a louder, punchy response.

Over the same period mahogany tops were commonly substituted for red spruce. When a mahogany back blank with exceptional tone was found, it became top wood instead. Quite a few J-45s and LG-2s were made this way. These mahogany-top instruments are brighter-sounding and have exceptional clarity of individual notes. In fact, for a number of reasons they are far superior tonally to the later LG-0 mahogany-top guitars of the same shape: LG-2s are older and have been played more; they have scalloped, high-profile "X-bracing"; tops were more carefully selected; their necks are more substantial; the LG-2s have solid sides, in contrast to the laminates of the

LG-0; and the LG-2 bridges are acoustically superior, the small rectangles having less mass.

These "Banner" LG-2s are handsome instruments. Whether topped with the usual spruce or the mahogany, they were finished with a sunburst. This finish on mahogany created a more reddish tone in the middle of the 'burst, because of the wood's natural coloration; spruce tops, on the other hand, moved from reddish yellow in the middle to a dark brown at the edge. The back, sides, and neck were all finished in a dark brown. The first LG-2s of 1942, like the Southern Jumbos and J-45s of the day, had a fire-stripe pickguard in a teardrop shape, multiple binding on the top and back, and the same rectangular bridge design as the J-45—Brazilian rosewood, with a saddle slot open at the ends and a very small pad on the underside. Machine screws passed through the bridge top and the pad, helping to hold things together. Pearl dots on the bridge hid these screws. Early bridge pins were black.

Changes on the LG-2 paralleled those of the J-45 and were dictated by the gradual depletion of materials during the War. In at least one way the smaller-body guitars had an advantage over the larger flat-tops: because of the smaller dimensions the LGs were less affected by shortages in top and back wood. It was not uncommon at the time for jumbo models to have four-piece glued-up tops. Also, the "Banner" disappeared from all Gibson guitars by 1947, leaving only the company logo, still in the old-style script, on the peghead.

In 1949 a ¾-size LG-2 was introduced. According to the 1950 catalogue, "This flat-top model is

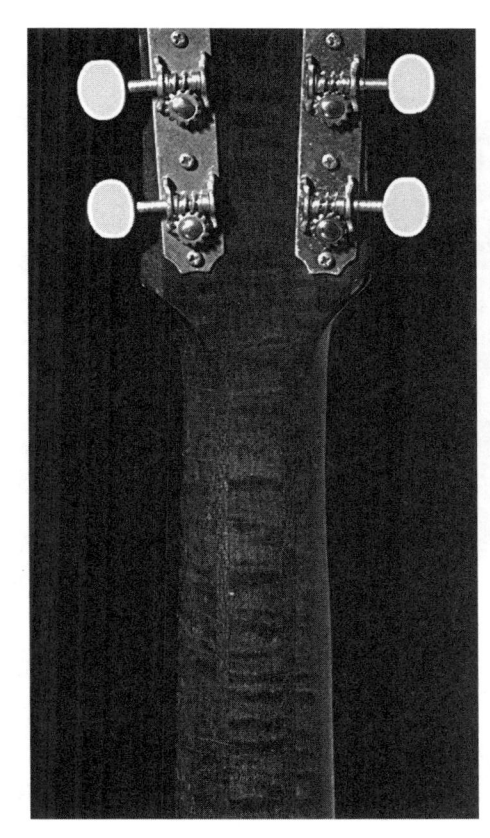

> A mahogany-top LG-2 "Banner" from 1943. During the War years necks were often built without truss rods.
>
> Three-piece maple necks were common just after WW II.

> "I bought the 1947 LG-2 at George Gruhn's store in Nashville in 1985, and it's my favorite guitar—the best acoustic I've ever owned. A great size and a great sound to match. Nothing beats this little LG-2. It sounds like wood; it sounds like a tree. Next I want an LG-0, an LG-1, and an LG-3—the whole family."
> —John Hiatt

The LG-2 3/4 on the left is '50s vintage; the cherry-burst was made in the early '60s.

Memphis blues star Furry Lewis and his B-25.

virtually a duplicate of the LG-2, except for its size. This three-quarter size is ideal for children or for players with small hands." The narrow-waisted miniature measured 12 $^{11}/_{16}$" wide at the lower bout, was 17 ¼" inches long, and used a 23" scale. One important difference between it and the grown-up: whereas the full-size guitar used "single-X" bracing, the ¾ version was constructed with ladder bracing. This model is fun to play—even for adults with regular-size hands—and it has found favor with collectors. The pickguard of the LG-2 ¾ retained the teardrop design until the model was dropped in 1968; otherwise, all feature changes follow those of the full-size version.

The Gibson script had evolved into a new block style in 1949. Probably in the early '50s the fingerboard was lengthened to accommodate a 20th fret. In the mid-'50s the tall, scalloped braces were changed to the low-profile design, and the longer pickguard with a single outward point in the treble bout replaced the original teardrop shape of mock-tortoise shell. By 1961 the dark sunburst was changed to the cherry sunburst. The LG-2 and its ¾-size offspring each listed for $115 in that year; for an extra $13.50 the player could get a decent soft case.

In 1962, after 20 years, the LG name ceased to exist (except for the mahogany-top LG-0), having been reworked into the B series. Overnight the LG-2 became the B-25. Changes between these two varied from superficial to important. For example, B-25s had white/black/white top binding, while the LG-2s managed with a simple white. Also, in this era the B-25s had laminated maple bridge pads, and many in fact featured what Gibson called the plastic "special bridge." Another difference involved the sides, which throughout the '60s were laminated on the B-25s. The thin, shell-pattern pickguard of the LG-2 was changed drastically, to a thick celluloid with a swirl pattern. Many of the mid- to late-'60s B-25s had the Gibson logo on the pickguard.

As inventory was gradually used up, the B-25s converted to the narrower neck around 1967, about a year later than the more expensive Gibson guitars. The cherry sunburst often faded on B-25s from this period; some from late 1964 to early 1967 faded excessively.

In 1968 the bridge took on a bottom-belly design, with the belly squarish and pronounced. The sunburst was also changed, becoming a distinct three-color combination, with the amber burst moving first to red and then to brown at the guitar's edge. The back, sides, and neck were finished in walnut.

By 1970 the bridge was non-adjustable, and the black peghead veneer was discontinued. The sunburst reverted to a two-tone, with a yellow 'burst surrounded by a rust-brown periphery.

By 1976 the B-25 was no longer listed in company literature. It is possible that some were built early that year, with the last six shipped in 1977. (This contrasts with sales of over 1,200 as recently as 1971.)

The LG-2/B-25 line served two generations well.

THE LG-3 AND ITS SUCCESSOR, THE B25-N

This most expensive representative of the LG series shares basic dimensions with the plainer members of the family: a body length of 19", a lower bout of 14½", and a body depth of 4½" at the endpin. And like the LG-1 and LG-2 it uses mahogany for its sides and back, with spruce on top. The exception, the LG-0, featured mahogany all around, including the top.

Gibson's 1950 catalogue is clear in differentiating the LG-3 from its relatives: "This flat-top model is virtually a duplicate of the LG-2 . . . the same dimensions and general appearance. However, the LG-3 has a beautiful natural finish spruce top, and a special selection of woods is used." In other words, the LG-3 bears the same relationship to the LG-2 as does the J-50 to the J-45: the LG-3 and the J-50 are built with "a special selection of woods," and their tops have a natural finish instead of a sunburst. (One small point of difference between the LG-2 and the LG-3 left unmentioned by the catalogue: the latter features multiple binding.)

It's difficult to pinpoint the exact date that the LG-3 appeared on the market. Earliest examples are "Banner" models with "ONLY A GIBSON IS GOOD ENOUGH" on the peghead, which dates them as 1946 or perhaps the latter part of 1945. The first alteration to the original instruments occurred in 1947 and involved dropping the "Banner," leaving the peghead bare except for the "Gibson" gold decal.

In the mid-'50s a 20th fret was added. Soon the scalloped braces measuring ⅝" tall were changed to a lower profile. Then, in about 1955, the teardrop pickguard was replaced by the longer Gibson-style 'guard with a single point. Uncertainty about dates and features of the LG models stems in large degree from the Gibson catalogues, which are notorious for their inaccuracy. For example, the early-1950s catalogues used a "Banner" LG-2 from the 1940s for the photo to accompany the LG-3 text and description. Also, while the 1956 catalogue clearly shows a teardrop pickguard on the latest LG-3, the guitar depicted is of 1947-1948 vintage, judging by the style of logo on the peghead. Meanwhile, though the 1959 catalog accurately shows the large, pointed pickguard and a contemporary "Gibson" logo, the '60 catalogue had reverted to the photo of a 1940s LG-3. Catalogue photos are not very good sources for accuracy of dating features; they hamper rather than help to pinpoint dates.

"Banner" LG-3, c. 1946.

1953 LG-3.

1957 LG-1, with ladder bracing. Tuner buttons have shrunk over the years, not an uncommon occurrence with Klusons.

1965 LG-1 with original plastic bridge.

Frets with larger crowns (tops) appeared in 1959. In 1961 the original rectangular, pin-style bridge became adjustable. Other features gradually changed as Gibson did. Frets were larger in 1959. In 1961 the bridge featured an adjustable saddle. About 1962 the bridge was again changed, to a top belly that retained the adjustable-saddle feature. Shortly thereafter, this bridge evolved to the top-belly adjustable bridge of plastic, a troublesome one that Gibson called, without irony, their "special bridge."

In 1963 the LG-3 was renamed B-25N, the differences being only the name and the new cherry finish rather than dark brown on the mahogany back and sides. Its neck was then changed, becoming narrower, with a 14-degree peghead angle, and its tuning machines were switched from nickel to chrome. The short scale of 24¾" was retained, however. The mock-tortoise shell pickguard was soon replaced by a thicker version with a swirl pattern, though in the same single-point shape. Later in the 1960s the Gibson "special" plastic bridge was dropped in favor of rosewood. The mahogany that was changed to cherry in 1963 again became walnut-brown. By 1970 the "X-brace" had become heavier, the bridge had been recast as a bottom-belly design, and the peghead veneer had been dropped. In another instance of name-changing, in 1971 the B-25N was promoted to the B-25N Deluxe.

It's likely that 1975, when 278 B-25s were shipped, was the last year this model was produced; six were shipped in 1977, but these were no doubt instruments that had somehow remained on some rack or shelf at the factory.

THE LG-1: BUDGET QUALITY

At the time of its introduction in 1947, the LG-1 was Gibson's least expensive flat-top. By adding this third member to the LG family—the more expensive LG-2 and LG-3 had appeared in 1942 and 1946, respectively—Gibson was attempting to capture part of the burgeoning lower-end market existing in the years after WW II. The 1950 catalogue identifies the market Gibson was going after: "LG-1—ideal for students or the guitarists desiring a low priced model. Selected materials and expert craftsmanship; same general specifications and general appearance as the LG-2. The LG-1 has a dark sunburst finish."

Externally, the difference between the LG-1 and the LG-2 was negligible—the amber center of the sunburst on the early LG-1s was smaller. The use of visually average woods on this model was made possible by the very dark sunburst finish, which covered imperfections better than a lighter sunburst or a natural top could. Internally, the difference was considerable: the more expensive LG-2 was "X-braced," while straight-across ladder bracing was used on the LG-1. Although ladder bracing characteristically produces a harder, less mellow tone, on a small-body guitar the difference between the two bracing systems is less noticeable.

Otherwise the LG-1 and LG-2 share numerous characteristics: spruce top and mahogany back and sides; one-piece mahogany neck; ivoroid binding and purfling ring; mock-tortoise shell pickguard in a teardrop shape; rosewood fingerboard (unbound) with pearl dots; rectangular rosewood bridge; and body dimensions of 14 ⅛" wide at the lower bout, 19 ¼" in overall length, and 4 ½" in depth at the endpin.

In 1955 the fretboard was lengthened from 19 frets to 20, and the larger pickguard with a single point in the upper bout was substituted for the teardrop. The fingerboard at the time was constructed on a 10" radius. Sides were usually laminated mahogany. Also, the rectangular bridge was modified: its size increased slightly during the mid-'50s, while the saddle slot changed from open at both ends to closed. Finally, frets with larger crowns were made standard on the LG-1 in 1959.

In the early 1960s (probably late 1962) the Gibson "special bridge" was used, replacing the standard and effective rectangle of rosewood. (See the LG-0 section for a discussion of the trials and tribulations with these plastic bridges.) By 1967 the neck was made narrower. Then a thicker pickguard was substituted for the thin shell-pattern 'guard.

The last couple of dozen LG-1s were shipped in 1968. At the same time Gibson changed the top on their inexpensive LG-0 from mahogany to spruce; no doubt they were cutting expenses by using up leftover tops from the defunct LG-1.

The LG-1 was one of their most successful flat-tops, coming close to the sales output of the LG-0, and in some years even outselling it.

1961 LG-0, the mahogany-top member of the LG series

LG-0: MAHOGANY TOP
←

The inexpensive LG-0 entered the market in 1958, tailor-made for a public wanting a guitar with the Gibson name but unable to afford the prices of elaborate models. The fact that the United States at that time was in the middle of a recession made the arrival of this new all-mahogany model all the more timely.

Gibson was by no means new to making decent guitars at budget prices. During the Great Depression the company built highly affordable L-series flat-tops, actually dropping prices to keep the factory busy. Also, the Kalamazoo budget brand was developed, a no-frills Gibson instrument with ladder bracing, no truss rod, fewer rounded contours, and no back binding. The Kalamazoo flat-tops had the Gibson quality and a low price tag.

It was in response to this growing atmosphere of diminished finances that Gibson developed the LG-0. Its body dimensions are the same as those of the LG-1, LG-2, LG-3, and CF-100 (Florentine cutaway design): lower bout, 14 ½"; body length,

19"; body depth at the endpin, 4½". This body style had been part of the Gibson line since 1942, when the LG-2 was introduced, and generally follows the dimensions of many classical guitars.

The 1960 Gibson catalog described the LG-0 as

> A top seller, favored by students, teachers, strolling players, and anyone who wants to have fun with the guitar. Brings you Gibson quality at Gibson's lowest price. Has slim, fast, low action one piece mahogany neck and adjustable truss rod . . . rosewood fingerboard and bridge . . . full size satin finish mahogany body. The small narrow neck is easy to finger, the action is easy, the tone full and round with deep bass quality.

The ad copy is accurate overall, though most players would differ with "deep bass quality"—the mahogany top and ladder bracing emphasize the mid-range tonal response, somewhat to the detriment of the bass. Bracing is identical to the spruce-top LG-1, while the two more expensive models, the LG-2 and LG-3, employ the "single-X" pattern.

LG-0 tops average slightly more than 1/10" in thickness. The bridge pads on the first LG-0s were rectangles of spruce, a wood that works well tonally with the mahogany top; the soft spruce created a problem, though, for the ball ends of the strings would wear out the pad prematurely. The LG-0 necks were identical to those of the other LG models, with the short scale (24¾") and the comfortable fingerboard radius that makes Gibsons play so well.

The following features distinguish the LG-0 from the LG-1, which was the next step up in cost: the LG-0 was built with a mahogany top, mock-tortoise shell binding top and back, natural finish, single black rosette ring, and a teardrop pickguard of thick black celluloid affixed to the top by three small screws. In spite of these differences, the resulting LG-0 was of a quality approaching that of fellow LG models. It played very well, producing a brighter and less mellow sound, and it cost less to construct, listing at $85 (1962 catalogue price), considerably below the $105 for the LG-1, $115 for the LG-2, and $127.50 for the top-of-the-line LG-3. Given the value per dollar, it's not surprising that the LG-0 was an excellent seller, with sales exceeding Gibson's expectations.

In 1959 the large-crown frets became standard issue on all Gibson flat-tops, the LG-0 included. Then in late 1962, in what can only be called a mistake, Gibson introduced their "special bridge" that was put on many models, from the LG-0 to the Southern Jumbo. The rectangular Brazilian rosewood bridge of the LG-0 was replaced by a molded one of hollowed-out black plastic, fastened on by four bolts and flat washers from inside the guitar.

The plastic bridge had two advantages: it was cheap to produce and equally cheap to repair. Most store owners of average ability could screw on a new bridge in a jiffy, an important point in 1963, when there were far fewer repair shops than now, and when most owners sent customers' Gibsons back to Kalamazoo for repairs if bridges pulled or split. Because Gibson was producing so many guitars, warranty repairs had become a major concern.

The "special bridge" turned out to be special only in the way that the Edsel was special. Many problems developed because of this bridge design. For one, it did not hold up well to string tension, and as soon as the top developed the normal twisting action, the plastic would start to crack, especially in the screw areas. This molded plastic couldn't offer the stability of a glued-on wood bridge: the guitar's top and bridge pad had to do it all. Thus, tops would develop serious belly problems immediately behind the bridge. Lightly constructed as they were, Gibson guitars needed all the support they could get in the bridge area. Plastic bridges were useless.

An additional problem involved the spruce bridge pads, which on the LG-0 were simply too soft. String tension put too much pressure on the three bolts attaching the bridge; the washers then would compress the spruce, allowing the bridge to lift slightly. This in turn exacerbated the pre-existing problems in the belly area of the instrument's top. In an attempt to correct these wrinkles, Gibson substituted mahogany for spruce bridge pads in the mid-'60s. This helped, but the real problem, the "special bridge," remained. By 1966 Gibson had finally scrapped the molded plastic and returned to a rosewood bridge with an adjustable rosewood saddle.

By 1963 the original black pickguard had taken on a "stretched" teardrop shape, like that on the soon-to-come Heritage, and was made of a thick, brown, swirly celluloid that was attached with three small screws. In late 1965 Gibson retooled and began producing a narrow neck with a 14-degree peghead angle; the less expensive models, including the LG-0, were the last to change, though, because existing neck blanks were used in constructing them. By 1969 the LG-0 mahogany top was a thing of the past, having been replaced by a spruce top and a bottom-belly bridge. The 1970 catalogue shows a new-style, black teardrop pickguard and a peghead with no veneer. The LG-0 at this time was being built with the new-style 1970s laminated mahogany neck. By then the LG-0 was no longer Gibson's least expensive flat-top, having been replaced at the bottom by the B-15.

Production of the LG-0 ceased in 1973, and the final three instruments were shipped in 1974. The model has begun to bring respectable prices on the vintage market and is no longer considered only as an inexpensive guitar. Because of excellent "miking" characteristics, it has found favor with some blues guitarists as well as acoustic rockers. The LG-0 is a good fingerstyle guitar and sustains well. Mahogany-top guitars produce an excellent "studio" tone—not better and not worse than a spruce-top version, just different. The very early LG-0s are the nicest and most desirable.

As a footnote, it might be interesting to compare the LG-0 to its Epiphone counterpart, the FT-30 Caballero. Other than slightly different peghead shapes and the Epiphone "E" on truss rod covers and pickguards, the two models are identical. This is not surprising, for the Chicago Musical Instrument Company owned both Gibson and Epiphone from 1957 to December 1969, when Norlin bought out CMI. Building two similar guitars at the same time and in the same factory must have offered certain flexibility to the company. Numerous other Epi/Gibson twins from this era exist, such as the mid-'60s Epiphone Texan, a quality round-shoulder jumbo much like Gibson's J-45. This overlap allowed the Gibson Company to franchise an Epiphone dealership in an area that already had its Gibson dealer.

F-25: GIBSON'S SMALLER FOLK GUITAR

Nineteen sixty-three was an excellent year for Gibson to introduce two guitars tailor-made for the folk market, the FJ-N and its smaller brother, the F-25. The folk music revival that had begun in the late '50s continued to blossom, resulting in further sales of "folk style" guitars. Joining the ranks of such established artists as Burl Ives, Josh White, and the Weavers were younger folk performers, including Joan Baez, Dave Van Ronk, and Peter, Paul & Mary, all of whom took a folk form a step further, making it contemporary, topical, and often political. Meanwhile, a folk/rock/blues genius named Bob Dylan appeared on the national music scene, and the times they were a-changin': the softer, less threatening traditional folk music had to share the stage with music of protest and injustice and inequality, music of civil rights and Vietnam, music of change.

1965 F-25, a lightly braced folk guitar.

Many of the more prominent advocates of The Movement were guitar players and singers, professional and amateur alike, in the folk genre. It was to this youthful, generally affluent group that Gibson wisely directed its F-25, a small-body instrument that could be played with either steel or nylon strings. Gibson's advertising of the day clearly states the three major selling points of this new model: "A fine quality folk instrument offered at an attractive low price. Gives rich, mellow tone, good response and power in a guitar that's easy to handle." The F-25 was folk, it was relatively inexpensive, and it was small ("easy to handle"), unlike the jumbo FJ-N.

Though Gibson had made gut-string classical guitars beginning in the late '30s, both its reputation and its expertise had been founded on its steel-string models. It was appropriate, then, that this new model was not a pure classical guitar, but a dual-purpose folk instrument—in the classical shape but capable of holding the greater tension of steel strings.

The new F-25 was designed along the body lines of Gibson's previous classicals, of which only the C series was in production in 1963, and also of the contemporary B-25, a steel-string guitar that had been introduced a year earlier and that was to serve as a useful model. With its classical shape, well-rounded bouts, a moderately wide waist, and deep ribs, the B-25 seemed little different from its folk/classical offshoot, the F-25, except superficially.

Visually, the biggest difference between the models was Gibson's use of huge, white pickguards on the F-25, as if shouting to the world that this was indeed a genuine folk guitar. To modern eyes these thin, celluloid 'guards might seem out of place on a classical/folk guitar, but at the introduction of the F-25 in 1963 international folk music was wildly popular, including flamenco music, which was played on guitars with pickguards/tapplates that surrounded the soundhole from both sides. Gibson hoped that what was good enough for Carlos Montoya, Sabicas, and other famous flamenco guitarists of the time was equally good for the American guitar-buying public. While the pickguard of the B-25 was large enough by normal standards, it was singular and seemed downright dainty in contrast to the double 'guards of its folk relative.

The F-25 and B-25 had necks of Peruvian mahogany, the standard Gibson non-slotted pegheads with a black veneer, the usual gold block script, and Kluson Deluxe tuners with white plastic buttons. For the feel of a classical, the F-25 featured a 12-frets-to-the-body neck (instead of 14), a neck width of 2" at the nut, and a flat rosewood fingerboard. Both models used a 24¾" scale and shared these body dimensions: 14½" wide, 19" long, and 4½" deep.

Sitka spruce for the top and Honduras mahogany for the sides and back were used on both models, and the bracing was identical. Because of the 12-fret neck of the F-25, the bridge had to be placed deep into the lower bout, with the soundhole and the "X-brace" in the same location as on the B-25. Gibson positioned the bridge and the laminated maple pad low in the "X-brace," almost to the tone bars. The bridge pad had to be an unusual shape because of its location in the top braces. Typical bridge bolts anchored the bridge to the top and the pad. This unusual design—with the 12-fret neck, braces forward, and the bridge deep in the lower bout—created a deep and rich tone with either steel or nylon strings. That this instrument sounded very good even with nylon strings says a lot about the light construction of the Gibsons at that time.

The rosewood, top-belly bridge of the F-25 was of pin design, unlike a true classical guitar; however, in true classical fashion the saddle was straight-across rather than angled, since pitch was true with the nylon strings without need of a compensating saddle. Bridge pins were white plastic, matching the pickguard.

The spruce top of the F-25 was given a natural finish, though during the first few years of production a sunburst option was offered. Its mahogany came only in a walnut hue.

Overall, these early F-25s were good guitars, with a pronounced classical feel, appearance, and tone, even strung with steel strings. For guitarists who on the one hand like the rich, warm tone and wide string spacing of a classical guitar but on the other want the punch and presence of steel strings, this model has remained in demand. The F-25 is a quite rare and an often overlooked instrument.

After six years of only minor changes, in 1969 the F-25 was drastically altered by Gibson. Gone was the standard Gibson peghead, replaced by a slotted version characteristic of classical guitars. The new peghead no longer had the black veneer, but it did retain the patented Gibson truss rod. Gone, too, was the well-rounded, classical body, discarded for the body shape of the Jubilee model. Though the dimensions of the revised J-25 remained the same, this was in fact a completely different body, with square, blocky bouts and a pudgy waist.

The bridge was inverted, becoming a bottom-belly design—tonally an unwise decision, considering how far back the bridge was located in relation to the braces. And retired were the white pickguards—the signature of the Gibson folk guitars. This new design lost not only the attractive classical appearance of the F-25, but it lost the wonderfully warm tone.

The F-25 lingered but briefly after this. It had disappeared by the 1971 listings, probably having been dropped by the company in 1970, when instruments shipped totalled only 46, from a high of 1,409 in 1964.

B-15: FOLK ECONOMY

From its introduction in 1967 until its demise less than four years later, the B-15 was Gibson's least expensive guitar—a basic student's model that initially listed for $110. A guitar at this price and of this simple construction seemed like a good idea on Gibson's part, for there were two important economic forces at work around that time. First, social unrest and the continuing "folk boom" had created a ready market for folk-style acoustic guitars. Secondly, the overseas guitar business was obviously intent on increasing its lower-end share of the American market.

It appeared to be a good time for introducing a new Gibson flat-top that could be purchased for not much over $100. Gibson's catalogue of the day shows that cost would be the model's market niche. The blurb, in its entirety, is as follows: "Responsive tone and rich appearance at an unbelievably low price. The contrasting black finger rest highlights the beautiful spruce top." Following the same economic logic, Gibson had seen its inexpensive but highly successful LG-0 model sell very well from 1958 until it was discontinued in 1970.

Gibson built the LG-0 and the new B-15 at the same time. Thus, for three-plus years these two models represented the company's economy guitars, with the LG-0, listing for $165 in 1969, about $40 more than the B-15.

The two models shared body dimensions, scale length, and materials. The differences in the B-15 were driven primarily by cost-cutting measures: an adjustable, rectangular bridge (rather than the more elaborate bottom-belly style in the LG-0); a satin finish; no binding; and simple neck construction.

The neck was built of laminated mahogany and featured an extremely narrow peghead, the most noticeable oddity of the B-15 and a result of Gibson's wish to avoid the expensive, straight-grained mahogany planks from which necks are customarily formed.

Despite Gibson's intentions and planning, cheaper foreign guitars began to corner the bottom of the market. These overseas products, though initially less expensive than the B-15, were essentially disposables, though the buying public by and large would not have known this until it was too late.

The imports characteristically used laminated woods, epoxy-type glues, plastic finishes, and neck/body joints that were next to impossible to repair properly; when these instruments needed fixing, and quickly they did, their problems were either inoperable or more costly than their value. For literally a few dollars more, these consumers could have owned a Gibson B-15, which with normal care would be playable today.

Though listed in the 1969 price list and the March 1970 catalogue, the B-15s had disappeared by the September 1970 price list. B-15s can be purchased very inexpensively. Although they will never make the lists of fine vintage guitars, they remain good student instruments and faithful traveling companions.

Flat-Tops with Pickups

Chapter Seven

CF-100/CF-100E: GIBSON'S FIRST FLAT-TOP CUTAWAY

Since their introduction in 1950 and 1951, respectively, the CF-100 model and i electrified version, the CF-100E, have deserved greater fame than has come to ther given their design features and the quality of construction. Gibson's 1950 catalogu tells us that this is a guitar with a difference:

> An innovation in the flat-top field—the CF-100 Gibson Cut-Away Flat-Top model. The modern cut-away design has been acclaimed by flat-top devotees, who are enthusiastic over the new playing ease offered in this instrument.

Although this model is favored by at least one major guitarist/vocalist—Leon Re bone—it has deserved a much larger following.

The CF-100 entered the market in 1950 as a small-body flat-top with a Florenti (sharp-pointed) cutaway. The body dimensions were the same as LG-series guita 14 1/8" wide, 19 1/2" long, 4 1/2" deep, and scaled at 24 3/4". Internally, too, the CF-100 mi rored the LG-2 and LG-3, with scalloped top braces in the "X" pattern and the typical tall, thin back braces. In addition, the woods used in its construction were all sol (non-laminated).

The spruce top was finished in a Cremona brown sunburst; its back, sides, and ne were Honduras mahogany. The Brazilian rosewood fingerboard, 20 frets in all, join the body at the 14th, and was edged with ivoroid binding, as were top and back. T fingerboard featured large block trapezoids (known as "Les Paul inlays," even thou the CF-100 preceded the Les Paul model by two years). The teardrop pickguard w made from a mock-tortoise-pattern celluloid. The bridge—rosewood, top-belly, wi a non-adjustable saddle—was of standard Gibson design.

The electric version, the CF-100E, was identical to its acoustic counterpart, exce that through its top, between the end of the fingerboard and the soundhole, w mounted a P-90 single-coil pickup. To accommodate this pickup, Gibson had to mo the soundhole more toward the bridge.

Gibson's better-known acoustic/electric, the J-160E, competed head-to-head with the CF-100E and outsold it—in spite of some points of superiority in the CF-100E. Namely, while the J-160E had a laminated top with the less productive ladder-style bracing, the CF-100 featured a solid spruce top that was supported by the sound-enhancing "X-brace." Also, the Florentine cutaway was an important advantage. The vogue of the CF-100 design finally arrived, but decades too late.

The CF-100 underwent few changes during its nine-year life. First, in about 1952, a pearl script replaced the gold decal logo on the peghead, joined by the Gibson pearl crown. Next, in the mid-1950s a larger pickguard shaped like those of the pre-War J-35 was substituted for the teardrop original. Probably in 1955 the scalloped bracing was changed: in profile this new, lower brace was shaped like an octagon without its bottom three sides. Although tonally responsive, this redesigned brace lacked strength, especially in the middle of the "X."

As Gibson advertising from the mid-'50s puts it, the CF-100 ". . . is designed particularly for the player who prefers the rich 'flat-top' tone but likes to use all the frets. . . . This model with a Florentine cutaway has won many friends among artists and amateurs alike." Sad to say, apparently not enough friends were won, or this innovative guitar would still be around. This model came 30 or 40 years too soon. Its designers would be amazed to see how wildly popular the acoustic flat-top with cutaways has become, especially with contemporary country performers including Garth Brooks, Lorrie Morgan, Joe Diffie, Clint Black, and scores of others.

J-160E: THE BEST OF BOTH WORLDS

Legions of aspiring young guitarists in the 1960s learned to play the beautiful guitar lead on "Norwegian Wood," one of the many Beatles recordings on which the Fab Four played a J-160E. Although its association with the Beatles makes this model one of the most famous in rock and roll history, as well as highly collectible, in its catalogue from the mid-'60s Gibson marketed the J-160 as a "jumbo flat-top electric guitar with adjustable bridge—for Country and Western Artists." To this day, though, John Lennon and George Harrison, not some Grand Ole Opry stars, are most immediately identified with Gibson's famous J-160E.

Gibson introduced this, their second flat-top electric, in 1954. (Their first, the CF-100E, entered the market in 1951.) The J-160E was based on the traditional round-shoulder jumbo body size and shape, like the Southern Jumbo, which in fact *was* designed for country and western artists. Contrary to popular opinion, the J-160E was of the same high quality as the Southern Jumbo but built with dual options in mind: it was designed to respond as an electric first, but it was to incorporate as natural a flat-top sound as possible. Because of its primary design as an electric—with a three-ply spruce top and lateral top bracing—the J-160E can't compete with top-of-the-line purely acoustic flat-tops, but as an instrument that offers the best of both worlds it succeeds beautifully.

1966 J-160E, the best-known of Gibson's electric/acoustic flat-tops.

Introducing such a guitar was an astute business move on Gibson's part. Acoustic rhythm guitars were the preference of rock, pop, and country performers in the '50s, thus guaranteeing the success of the J-160E. Its introduction and subsequent high sales no doubt helped kill Gibson's smaller CF-100E, a quality predecessor similar in features but with a cutaway solid spruce top and "X" top braces.

Gibson's chief competitors, the C. F. Martin Company, knew a good thing when they saw one, and four years after the J-160E introduction they brought out their dreadnought acoustic/electrics, the D-18E in 1958 and the D-28E in 1959. Martin's natural advantage—of studying the J-160E so as to bring a competitive product to market—wasn't enough to help them produce a superior acoustic/electric combination. The Martin creations, of good quality, are generally considered inferior to those of Gibson: they play poorly, they lack the tonal qualities, and they are aesthetically disunified.

Custom twin pickguards on a 1964 J-160E.

The comparative sales figures prove Gibson's edge. By the time Martin brought out their D-18E, Gibson had already shipped over 1,600 J-160Es. In the six-year period that Martin built their D-18E and D-28E, they sold only 540 of these models, combined. Gibson had effectively cornered the market on high-end flat-top electrics with its J-160E.

Except for the two control knobs on the right side of the lower bout, the exterior of the J-160E looked much like numerous other well-constructed round-shoulder jumbo models that Gibson had made over the years. The plywood Sitka top featured a traditional brown-to-amber sunburst. All J-160E round-shoulder guitars were sunburst. The original J-160E had a solid mahogany back and laminated mahogany sides, typical of many Gibsons of the day.

The one-piece mahogany neck had the usual 17-degree peghead angle; the bound Brazilian rosewood fingerboard was inlaid with pearloid trapezoids (in the style of the CF-100E); on the peghead were a crown inlay and the company logo in pearl script; the individual Kluson tuners with white buttons were soon changed to the keystone style.

The pickup was a P-90 single-coil with adjustable polepieces installed with the coil beneath the top, with only the small plastic plate and polepieces above the soundboard. The jack is in the side of the body, close to the tone and volume controls; the knobs were whatever was being used at the time on other electric models made by Gibson.

The plywood top and the ladder bracing both helped to keep the amplified J-160E from producing unwanted frequencies. This lateral-bracing pattern served another purpose. Because the longer neck met the body at the 15th fret, there was room to place the pickup between the soundhole and the fingerboard. Accordingly, the bridge had to be moved forward; in fact, with Gibson's 24¾" scale, the bridge was too far forward for any appropriate use of an "X-brace."

The Brazilian rosewood top-belly bridge was in the style of the period but was designed with a highly unusual adjustable saddle—this was the first Gibson adjustable bridge on a flat-top. The saddle could be lowered or raised by turning two nickel-sized wheel screws, one at each end of the

Flat-Tops with Pickups **109**

the larger-crown frets on all models. At that time the J-160E also switched to the conventional adjustable bridge. The 1970 catalogue shows a bottom-belly adjustable bridge (the inversion probably happened in 1968, when the other Gibson flat-tops underwent the same change) and a pickguard shared with the J-45s of the late 1960s. Quick mention should be made of some custom J-160Es of that era: they were built in a sharp-edged (Florentine) cutaway style and, though attractive, look like oversized CF-100Es.

Exactly when the J-160E changed to the square-shoulder jumbo shape is unclear, but this occurred sometime between 1969 and 1971, though the 1970 catalogue photo depicts the round-shoulder variety. (Gibson's catalogues have been notoriously inaccurate over the years. For example, catalogues through the 1960s show the same 1954 J-160E; the 1959 catalogue omitted the J-160E completely, though 179 were sold that year.) By 1970 all other round-shoulder Gibson models had been converted to the square-shoulder style, and while it is possible that Gibson made only the J-160E in a round-shoulder into 1970, it's far more likely that an old photograph was used for the 1970 catalogue.

The last year of the production model was 1978, with one straggler shipped in 1979. No electric/acoustic in history has been more important than the famous J-160E.

> 1956 J-200 custom with original Tune-O-Matic bridge. J-160E electronics were factory-installed into various flat-top models.

bridge. How low could it go? Low enough to disappear from view, leaving a vacant slot where the saddle was.

The J-160E underwent minor changes, such as substituting different volume and tone controls. When other Gibson electrics would be switched to a different style, the J-160E got the hand-me-downs. The sunburst finish also followed the lead of other flat-tops, such as the J-45 and Southern Jumbo, so that in the mid-'60s cherry sunburst J-160Es were made, although it's uncertain how many or for how long.

As Gibson made feature changes in other models, the J-160E followed suit. For example, double soundhole purfling rings were introduced, followed by the narrowing of the neck and a 14-degree peghead angle. Then nickel-plated tuners were switched to chrome. In 1955 the larger 20-fret fingerboard was put on the J-160E and on the other short-scale Gibsons. In 1959 Gibson went to

LES PAUL JUMBO: AN ELECTRIC/ACOUSTIC ODDITY

It's as if students in a "How to Name a Product" course at the local community college were given an electric/acoustic flat-top, designated Model X, as a project. The goal: to come up with a name that yields the greatest sales. After rejecting all the words that connote power or beauty or adventure or harmony because they've already been used, words such as Emperor and White Falcon and Explorer and Silvertone, the class decides to keep things simple: Model X should be renamed to reflect its size. Jumbo is good, but by itself the word won't do much to sell guitars. Add name identification, an endorsement. Two of the most famous guitar players come to mind. One of them, a fellow named Chet, endorses for a rival company,

Gretsch, so he's spoken for. The second name, another guaranteed luminary, has proven selling power. It doesn't matter that this guitarist for decades has been synonymous with solidbody electrics, not flat-tops. But what's in a name? In this particular name, everything.

With a reputation unsurpassed in the history of the modern guitar, the extraordinary Les Paul is chosen—jazz guitarist supreme, electronics wizard, inventor, recording studio pioneer, electric guitar prime mover, the ultimate innovator. His was the perfect name, but not for this guitar that can best be characterized as an oddity.

Although the Les Paul Jumbo was constructed using the same body size as the other square-shoulder Gibsons of the day, it looks like a guitar designed by committee. The Venetian (soft) cutaway is extreme, with the lowest part actually beneath the last fret (the 19th) of the fingerboard. A bound spruce top rests conservatively upon sides and back of rosewood; the standard Gibson peghead features the logo decal in gold script, beneath which is a 14-frets-to-the-body neck with dot inlays.

Nothing else about the top is usual. Located directly beneath the fingerboard is a low-impedance pickup in the shape of a round-cornered rectangle; with its mounting flange the pickup occupies so much space that it nearly touches the bottom of the fingerboard above, the soundhole below. The four control knobs follow the contour of the lower bout, on the treble side fencing in the on/off switch. The squat pickguard of mottled celluloid is shaped like Pac-Man, ready to devour the purfled soundhole. Because of the area occupied by the pickup, this soundhole is pushed abnormally close to a bridge typical of the period: low-profile, bottom-belly, with adjustable saddle.

Judging from the Gibson shipping lists, this model was available from late 1969 through 1973, although of the 139 total instruments, 132 were sent to dealers in 1970 and 1971 only. The Gibson catalogue and price list of 1971 mention the LP Jumbo as having bookmatched maple back and sides and a price of $595.

The guitar was short-lived, probably because it couldn't compete with Gibson's own J-160E, an electric/acoustic of attractive lines.

Square-Shoulder Jumbos

Chapter Eight

THE HUMMINGBIRD: GIBSON'S FIRST BIRD OF PARADISE

The Hummingbird is numbered among those elite guitars that look like no others, that are unmistakably individual and unique. Of all the models in the history of Gibson acoustic flat-tops, probably the venerable J-200 alone is more immediately identifiable than this peerless 'bird of paradise. The rapid growth of both the reputation and the religious following of the Hummingbird is all the more remarkable in light of the model's relative youth. This guitar proves that something other than age and longevity are needed in elevating a model to "vintage status."

Gibson introduced the Hummingbird, their first square-shoulder guitar, in 1960. Their goal: an instrument designed for vocal accompaniment, one whose warm and honeyed tone would complement the voice, not overpower it. In reaching this goal Gibson employed a radical design that resulted in an instrument more boxy than its round-shoulder predecessors, which had been part of the company line since 1934, when the Jumbo was introduced. Although in catalogues of the time the Hummingbird was listed as sharing dimensions with the round-shoulder guitars (16 ¼" wide at the lower bout, a body 20 ¼" long and 4 ⅞" deep), its body was actually smaller than this. Given Gibson's history of inaccuracy in catalogue specs, this discrepancy was most likely an oversight.

In fact, this new body differs considerably not only from the Gibson round-shoulder shape but also from the dreadnought body of rival C. F. Martin Guitar Co., in spite of its visual similarity to the latter. The following table gives the actual dimensions of the Hummingbird (and other square-shoulder Gibsons to come), the slope-shoulder models, and the Martin's dreadnought size (in inches):

1962 Hummingbird with maple back and sides. Except for a few batches of maple 'birds made in 1962 and 1963, mahogany was used for this model.

	Square-Shoulder Gibson	Slope-Shoulder Gibson	Dreadnought Martin
Body length	19 7/8	20 3/8	19 15/16
Lower bout width	15 15/16	16 1/8	15 3/4
Waist width	11 1/8	10 11/16	10 3/4
Upper bout width	11 5/8	11 5/8	11 7/16
Body depth, rear	4 15/16	4 7/8	4 7/8
Body depth, front	4	3 13/16	3 7/8
Soundhole diameter	3 15/16	3 15/16	4

The above shows that the new Hummingbird body was significantly wider at the waist and deeper in the bouts than the Martin dreadnoughts, in spite of apparent similarity.

Gibson's advertising copy accompanying the introduction of the new Hummingbird offered praise through hyperbole:

> A fabulous acoustical guitar—one of the finest ever made for voice accompaniment. The sound is big, and round, and full, with the deep rumbly bass so prized by guitar players. There's plenty of showmanship for the player in its wonderful resonant tone and carrying power, and in its striking beauty, too.

The price and quality of this new model were appropriate for a guitar second only to that of the J-200 among Gibson flat-tops. Its top was choice Sitka spruce, finished only in "incomparable cherry-sunburst color," according to the sales brochure. The soundhole, which retained the relatively small 3 15/16" diameter of the earlier round-shoulder bodies to enhance bass response, featured two groupings of alternating white/black purfling in the mode of the Southern Jumbo and J-200. Binding around the top and the back was also an alternating white/black design. The Honduras mahogany of the sides and back helped to create a warm, bassy, mellow sound characteristic of guitars built with this wood. The Brazilian rosewood bridge was a top-belly, adjustable design; the bridge pad beneath was of three-ply maple construction, typical of the day's flat-tops.

On a peghead angled to the neck at 17 degrees were the Gibson logo and crown in pearl, balanced by pearloid keystone buttons on the gold-plated Kluson tuners. The truss rod cover was a simple black with white edging. Gibson described the short-scale (24 3/4") mahogany neck as "new, extra-slim . . . for fast, low action." Inlaid in a bound rosewood fingerboard were twin parallelograms of pearloid. Gibson designer Hartford Snyder created the Hummingbird's single greatest mark of distinction, its single most prominent point of uniqueness, the pickguard. Within the thick, oversized piece of celluloid shaped like a dragon's back, a hummingbird hovers among blossoms, vines, and ferns, in engraved ornamentation. And at the top, minding its own business, is a generic butterfly. No matter what the viewer's aesthetic sense, dull this pickguard is not. To the uninitiated (i.e., those eventual Hummingbird lovers who need a while longer to be converted) this gewgaw is ostentation rather than adornment, gaudy more than gorgeous. But to the many true believers, the Hummingbird pickguard could be mounted, framed, hung on the wall, and admired as artwork.

Internally, the Hummingbird retained the low, thin top braces that Gibson had used on the jumbo models since the mid-'50s and the slim back braces featured on most flat-tops since the '30s. The "single-X" top brace, in the 102-degree spread employed by Gibson when a warm and rich tone was desired, was glued close to the soundhole, at a distance of 5/8" to 7/8" from the aperture. The tonal results from this light bracing were excellent.

This new model was not only more visually stunning than the competition of the time (especially that of other guitar companies), it offered superior playing capabilities. The Hummingbird certainly gave the public what it wanted: sales jumped to 595 in 1961 from 156 the previous year. In fact, the model was selling so well that Gibson expanded the Hummingbird concept, creating the Dove, which was based on the same body as the Hummingbird, but had maple back and sides, a long-scale neck, and different external components. The Dove cost approximately 35 percent more than the Hummingbird and filled the price slot between it and the top-of-the-line J-200. Because the Dove was so similar to the Hummingbird, however, most buyers didn't spend the extra 35 percent; they kept buying the Hummingbird instead.

According to Gibson employees of the time, some of those guitarists who bought Hummingbirds unknowingly got partial Doves. When this second bird of paradise was introduced, in 1962, Gibson apparently produced more Doves than they had orders for. Consequently, from time to time they would pull a batch of incomplete Doves from the rack and finish them with Hummingbird trappings, for the Hummingbirds continued as hot sellers.

As a result a number of maple, long-scale Hummingbirds were made in 1962 and 1963, and these are exceptional-sounding guitars. The late songwriter/guitarist Steve Goodman ("City of New Orleans") owned one of these maple Hummingbirds, which became his main guitar for a decade and the one he described as "the first guitar I ever loved."

Whether as pure Hummingbird or as the Dove hybrid, the model quickly established itself as a guitar of choice, as the shipping totals for the first decade attest:

Year	Total Shipped
1960	156
1961	595
1962	503
1963	1,461
1964	1,283
1965	1,522
1966	891
1967	1,738
1968	2,213
1969	1,595
1970	1,335

By 1962 the price had risen to $250 plus $50 for the standard hardshell case of the era, a black arch-top version with a yellow plush interior and small brass latches. In 1963 a natural-top option with cherry-stained sides and back of mahogany was added to the original cherryburst, and by that year the longer scale had been instituted. About this time the original pickguard, which had extended nearly to the bridge, was slightly reduced in size, while the price increased to $265. The folk music revival was in full force, leading to a tripling of Hummingbird sales from 1962 to 1963.

By 1965 the Hummingbird had been relegated to number five in the Gibson lineup, according to price, behind the J-200, Dove, Heritage, and Everly Brothers guitars. Also in this year many changes were made in the Hummingbird. One of the more unusual involved triangles or rectangles of black paint on the guitar's sides, next to the neck heel. According to employees at the time, Gibson resorted to this literal cover-up when the first ply of the mahogany laminate was sanded through, near the dovetail block, prior to the neck set. (Many Hummingbirds had laminated sides.) The black lines were painted just prior to the final coat of clear lacquer and proved a simple way to cover a production mistake by embellishing it. It is

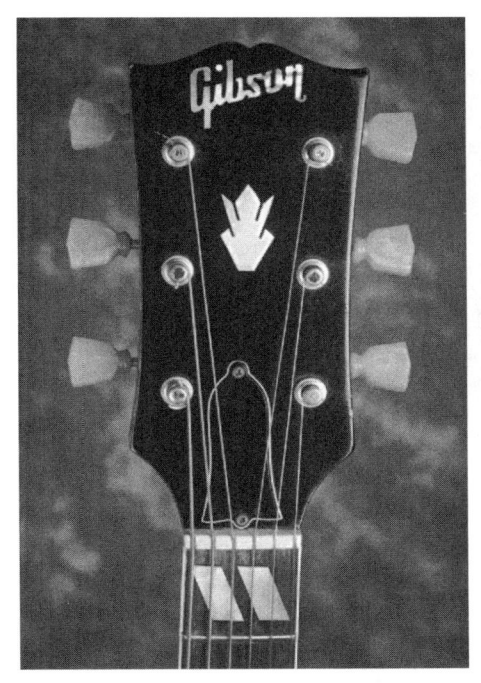

In late 1965 Gibson changed neck machines. At the same time the peghead angle was reduced to 14 degrees from 17 and a slimmer, more shallow neck was created.

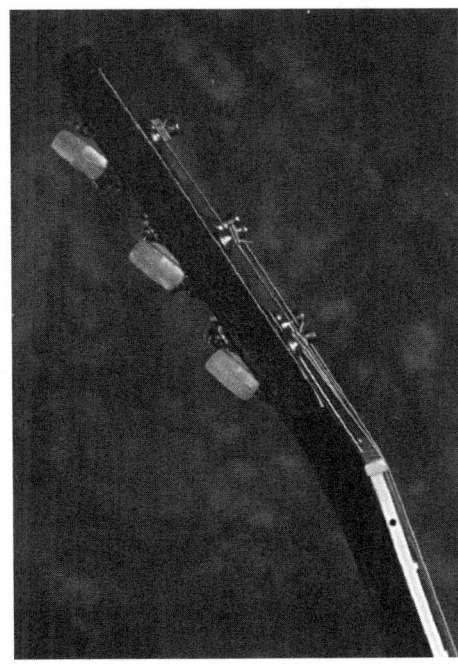

possible that this efficient method of cosmetic correction was used even before 1965.

That year also saw a neck change, in which the peghead angle was reduced to 14 degrees from 17 and the neck was made more narrow, two modifications that affected the entire flat-top line at that time. Also, chrome plate supplanted nickel that year. (Nickel has a yellow hue, chrome more of a blue cast.)

An unexpected change that spread across the period from 1964 through 1966 was the fading cherry sunburst. For some reason the reds that Gibson had begun to use were unstable, fading to various shades of light red, in some instances so much so that at first glance some tops look natural (and not at all unattractive). In '66 the list price of the natural-finish top was $325 and $310 for the cherryburst, with hard-shell cases at $62. An identifying feature of that year's Hummingbird is a pearl "Gibson" set higher on the peghead than was customary.

During 1967 and 1968, in a short-lived experiment, pickguards were attached by tiny screws rather than glued; also, some nickel-plated tuners were found on the 'birds. In 1968 the top-belly bridge was replaced by a squarish bottom-belly design; the adjustable saddle was retained. At this time some Hummingbird tops were also finished with the traditional dark brown sunburst instead of the trademark cherryburst.

The last year for the ultra-light Hummingbird construction that produced such excellent sound was 1968. Near the end of that year Gibson initiated major changes intended to increase production while keeping warranty work to a minimum. Thus, the braces on both top and back became large and bulky, as did the solid-wood bridge pad.

At this time the neck began changing subtly, becoming wider, with a less rounded heel and a longer, wider peghead; the "crown" inlay grew, and the "i" in "Gibson" lost its dot.

In or about 1970 the solid mahogany neck was replaced by a three-piece mahogany laminate. This change cannot be specifically dated, however, for existing stocks gradually had to be depleted. It was also within this general time frame that Gibson changed its methods for gluing braces. This new system had production advantages, but accompanying it was a major flaw that appeared only after a guitar's finish started to darken with age: on instruments with natural-finish tops the outline of the bracing pattern became increasingly visible on the guitar's exterior. This is a common flaw, for over 5,000 Hummingbirds were made from 1968 through 1970.

> 1966 Hummingbird with the high-set script common that year.

> "The best rock acoustic guitar ever made was the Hummingbird. Period. Ask Keith Richards or John Mellencamp. It's like the enlarged high-hat, that extended high-hat sound—you get that Hummingbird chugging and all hell breaks loose. You hit the magic pocket.
>
> My first good acoustic guitar was a Hummingbird, which I bought new in 1968 and dearly loved. It was stolen from me and never returned."
>
> —John Hiatt

By no means was this the only quality-control problem at the time, for Gibson had entered its period of darkness. The new owners, the Norlin Corporation, understood short-term profits better than they understood what it takes to maintain a reputation for excellence that had been over 70 years in the making. The period that began in about 1968 gradually worsened until recovery arrived in the mid-'80s, in the form of another change in management.

During this period the beautiful old Kluson tuners with the pearloid keystone buttons were dropped for tuners with metal buttons. Then a white butt wedge and heel cap were added. Although the 1968 to 1971 Hummingbirds remained classy guitars, they sounded and felt different from their predecessors and were a clear cut beneath them.

By 1969 most fingerboards and some bridges had become Indian rosewood instead of Brazilian. In the early '60s Brazil had placed an embargo on exporting rosewood logs and had stipulated that all logs had to be sawed in Brazil. For two major reasons this in effect eliminated the excellent Brazilian rosewood from the market: first, the price rose drastically; additionally, this exceptional lumber more often than not was slab-sawn, rendering the wood less useful for instrument construction, which usually required quartersawing. Then began the destruction of South American rainforests, with grazing cattle winning over rosewood. The Brazilian rosewood that Gibson had stockpiled was used for bridges; accordingly, many later Gibsons have Brazilian bridges but Indian rosewood fingerboards.

With 1970 came other minor changes. Gibson replaced the black-stained holly peghead veneer with a black fiber to avoid weather checking. Also, on the back of the peghead they began stamping not only each instrument's serial number but "Made in U.S.A.," a move to cultivate patriotism in a politically anxious year as well as to distance Gibson's well-made guitars from the occasionally shoddy imports.

Because of very high consumer demand and subsequent increased production of guitars during the 1970s, quality materials grew increasingly scarce, not only at Gibson but at Martin and Guild, too. As a result many less expensive models were given inferior woods, and at the same time production techniques were changed in order to expedite productivity. Profits increased at these three major flat-top manufacturers, but quality suffered.

In 1971 Gibson began building all their flat-tops, Hummingbirds included, with their patented "double-X" bracing pattern. Throughout the "double-X" period (1971 until 1984), two versions of this pattern were used, neither of which was what might be called tonally responsive. The main "X" was moved back from the soundhole almost ½", with the angle of the "X" reduced to about 95 degrees. The Hummingbird was quickly losing its famous mellowness; this bracing system accelerated that loss.

In the same year the twin-parallelogram pearloid inlays in the fingerboard were replaced with rectangles. Also, the bridge became flatter and less contoured and was no longer adjustable. As a result, for the first time in Gibson's history necks were underset, partly in compensation for the flat, thinner bridges.

From 1975 through 1977, serial numbers were applied not through stamping but by decal on the back of the peghead. Any refinish work would, of course, eliminate the serial number. Pegheads of this period featured flat-bottomed truss rod covers. Neck heels had been changed to a French style but were poorly contoured, with the lowest part of the heel forming an obtuse rather than a right angle. All woods were solid during this period, except for the huge diamond-shaped bridge pads.

Gibson switched to a three-piece maple neck at this time, perhaps because of the huge number of guitars being made then and a resulting shortage of mahogany thick enough for necks; perhaps, too, it was just a cost-saving move, domestic laminated wood costing less than imported. Volutes then appeared on the backs of necks to protect against broken pegheads, a problem that the heavier electric guitars were susceptible to when the instruments accidentally tipped over.

Finishes were being sprayed over soundhole purfling and back strips. Oddly, some Hummingbirds of this era appeared with pearl dots in the extremities of the pickguard. Gibson must have had some leftovers from 1967, perhaps those whose screw holes had been misdrilled. It would have been a simple task to fill holes with small pearl dots. Gibson, which had produced many of the world's best and most beautiful guitars, was at this time drifting, having lost connection with their rich history. The guitars they were producing were not worthy of the company's reputation. Quality control lost and quantity control won.

By popular demand Gibson dropped the peghead volute by 1981, but no other major changes were made until 1984, the year that flat-tops began to be made in Nashville. By then, however, serious damage had been done to the Gibson name.

In or around 1983 Gibson had designed a Hummingbird much like the beautiful originals and planned to build reissues in the Nashville factory. Gibson's Abe Wechter and Tim Shaw had carefully studied the old Hummingbirds and hoped to restore this famous model to its former glory. These new guitars were built of solid woods and were braced more like those of the early 1960s. These braces were a little taller and tapered at the ends, though; Gibson felt that they didn't have the skilled labor force necessary to scallop braces with controlled expertise at the new factory.

In 1984 Gibson celebrated its 90th anniversary by adding the following to the lineup: the reconstituted Hummingbird, J-200, J-45, and Dove models, and the brand-new J-25 guitar. With this move Gibson not only added quality to their line of flat-tops, but they also reduced their flat-top models to only five, a useful number for a company concerned with cost containment during an expensive transition period at the new Tennessee facility.

These new Hummingbirds reinstated numerous features of the 1960s 'birds, such as twin-parallelogram inlays, a top-belly bridge, and a 24¾" scale. Due to the availability of stocked parts, the necks on these reissued Hummingbirds retained the double dovetail designed by Richard Schneider in the mid-'70s. Binding was put on the fingerboards with a mortised slot to make construction easier. Overall, these were not excellent copies. Nevertheless, this attempt represents a significant time in Gibson's history—a first step in the return to quality of years past. Since the purchase of Gibson by a trio of investors in 1985, the Hummingbird and all Gibson flat-tops have continually improved to the present excellence coming out of the Gibson/Montana factory in Bozeman.

A separate section dealing with construction and repair issues is needed for a complete discussion of the Hummingbird, whose quality has varied widely over the years. Here in a nutshell are the fluctuations.

The Hummingbirds built between the model's introduction in 1960 and 1967 are the most prized. While those from 1968 through 1970 can be good, characteristically they are without the warm, mellow tone and the feel of the earlier ones. From 1971 until 1984 the Hummingbirds (and all other Gibson flat-tops) were simply a cut beneath those guitars that came before and those that came after. The Hummingbirds from 1984 to 1989, the Nashville years, are decent instruments, though some developed problems because of the Tennessee humidity; individual guitars can be very good instruments, and at a good price. Each of these groupings mentioned above deserves discussion, merits and demerits alike.

1972 Hummingbird.

Hummingbirds built from 1960 through 1967 are the most desirable, for a number of reasons. Being so lightly built with the wide-angle forward bracing, they yield a distinctly sweet tone. Their one-piece mahogany necks are user-friendly and great to play on, and those who like the narrow-neck Gibsons should look for those built from mid-year 1965 through 1967, when all had 14-degree peghead angles and the long scale that produced a tight, punchy sound for full-chord playing.

Problems developing in Hummingbirds of this era are usually related to the top sinking in the soundhole/shoulder region. Among the probable causes are these:

- Poor-quality bracing spruce susceptible to splitting
- Braces that can fail because of sloppy gluing
- Adjustable bridges that were often set too high by owners wanting to create greater volume or to avoid string buzzes. Excessively high action could lead to the fulcrum effect, which can badly twist a lightly-made top.
- Bolts in the bridge that will partially retain it, even after the glue has failed, resulting in a twisted and distorted top
- Laminated bridge pads that come loose because they cannot flex properly or because they were improperly glued

These problems rarely develop on Hummingbirds that are played and maintained properly. However, the level of sophistication about guitars and the number of savvy repairpersons 30 years ago were not what they are today. Any one or combination of the above problems leads to a top that will sink in front of the bridge, an area vulnerable because these guitars have lightly built tops and braces, "X-brace" angles of about 102 degrees, and an "X-brace" located only about ⅝" to ⅞" from the soundhole's edge.

Another problem common to the Hummingbird of this era is the bridge, which was made of Brazilian rosewood, a substance prone to splitting. A couple of design flaws exacerbate this problem: the bridge pins are too close to the rear edge of the bridge, leaving too little wood there for strength; and the adjustable saddle, because it is wide and offset (compensating), does not permit a sufficiently large area on the front/treble side of the saddle, which again encourages a bridge to split.

Some repair shops remove the bridge bolts and adjustable saddle, filling the remaining slot with Brazilian rosewood and then rerouting for a new bone saddle. This alteration definitely improves the tonal response; however, it should be carried out only after careful consideration, for the Hummingbird will no longer be "original." By the same token, for originality's sake Brazilian rosewood should be used if a new bridge is needed, and the pearl dots covering the bolt heads retained.

Other repairs intended to enhance tone involve the removal of the two brass nuts that are inset into the top to receive the bridge bolts. At the same time the bridge plate is often replaced with a smaller one of solid hard maple.

Hummingbirds of this era deserve a good inspection with a mirror and light, on occasion. Loose, cracked, or sinking braces should be searched for, as should bridge shortcomings. Long-scale Hummingbirds seem to suffer an inordinate number of these problems. Fortunately, Hummingbirds were made with excellent neck-sets, so that repair in this area is seldom needed.

Fewer problems faced the Hummingbirds built from 1968 to 1971, because of heavier braces and a different bridge design. Sadly, there is a corresponding tonal loss. Also, Gibson in these years used large, thick bridge pads of solid maple or beech that were much too large, resulting in the same inflexibility problems as the previous, smaller laminated ones. With not much success Gibson then attempted to correct this by cutting grooves into the pads, following the same direction as the top grain.

The 1971 to 1983 Hummingbirds have been besieged by a multitude of problems: the "double-X" bracing system was too rigid; neck-sets were poor; neck laminations have separated; bridges were built too thin; and loose bridge pads have proved a nightmare to remove, for they are surrounded by braces on all four sides.

Frankly, workmanship and design in this era failed to measure up to Gibson's standards. The shortcomings can, of course, be rectified, but at considerable expense: some owners have had the rear, smaller "X-braces" removed and replaced by angled tone bars, the bridge pad removed and replaced by a small one, top braces scalloped, the neck reset at a more pronounced angle, and a taller bridge made. These operations do indeed improve the tone, but it would have been easier and cheaper simply to find a Hummingbird from a different period.

The Montana Hummingbirds represent a refreshing return to the merits that marked the first few years of the model. Quality control is excellent, and design changes have helped greatly in producing instruments with superior tone and playing characteristics.

The first Hummingbirds are quickly becoming popular on the vintage market, for a number of reasons: 1930s-, 1940s-, and 1950s-vintage flat-tops are now beyond the means of many individuals; the early 'birds made a strong impression on baby-boomers, who now can afford what they coveted in the 1960s; they are stunning stage guitars that play effortlessly and yield a sweet sound.

It's no wonder that the Hummingbird is second only to the J-200 as the longest-running Gibson flat-top in continuous production.

The unforgettable pickguard, 1965 Dove.

THE DOVE: GIBSON'S OTHER BIRD OF PARADISE

Although predicting which moderately priced current models will find favor as collectors' favorites is uncertain at best, it's a good bet that the demand for Dove guitars built from 1962 to 1968 will continue to increase quickly. Like the Everly Brothers model, the Dove has begun attracting a special group of musicians who want a guitar with a great neck and bold looks, one with wonderful rhythm capabilities and tonal qualities that are superior for backing up vocals. The Dove fills this niche perfectly. Gibson's 1991 reissue catalogue says this: ". . . The Dove has been considered the most beautiful acoustic ever built in Gibson's long history of original designs. . . . Unmistakable features . . . have made this model one of the most sought after in today's renaissance of acoustic music." Although beauty can be in the eye (and ear) of the beholder, the Dove is quickly coming into its own as an eminently playable and collectible instrument.

Gibson introduced its first square-shoulder jumbo guitar in 1960, in the form of its highly successful Hummingbird. This model had been designed primarily for vocal accompaniment, the goal being a warm, smooth-sounding, mellow instrument that complemented rather than overpowered the voice. After assessing the public's reaction to this model, Gibson expanded upon their success by creating a similar guitar, but one with a very different personality. This new model was the Dove, which in costing more than the Hummingbird but less than the J-200 was intended to fill a void. When introduced in 1962 the Dove served as a cross between its two famous predecessors: it featured a maple back and sides and the long scale, like the J-200, but with the same body dimensions, construction design, and vocal-accompaniment qualities as the Hummingbird.

Shared characteristics of the Hummingbird and Dove include body dimensions, bracing system, twin-parallelogram fingerboard inlays of pearl, individual nickel-plated tuners, cherry finish, peghead design, and one-piece mahogany neck. After these, though, the two models follow diverging paths.

The Dove is most noticeably different in the design of its pickguard, on which a mother-of-pearl dove sits upon a branch amid a garden of wild roses, the whole peaceful scene hand-engraved into a large, three-pointed cutout of celluloid, with two points directed to the bridge, the third rising skyward, toward the upper bout.

Dove pickguards are a story of their own. The first were hand-engraved, painted, and inlaid, but to reduce costs Gibson began to mold them. Then the company stopped making them entirely, ordering them instead from a supplier in Germany. A pantograph (a machine that simultaneously creates duplicate designs) was purchased, which in effect combined hand and machine work. Surviving all the changes was Maudie Moore—from 1964 to 1980 Gibson's chief pearl cutter, inlayer, and engraver at the Kalamazoo factory. Not only did she hand-make many of the fancy Dove, Hummingbird, and J-200 pickguards, she did custom pearl work for the Nashville-made Gibsons.

Nearly as unusual as the Dove pickguard is its bridge, a unique winged design created specifically for the Dove (though used with slightly different trim by the J-200 in the 1970s). Its pin holes follow a slight downward arc, the cusps pointing to an inlaid pair of symmetrical pearl wings in flight. (This arc and the Dove's Tune-O-Matic adjustable saddle were shared with the J-200's "moustache" bridge.)

It's interesting to see how Gibson designed the Dove to possess a sound somewhat different from the Hummingbird's, yet with its full, rich, mellow tone and good overall balance. The sides and back woods make a tonal difference: the Dove's maple back and sides, in contrast to the Hummingbird's warmer mahogany, yield a louder, crisper sound, but one that dampens more quickly. Also, the bulkier bridge, with the metal Tune-O-Matic saddle, subdues the sound while making it metallic.

Early 1965 Dove, the more expensive of Gibson's two "bird" flat-tops.

Overall, the Dove's tone is very pleasant, particularly in the lower end of the scale; however, it does lose some of the ringing trebles normally associated with Gibson flat-tops when it's played up the neck.

These early Doves, like other Gibsons from the period, are constructed lightly, resulting in excellent tone and volume. There is a trade-off: when internal problems such as loose braces or bridge pads are left unattended, the tops can develop a slight sinking that starts in front of the bridge and continues into the shoulder region. The longer scale exacerbates this tendency.

Peghead, 1965 Dove.

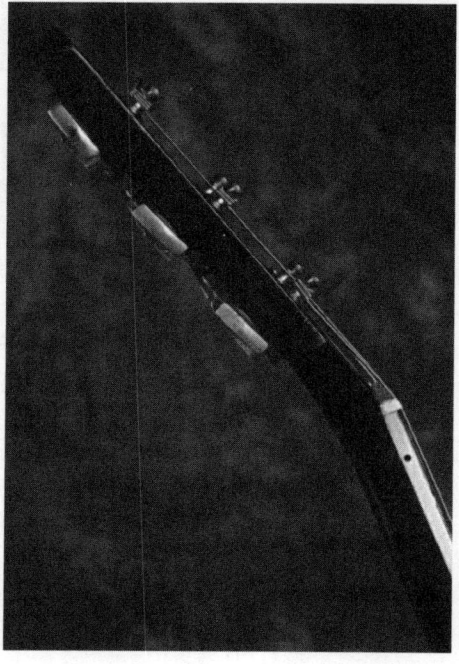

As a sign of Gibson's reticence to mess with success, the changes in the Dove were subtle and gradual. First, in 1963 the Dove N became available, which had the original cherry finish on its back and sides, but a natural top. By 1965 the Grover Rotomatics of the earliest guitars had been phased out in favor of Grover individual machine heads with metal keystone buttons. At about this same period the black truss rod cover with white border interchanged colors. Then the backs and sides were constructed of maple laminates. Finally, in late 1965 the necks were narrowed and the pegheads set at a 14-degree angle.

The Dove then remained relatively unchanged until 1968, when alterations of a larger scale began:

- Bracing on both the top and back was made heavier
- Pickguards were attached by screws (on some only; later, inlaid pearl dots covered the screw heads)
- Pegheads were enlarged
- Bridge pads became solid maple and huge
- Grover Rotomatics were restored as tuning machines
- Adjustable rosewood saddles replaced the Tune-O-Matic metal version

At some point in the early '70s, the neck was changed to three-piece laminated maple from mahogany of a similar design and widened in the process. At about the same time, the back and sides again were made with solid maple, rather than veneer.

In 1971 two important changes were made. First, the Dove was given a flatter bridge with a non-adjustable saddle. More important, it was built using Gibson's patented "double-X bracing." The company marketed the "innovation" this way:

> . . . Our patented "symmetrical bracing" gives Gibson a light, yet extremely sturdy construction. It allows the wood to resonate freely for the fullest possible tone production. And it still supports the instrument with the kind of strength that has enabled Gibson guitars to perform flawlessly year after year.

This bracing pattern also killed sound. (Because changes in the Hummingbird and the Dove were shared, consult the Hummingbird section for more details.)

Gibson reverted to the general construction design of the original early-'60s Doves in 1984. Although a considerable improvement over the uneven product that had been built since 1969, they were not excellent copies of themselves. However, Dove guitars of high quality—the Gibson/Montana "Limited Editions" reissues—were only seven years away.

Some feel that the early Dove is among the most beautiful guitars ever built, from its graceful peghead, pearl inlays, multiple binding, curly maple body, and cherry finish to its unique and elaborate pickguard, engraved with wildflowers and inlaid with a pearl dove. After some difficult times at Gibson, this model that has been in continuous production for over 30 years is again being built to the high standards that its reputation deserves.

THE SQUARE-SHOULDER SOUTHERN JUMBO: A.K.A. THE SJN COUNTRY-WESTERN & SJ SOUTHERNER JUMBO

In late 1962 the round-shoulder body that had characterized the Southern Jumbo since its introduction in 1942 was changed to its square-shoulder design. The body shape of this revamped Southern Jumbo model was not new, however, having been used on the very popular Hummingbird since its birth in 1960. By the end of 1962 the Dove had swelled the Gibson square-shoulder Jumbo lineup to three, although it featured maple back and sides in contrast to the mahogany of the other two.

Structurally, this reshaped Southern Jumbo was built very much like the Hummingbird but retained most of the general physical features of the round-shoulder SJ, a model that had become much revered ever since its introduction in 1942. Probably in an attempt to create an "image" for two targeted consumer groups, Gibson eschewed rational and meaningful names for the two new versions of the well-known Southern Jumbo. Version one should have been called the Southern Jumbo N (for natural finish), and the second simply Southern Jumbo, which for its life had come with a sunburst as the standard finish and thus needed no further elucidation. Instead, Gibson marketing produced these:

[the SJN Country-Western]

Country-Western artists have no greater favorite! They praise the SJN's traditional jumbo size and shape, its deep resonance, powerful tone and deluxe appearance, and its Gibson quality.

[SJ Southerner Jumbo]

A special favorite with southern balladeers, but preferred by many Country-Western stars, too, especially for its dramatic appearance. The SJ has all the outstanding features, the tonal response, and quality workmanship of the SJN.

Gibson catalogue, 1962

Blues musician John Hammond Jr. playing his square-shoulder Southern Jumbo.

1965 Country-Western.

Muddy Waters, the "father of electric blues," playing his mid-'60s square-shoulder Southern Jumbo.

1966 Southern Jumbo in the square-shoulder body shape.

It's unlikely that any potential customer would be influenced, for good or for ill, by these blurbs of advertising copy.

By far the most desirable of the square-shoulder SJs are those from 1962 to 1968, a period in which their bodies were lightly built, with top bracing wide-spread and set forward. The SJ/SJN stayed with the 24¾" scale throughout this period, though in 1965 a switch was made to a narrower neck, in keeping with the other Gibsons of the period.

In late 1968 the model began a series of gradual changes that ended three years later in a very different guitar. Three changes affected tone: first, a bottom-belly bridge (which the original 1940s Southern Jumbo featured) reappeared; then the ultra-light braces were traded for bulky, heavy braces that surrounded a huge, solid-wood bridge pad; finally, the scale was lengthened to 25½".

Other changes were more aesthetic and less tonal. The peghead was lengthened, slightly but noticeably; the three-pointed pickguard—made of thin tortoise-pattern celluloid in the style of the Hummingbird's, only smaller—was exchanged for one of a teardrop shape; the neck block became a two-piece construction, offering more support under the fingerboard tongue; the fingerboard and bridge became East Indian rather than Brazilian rosewood; the bridge took on a shapelessness and became non-adjustable; and the one-

"*T*he guitar I play around the house is an SJN that I bought used in 1966. It was my main guitar throughout my folk club days, until it got smashed by the airlines. Of course I got it fixed, because of its unbelievably sweet tone. I wrote "Prayer in Open D" on my SJN, and then I used the guitar in the studio when I recorded the song."

—Emmylou Harris

piece mahogany neck was switched for a wider, laminated version.

Gibson's patented "double-X" top bracing was incorporated into the SJ duo in 1971. By 1973 the models had suffered yet another name change, being upgraded, through word inflation only, to the SJN Deluxe Country and Western Jumbo and the SJ Deluxe Southern Jumbo.

By 1976 this noble model was no longer listed in Gibson literature, thus ending a legendary guitar—after a musical life of 34 years.

FJ-N: CHILD OF THE SIXTIES

In the early '60s Gibson began to design a guitar they hoped would capitalize on the folk music boom sweeping the land. The songs that the Carter Family made famous to a relatively narrow, predominantly rural audience in the late '20s and '30s were revivified after WW II by Woody Guthrie, Cisco Houston, and others, and they in turn influenced Pete Seeger and the Weavers, urban contemporaries who brought the music to a national record-buying public. By the late '50s and early '60s the third wave of American folk performers, led by the Kingston Trio, began recording, to astounding success. Such folk groups as the Brothers Four, the Limelighters, and Peter, Paul & Mary saw their songs reach the top of the pop charts week after week.

Meanwhile, a more "hip" audience—urban and college-educated—listened not to the commercial groups but to Oscar Brand, the Seegers (Pete, Peggy, Mike), Theodore Bikel, Odetta, Elizabeth Cotten, John Jacob Niles, Bascom Lamar Lunsford, and an unknown guitar genius, Arthel "Doc" Watson, who debuted on a Folkways Records sampler in 1961.

And into this frenzy of folk music came the FJ-N, referred to by Gibson as the "Jumbo Folk Singer Guitar." Introduced in 1963, the F (Folk) J (Jumbo) N (Natural finish) was intended as an all-purpose folk instrument that would satisfy those who wanted a steel-string guitar as well as those who preferred the sound of gut (nylon) strings. Gibson had built classical guitars off and on since 1938, namely the GS (Gut String) line and the C (Classical) Series, but these had been 14½" small-bodied instruments not targeted for the folk audience. With the FJ-N, the company offered to fans of folk music a 16"-wide, square-shoulder jumbo that had received the official sanction—at least in Gibson's advertising—of genuine "folk." No matter that Woody Guthrie had played his music on a WW II Southern Jumbo or that Doc Watson and Bob Dylan (Woody's most famous disciple) had preferred older Gibsons, a vintage J-35, J-45, or J-50. The FJ-N was clearly marketed to a different audience.

The body shape places the FJ-N into the family of Southern Jumbos, Hummingbirds, and Doves of the day—the typical wide-waist, square-shoulder Gibson jumbo, bound in white with a black inner purfling strip on the top of a body measuring 16" wide, 19⅞" long, and 4 15/16" deep. The top was finished natural, and the back, sides, and neck were either a walnut-brown hue or a dark red. As if to leave no doubt that the FJ-N was a folk guitar, Gibson added two large, white vinyl pickguards, the top one adding even greater protection for that folk musician whose exuberant style (for example, flamenco and calypso) might otherwise have damaged the soft spruce top.

Two features of the Peruvian solid-mahogany neck distinguish the FJ-N from its relatives, however; the "folk" width at the nut is a full 2", and the neck joins the body at the 12th fret rather than the 14th. Otherwise, the FJ-N trim package has much in common with the Southern Jumbos of the day: the pegheads, with pearl crown inlays and logos, are identical, as are their Brazilian rosewood fingerboards featuring the twin-parallelogram pearl design and white celluloid binding. Both models also share top-belly pin-style rosewood bridges, the saddle of the FJ-N being uncompensated—that is, parallel to the nut—for nylon-string intonation.

Lightly constructed bodies characterize Gibsons from this period. The FJ-N, with its big body, mahogany back and sides, and deep-set bridge made for a resonant, balanced, and tonally responsive folk guitar, just as advertised. By the mid-'60s, the popularity of nylon-strung guitars had waned and steel-strings were the clear choice of most guitarists. Although the FJ-N was a true dual-purpose guitar, nylon or steel, it was susceptible to damage that could result from heavy-gauge strings ("boomers") on its light, relatively delicate bracing.

The last year for the FJ-N was probably 1967; at least this model had disappeared by the June 1968 price list, after approximately 600 instruments had been sold. Gibson had undertaken a large-scale redesigning of its flat-tops in 1967 and 1968, when it moved to much heavier bracing. No doubt the FJ-N had by that time become expendable as its sales figures reflected the public's loss of interest in folk music.

THE HERITAGE: FOLK MEETS COUNTRY

By the mid-'60s two distinct and definable guitar-buying markets—folk and country-western—had converged. The Gibson Company, which over the years had done well in reacting to consumer demand (if not in fact creating demand), decided to spend some time at the designing board. The goal? To create one guitar that could appeal to both markets—as well as attract the bluegrass fans. Followers of bluegrass were rapidly increasing in numbers, due especially to Lester Flatt and Earl Scruggs, whose "Ballad of Jed Clampett" tasted of bluegrass, though imperceptibly. This theme song for the nation's number-one television show, *The Beverly Hillbillies*, itself went to #1 in the country-western charts, in the process tuning in a whole generation to Jethro, Ellie May, Granny, and Jed, and, more important, to a new genre of music.

Gibson's very reasonable idea was to create a single model that would be embraced by those diverse musicians who followed folk, country, or bluegrass. The Heritage resulted, designed to offer much to many: to the folk market, simplicity of appearance with quality; to the country segment, a dreadnought for a big sound and rosewood for a smooth "thump" in backing vocals; and for the legions of new bluegrass players, a strong competitor to Martin's D-28, a model that had become the preeminent bluegrass guitar, just as Gibson's Mastertone had become *the* banjo and its F-5 *the* mandolin.

It was thus with considerable foresight and great expectation that Gibson introduced the Heritage in 1965—a square-shoulder jumbo with a spruce top and Brazilian rosewood book-matched back and sides, tortoise binding front and back, and the long 25½" scale. This guitar's image was to be of elegance and simplicity, two characteristics that had served the C. F. Martin Company well for over a century. The Heritage featured an ebony bridge with an adjustable ebony saddle; its unbound fingerboard was of the same wood, with pearl dots as markers. Like the Martins, the

Early 1968 Heritage with replacement bridge and tuners.

Heritage came in a natural finish, and its pickguard was mock-tortoise shell, in an elongated teardrop shape that it shared with Gibson's student-model LG-0.

Everything else about this model is all Gibson—the top-belly adjustable bridge, Gibson's advanced bracing, and the sleek neck with the pronounced fingerboard radius and patented truss rod. The neck is one-piece mahogany; individual tuners are nickel-plated, with metal keystone buttons, the same tuning machines used on the Dove model of the day. In a minor way only, Gibson kept with its reputation for visual flair via its truss rod cover, black with a white border and an inscribed "custom." (The cases from 1965 to 1967 added a touch of vividness, too—a somber black exterior with a lively yellow-orange plush within.) The peghead logo was understated, featuring the gold block script common in less-expensive Gibsons.

At its introduction the Heritage was the third-most-expensive model among the Gibson flat-

Folksinger and Lovin' Spoonful member John Sebastian with his early Heritage.

tops, with only the J-200 and the Dove costing more. Prices in June of 1965 are as follows:

J-200 N	$505.00
J-200	$490.00
Dove N	$385.00
Dove	$385.00
Heritage	$349.50
Everly Brothers	$330.00
Hummingbird N	$285.00
SJN	$220.00
SJ	$220.00

By 1968 the bridge had evolved into a bottom-belly design; the back and sides were Indian rosewood. Somewhat later, multiple body binding with a white outer layer was substituted to dress up a model that had intentionally been kept relatively unadorned. Then, by 1969, the Heritage became affected by the same overhaul that touched all Gibson flat-tops of the period. Market demands and quality control no longer drove changes; instead, "innovations" appeared only when they benefited Gibson's manufacturing efficiency and the bottom line.

By 1969 and 1970 the Heritage had entered a gradual metamorphosis. Tone and volume became restricted by its large braces, aided and abetted by the bulky bridge plate, all of which compromised the model's "fat" tone. A black, overweight pickguard supplanted the regal original. The simple and proportionally harmonious peghead became elongated; the original decal logo was replaced by mother-of-pearl, and beneath it was a thin, vertical diamond with a curlicue on each side, also of pearl. At least the neck retained the slimness of the very playable original. Despite these changes that rendered the Heritage a quite different guitar from what was intended, the Gibson Company pursued the original marketing strategy, as this 1970 ad copy attests: "A fine rhythm guitar preferred by both folk and country western artists. The Heritage features excellent tonal balance and a strong, brilliant sound."

In 1971 the Heritage was to suffer additional, more drastic changes. Along with other Gibson flat-tops, this model's bracing was changed to the "double-X" design, which deadened sound, in part because of this system's huge, diamond-shaped, laminated bridge pad. The bridge itself, while remaining ebony, took on a new pointy-cornered shape, like that on the J-200 of the same year. Curlicue mother-of-pearl inlays appeared. At the same time, the neck became wider: 1 $^{11}/_{16}$" wide at the nut. Finally, large blocks of pearl were inlaid in the ebony fingerboard.

By 1973 or 1974 another series of changes had arrived:

- Fiber bridge-pin insert added
- "Heritage" inscribed on the truss rod cover
- Necks switched to three pieces of mahogany
- Purple plush interior for cases, with Gibson block-style logo silkscreened on outside
- Binding added to the fingerboard
- Body binding switched to black
- White/black/white soundhole purfling
- Metal keystone buttons used on most Heritages of this period
- Bell-shaped truss rod covers changed to a flat-bottom, three-screw design

By 1975 the body binding reverted to the tortoise celluloid with white/black/white purfling. At decade's end white binding was again used, with black/white/black purfling. The bottom of the neck's heel formed an obtuse angle rather than the standard one of 90 degrees. Tuners were Schallers specially made for Gibson. The truss rod cover was changed back to the traditional bell shape. Guitar cases of this period were black, with larger latches and an interior of maroon plush.

1972 Blue Ridge.

The Heritage was discontinued in 1982, having met at least some success in filling its intended niche as a much-to-many guitar. Music and buyers' tastes had changed radically over the 17-plus-year life of the Heritage; this fact, combined with the many changes in this model's personality and design, led to its demise.

THE BLUE RIDGE: ECHOES OF BLUEGRASS

When Gibson redesigned their square-shoulder jumbos for 1968, they brought out a new model, the Blue Ridge. As its name implies, this model was designed to appeal to bluegrass musicians at a time that the genre was becoming a major market to makers of guitars, mandolins, and banjos. Gibson's reputation in making the latter two instruments was unequaled, leaving the guitar as the target area in the company's attempt to attract some of the customers who liked the appearance of Martin's dreadnought series.

The Blue Ridge was basically a stripped-down version of the Heritage, a model that had sold decently since its introduction in 1965. In price the Blue Ridge was sixth in line, behind the J-200, Dove, Heritage, Everly Brothers, and Hummingbird, listing for $100 less than the Heritage and $40 less than the Hummingbird. It was chiefly by its low price that the Blue Ridge distinguished itself; with its typical square-shoulder body, it presented the same body shape as five other Gibson models of the time. Accordingly, in its catalogue Gibson tried to capitalize on the cost factor of the Blue Ridge: "This new Gibson model features the ultimate in performance and visual elegance at a popular price."

Upon its introduction in 1968, the Blue Ridge was an attractive, solidly constructed guitar: a top of solid spruce in a natural finish; back and sides of a two-ply rosewood laminate with an inner skin of maple; a rosewood top-belly bridge with an adjustable rosewood saddle; a long-scale rosewood fingerboard with pearl dots; a narrow, one-piece mahogany neck standard with most Gibson flat-tops of that vintage; a body bound in white ivoroid, with double purfling rings around the soundhole; a black pickguard in the teardrop shape; and large, "single-X" bracing that Gibson was to use from 1968 through 1970.

In 1969 the bridge was changed to a bottom-belly adjustable design, though a year later it became non-adjustable. In 1973 a low-impedance pickup became optional. Gibson made wholesale changes in construction in the 1970s affecting all flat-tops, the Blue Ridge included (see the Hummingbird section for generic changes).

The Blue Ridge sold well from 1969 through 1975—over 5,000 instruments, in fact—but sales fell sharply as the bluegrass craze waned. Also, for not much more money a Hummingbird could be purchased, and for *less* money the well-known Southern Jumbo was available.

The model ceased to exist in 1979.

THE J-45/J-50 SQUARE-SHOULDER

After 35 years of satisfying their customers, in 1969 Gibson dropped production of all its remaining round-shoulder jumbo models. The famous J-45, which had been around since 1942, and its natural brother of 1947, the J-50, were redefined as much different guitars from the round-shoulder versions that had been so popular for so long. By being forced to take on the square-shoulder shape these venerated models changed personalities greatly.

On the practical (and profitable) side, with this change in body shape Gibson could make all their flat-tops, except for the top-of-the-line J-200, in the same mold—literally. All scale lengths became 25 ½", a move that in turn standardized neck construction. This unquestionably improved manufacturing efficiency; however, it did little but harm to the quality, playability, and remarkable history of the jumbo-style guitars.

The revised versions at first featured ivoroid binding and a plain pickguard of black celluloid. Internally, this model was overly built, with heavy-duty "double-X" bracing. Ironically, these recast versions were given promotions—advertisements referred to them as the J-45 Deluxe and the J-50 Deluxe. And in 1971 the adjustable, bottom-belly bridge changed to one with a stationary saddle.

These were profitable times for guitar makers, thanks in large part to a resurgence in the popularity of folk music that accompanied the social protest of the late '60s. Gibson had been purchased by Norlin, a company that had no feeling for the music business and that was interested in profits only. Sadly, Gibson's great name and heritage quickly began to suffer, and so did the quality of their guitars. J-45s and J-50s declined in tone, playability, and appearance, while their prices jumped as much as 10 percent annually.

To energize flagging sales, by 1975 Gibson used four-ply binding with the outer layer of tortoise grain on the tops and single-ply tortoise binding on the backs. By 1981 the bodies of these two models were again wrapped in white binding.

Sales of the J-45/J-50 plummeted, to a combined total of fewer than a thousand in 1979 from more than five times that in 1971. The model was dropped from the Gibson line in 1982. (See the J-45 section for the 1984 re-emergence of this model in its original round-shoulder shape.)

J-40: BIG SOUND, SMALL PRICE

Through the dozen years of its life, the J-40 brought to the guitar-buying public an inexpensive, large flat-top. Coincidentally, 1971 marked the debut of this model and also the "double-X" bracing system found in this and other models. Selling at under $300 at its introduction, the J-40 yielded a big sound for a reasonable price.

This jumbo was built in the square-shoulder design exhibited by numerous other Gibson models contemporary with it, including the Gospel, Hummingbird, J-50, and J-55. The finishes varied: a natural spruce top with walnut-toned back and sides of solid mahogany was the most popular; cherryburst was an option.

Typical with this model during its first few years, "Gibson" in gold script was emblazoned on a peghead free of a veneer overlay; individual deluxe Kluson tuners with metal keystone buttons were standard. The peghead itself, pitched at 17 degrees, was strengthened by a volute. The Indian rosewood fingerboard was left unbound, with dot inlays marking the frets. Like the back and sides, the neck was mahogany—a single piece rather than a glued-up laminate. The first J-40s have black teardrop pickguards without the traditional Gibson teardrop contours. The bottom-belly, non-pin bridge is Indian rosewood and "shapeless." This design was easier to build, easier to repair, and easier to change strings on, but sadly not productive of the tone and volume associated with a pin bridge.

Within a couple of years, the J-40 neck became a three-piece maple laminate. In general, Gibson necks were interchangeable during that period, model to model. Soon, the black pickguard was dropped in favor of the larger version, similar to those used from the mid-'50s to the early '60s, giving the J-40 a more traditional Gibson look. Also, to re-create that traditional look the company by 1977 began to reintroduce a black peghead veneer.

Gibson discontinued this model in 1982.

Overall, the J-40 did well enough as an inexpensive, functional guitar. It cannot, of course, be compared favorably with the higher-quality Gibsons, Martins, and other expensive flat-tops. What this model lacks in class it makes up for in basic functional value. A selective buyer can often find an excellent J-40 at a reasonable price.

THE GOSPEL (ACCORDING TO GIBSON)

Gibson added two new models in 1972, the J-55 and the Gospel. Other than a difference in price and details, these two durable guitars were nearly identical. Both were built on the square-shoulder body shape and employed the 25 ½"-long scale with "double-X" bracing, and both featured a unique arched back of laminated wood—mahogany in the case of the J-55, maple for the Gospel. List price for the J-55 was $390, while the Gospel retailed at $495 (1973 prices; for the sake of comparison, the J-200 that year sold for $695).

Gibson's reasons for selecting "Gospel" as the name for the new model can only be guessed at. It's certainly possible that they were attempting to sell guitars to the relatively large and solid audience that followed gospel music, but it's just as likely that the company decided simply to choose a word with positive connotations, one that would be well received, especially in the South, where nearly every musician, regardless of color, grew up listening to church music. In any case, the only genuflection the model makes to its name is the decal of a flying dove on the peghead. Atop the dove, on a black overlay, is the standard "Gibson" script logo, amid individual tuners with keystone metallic buttons.

Typical of Gibsons of this period, the neck was laminated maple. The ebony fingerboard was unbound and had simple pearl dots. The bridge, also of ebony, was of the bottom-belly, pin design. The black wood of the bridge and fingerboard contrasted well with the natural finish of the spruce top. Gibson used a four-ply binding on top, with a tortoise edge; this binding nicely set off the natural top from the maple sides. Matching the binding was a tortoise pickguard, contoured to the body shape, with an outward point in the upper bout.

The Gospel is a punchy-sounding guitar, somewhat louder than most 1970s Gibsons with "double-X braces" because of its larger sound chamber resulting from the arched back.

It was discontinued in 1980.

J-55 SQUARE-SHOULDER: FAMOUS MODEL, NEW SHAPE

In the early '70s Gibson lovers must have had their hopes raised when hearing that the J-55, one of the great flat-tops in company history, was to be reintroduced. "Reactivated" might be a better word, for during that low period in Gibson history a reissue of a revered model from the early '40s would have been like a savior coming to the rescue.

This 1973 J-55, however, shared little more than the name with its famous pre-War predecessor, and differences between the two guitars outnumber the similarities. Although a reincarnation this model was not, Gibson presented a sturdy, square-shoulder (in contrast to the original's slope-shoulder body), useful guitar.

Dimensions of the J-55 were typical of other contemporary square-shoulder Gibsons. With their three-ply arched backs, though, the J-55s differed from other mid-'70s Gibsons. In the construction of the backs, three sheets of veneer were laminated and then put into a press to create the arch. In so doing, Gibson strove to further the square-shoulder, thick-waisted body's natural sympathy to the bass resonances. This design feature had been used previously on Guild's successful D-25.

The model featured a natural spruce top on walnut-finish mahogany back and sides, a laminated maple neck of a 25½" scale, an East Indian rosewood fingerboard with pearl dots, and the flat, thin, pin-type rosewood bridge used on most 1970s Gibsons. A gold decal with "Gibson" in script adorned the peghead, balanced by chrome-plated individual tuners. Its mock-tortoise shell pickguard, with a point in the upper bout, typified many Gibsons built since the mid 1950s. The body binding, which began as tortoise, by 1981 had become white with black accent purfling.

Upon its introduction in 1973 the square-shoulder J-55 retailed for $390 (and $95 for a hard-shell case); the price had more than tripled by 1982, the last year the guitar was offered. Though relatively short-lived, it still outlasted by two years the similar but fancier Gospel model, which was also introduced in 1973.

Like all Gibsons from that era, the J-55s are sturdy, quite well-constructed guitars but lack refinement. On a positive note, used versions can be found at prices comparable to new overseas guitars. And the Gibsons are clearly the better deal.

J-35 SQUARE-SHOULDER: A FAMOUS MODEL REDESIGNED

By introducing the J-35 in a square-shoulder shape mid-year in 1985, Gibson no doubt was trying to bring an additional model to market at little start-up expense. This plan showed economic common sense, for the J-35 shared so many characteristics (and parts) with the popular Dove model. In fact, these two were the only Gibson models at the time to feature the square-shoulder design with maple backs, sides, and necks. The J-35 square-shoulder was thus a plainer, less expensive version of the Dove.

In offering the square-shoulder J-35 Gibson gave itself more manufacturing flexibility, by creating an outlet for parts that were good but not of high enough quality for the more expensive and ornate Dove. This new J-35 model would also have offered the company numerous options in the case of production overruns on various components of the Dove. Like the Dove, J-100, and J-200, the J-35 used a long-scale (25½") maple neck; all other parts were standard from most models. This "interchangeable parts" approach allowed Gibson to produce a low-cost guitar without having to retool or create any special parts.

The result is an attractive guitar. Starting at the top, the peghead has a traditional black overlay with a gold block script and is pitched at 17 degrees. The truss rod cover is black with a white border. Tuning machines, as on all Gibson flat-tops from that period, have pearloid keystone buttons. On the solid-maple neck is an unbound rosewood fingerboard with pearloid dot inlays. The rosewood bridge is of the top-belly pin style. The mock-tortoise shell pickguard has the standard teardrop shape. Nearly all square-shoulder J-35s are finished with a cherry sunburst. Their tops and backs were constructed with a slight arch to provide greater strength and response.

As is the case with other Gibson flat-tops of this period, the J-35s have suffered numerous problems because of excessive humidity during construction. Better climate control was needed for stability of the instruments, and especially the flat-tops, produced in the Nashville factory.

Gibson constructed few of the square-shoulder J-35s over the two-year production run, and thus the model is relatively rare. These reasonably priced guitars can be sleepers on the market. Be aware that this J-35 is often mistaken for such guitars as the J-40 and J-50 from the "double-X" period, or for the less expensive J-30, a contemporary of the J-35.

J-30: A HUMMINGBIRD WITHOUT THE PLUMAGE

Hank Williams said (and sang) it best—"Praise the Lord, I saw the Light." In a business rather than religious sense, Gibson saw its economic light in 1984: musicians didn't like the flat-tops that this venerable and revered nameplate had made throughout the 1970s and into the '80s. And this facing of reality was a turning point of great consequence to the company. Fortunately for legions of faithful followers, it wasn't too late to turn things around.

Fact: players wanted the older Gibsons. Because of the finite number of these older guitars available, Gibson did the next best thing—they started producing copies of their older models that had been loved by guitar players for decades. At first the copies were not remarkable, but they showed that the people running the company finally realized what musicians had wanted for years. It was a significant start.

When these reissues appeared at the 1984 NAMM show, people in the business were less impressed with the quality of the instruments than with the fact that Gibson was finally trying to set things right. It should be noted that the flat-top operation had recently been moved to Nashville, so in many ways the company was starting over and needed time to get the bugs out. They had many new workers and a climate much more humid than that around Kalamazoo.

In their initial offerings Gibson stuck to the tried and true, reissuing the Hummingbird and Dove models, both similar to the 1960s versions, as well as copies of the 1950s J-45 and J-200.

In 1985 they introduced a new model, the J-30. Basically a stripped-down Hummingbird, this new guitar allowed Gibson to produce an instrument with the same feel and sound as their famous 'bird—at about two-thirds the cost. That year's catalogue marketed the model this way:

> Gibson J-30—The all new combined with the old style Gibson acoustic. People always talk about the old '50s Gibson flat-tops and how great they were. Well, here they are! Single-X bracing on the finest solid spruce top money can buy. Book-matched solid mahogany back and rims, rosewood fingerboard on a '50s style slim mahogany neck. If you want sound with a comfortable feel and price, too, this is the one. Available in antique walnut, wine red, and vintage cherryburst.
>
> PRICE: $532.00

Here are a few specs: the scale was 24¾", like the Hummingbird of that time; the back, sides, and neck were mahogany; the fingerboard was unbound, with dot inlays; a gold decal in block script graced a peghead that had no further ornamentation; the pickguard was the old-style teardrop in mock-tortoise shell.

For numerous reasons these early Nashville guitars had many problems; because of all the company had gone through in the previous decade, because of losing a trained work force, and because of uncontrolled humidity in Tennessee. But the true Gibson renaissance wasn't far away: it appeared in the form of the Montana Division, in June of 1989. Since then the J-30 and other models have evolved into guitars of predictable quality.

THE JG-0 AND THE JG-12

Both as a 6-string guitar (the JG-0) and as a 12-string, the JG model that Gibson introduced to the public in 1970 was an inexpensive square-shoulder jumbo that shared a body size and shape with that year's Jubilee, Heritage, Blue Ridge, and Southern Jumbo, to name just a few. Gibson hoped the JG's affordability would produce strong sales at a time of continued popularity in folk music and growing interest in bluegrass.

The JG models featured natural tops of spruce upon mahogany backs and sides. Trim was minimal: only a simple celluloid strip edging the top and the back left unbound; simple dots on the rosewood fingerboard; the company logo, in decal form, on an otherwise bare peghead.

In 1970 nearly 200 of the JG-12 model sold, a decent number; for whatever reason, Gibson dropped the 12-string version after only one year. The JG-0 did better, with over 500 being sold from 1970 through 1972, the last year of its construction. Although seventeen instruments were shipped in 1973 and one in 1975, it's likely that these were orphans left in the factory in 1972.

12-Strings

Chapter Nine

Ian Tyson of Ian and Sylvia with an early B-45-12.

B-45-12: GIBSON'S REVERED 12-STRING

It's the one that Canadian folksinger-superstar Gordon Lightfoot loves; it's the one that guitar phenomenon Leo Kottke has said is the best 12-string he has ever played. And these two ought to know, forming as they do two-thirds of what can be considered the triumvirate of famous 12-string players. The final third, of course, is the great Leadbelly, who died in 1949, before this model appeared.

In a *Guitar Player* magazine interview, Leo Kottke explains why he so treasures the 12-string B-45:

> I prefer one [a 12-string] that has mahogany rather than rosewood because the note sounds warmer, more apparent, friendly, more musical. That's true of any guitar, but especially true of the 12-string. You get more high-end ring with a rosewood 12-string, and you don't need much of that.

> I really like the B-45 for its adjustable bridge. ...Now I'm becoming convinced that a 12-string should be built with an adjustable bridge, suspended on a couple of screws, because without one the bridge destroys a lot of sustain.

Kottke knows that much of the basic (6-string) guitar-tone theory needs to be thrown out the window when trying for good 12-string tone. Too much treble, too much ringing, too much harpsichord sound: these all often make a 12-string overpowering, with the notes unfocused and indistinct. It's in solving these problems inherent in 12-string guitars that the early B-45-12s excelled, for their many unique features made the model warm, rich, and controllable, more like a 6-string.

However, the construction design that made the very early versions of this model so excellent tonally—to some minds the best 12-string ever—created problems in the instrument's very survival. In short, that which made it good also made it fragile. With this in mind, Gibson recommended that their early 12-strings be tuned down a whole-step and built them very lightly. Buyers didn't always heed Gibson's advice and often cranked them up to standard 6-string pitch or used heavy strings, destroying the instruments in the process. Gibson made attempts to correct this weakness, first by adding a tailpiece and then by beefing up the construction. Neither solution produced instruments equal to the earlier lightly built, pin-bridge models.

Built along lines similar to the revered J-45, at its introduction in 1961 the B-45-12 featured a handsome, 16¼"-wide round-shoulder body with a stock cherry sunburst finish on its Sitka spruce top, as well as on its mahogany sides and back; triple-bound celluloid edged the top and a single strip the back. The Brazilian rosewood bridge was small and rectangular, adjustable by means of an ebony saddle; a trapeze tailpiece made string-pins unnecessary. The pickguard of mock-tortoise shell material was cut into a shape reminiscent of that on the Super Jumbo 200.

The elongated peghead was remarkable for its size and its two pearloid triangles, inlaid vertically, base to base. Enclosed Kluson tuners—very light in weight in order to keep the guitar from becoming peghead-heavy—were fitted with white plastic buttons. The 14-frets-to-the-body neck, built on the 24¾" scale and formed from one piece mahogany, makes use of a single truss rod. A typical 2"-wide neck provided comfortable playing, with an unbound, highly arched fingerboard of Brazilian rosewood marked with pearl dot inlays.

Major changes came within a year. When Gibson switched their Southern Jumbo model from round- to square-shoulder in late 1962, the B-45-12 no doubt followed suit. As Leo Kottke says, this new, boxier body creates the unique Gibson 12-string tonal response: "The B-45 has a 'quack' sound, more presence, more apparent level." This new body shape was about ¼" narrower than its predecessor but wider in the waist and shorter by an inch. Bracing followed the small, non-scalloped style, typical of the late 1950s and 1960s. To take the pull of 12 strings, two parallel longitudinal braces were added, one on each side of the "X-braces." Gone was the tailpiece bridge arrangement, replaced by a top-belly rosewood design with standard bridge pins, an adjustable saddle, and a laminated maple bridge pad.

A small but hard-core group of aficionados seeks out these square-shoulder, pin-bridge B-45-12s made in the early '60s. Sadly, there aren't many of these instruments around (and in good shape), for a combination of light construction and consequent abuse has resulted in structural failures of this fine model, and most of these surviving guitars have not only suffered structural damage but have also had improper repair. (It should be said that 12-string guitars of Martin and Mossman often suffered similar fates; even the heavy-duty Guild 12-strings have had problems. Twelve strings exert so much tension on a guitar that something often gives.)

Starting in 1963 Gibson offered its big 12-string in both the standard cherry sunburst and also as the B-45-12N, which retained the cherry on the back and sides but featured a natural top. Then in about 1964 the model began undergoing considerable modification. First, the bridge was changed to a non-pin version that required the strings to be inserted into holes at the end of the bridge. Then, in an attempt to make these guitars more sturdy, Gibson reverted to a tailpiece to keep the bridges from pulling up from the top. The bracing, however, was designed to take up-pull from a non-tailpiece pin bridge. Subsequently, when the guitar was strung to standard pitch with heavy strings, or the adjustable saddle was raised too high, or a brace/bridge became loose, the top would gradually cave in. Some owners have removed the tailpieces and converted their bridges to a conventional pin-style in an attempt to pull the sunken bridge back to its original plane.

The mid-'60s tailpiece versions used bridges the same size and shape as the pin design. Because all the mass of this bridge was made unnecessary by the tailpiece, a smaller, rectangular bridge was soon substituted, glued to the top as if it were pin-style.

By 1970 Gibson had redesigned their big 12-string, once again reverting to a pin bridge, but this time one with a pronounced bottom belly. Gibson had also converted the B-45-12 to a 25½" scale. The cherryburst finish had been replaced by a dark sunburst, with walnut stain on the mahogany. The natural finish (B-45-12N) continued as an option.

Next to go was the long, pointed pickguard, replaced by a black teardrop; following this was a 14-frets-to-the-body neck, which gave way to a 12-fret. In general, B-45-12s of this era were typical of the 1970s guitars: overbuilt, with workmanship that fell far short of Gibson's reputation.

It's not clear when this renowned model was discontinued, probably 1980. The last catalogue appearance of this grand 12-string was 1976.

Because so few of the great, early versions have survived, you will be lucky to see one. Gibson chose this model as one of its excellent reissues in its "Limited Editions" series that began in 1991, but as of this book's printing Gibson builds no 12-strings as production-line instruments.

THE B-25-12: GIBSON'S SMALLER 12-STRING

Gibson's first 12-string guitar, the B-45-12, was introduced in 1961, retailing for less than $190. The next year a second 12-string, the smaller B-25-12, appeared, selling for about three-quarters the cost of its predecessor. The company catalogue referred to this addition as "a traditional grand concert size instrument," which, at 14½" wide, 19" long, and 4½" deep, had the same body size as the LG- and B-series Gibsons.

This well-constructed guitar featured a 20-fret neck of one-piece Honduras mahogany with 14 frets to the body, pearl dots as fret markers, and an overlay peghead with only the traditional block "Gibson" script in the form of a gold decal. The trim effectively contrasted with the mahogany back and sides, with triple binding around the top, single celluloid on the back, and a mock-tortoise pickguard with a single point in the upper bout. The large adjustable bridge was a top-belly pin design of rosewood, with two pearl dots covering up the heads of the bridge bolts. Tuning machines were six-on-a-plate Klusons, nickel-plated with white plastic buttons. The standard finish on the spruce top was cherry sunburst, though the B-25-12N (natural) was an option. Sides and back were also finished in cherry. (The Epiphone line of Gibson included a version of the B-25-12N during the 1960s, the FT-85 Serenader, which sold at approximately the same price.)

The bridge began a series of changes in or around 1964, when it was altered to a top-belly non-pin style, the strings being inserted and anchored through its end. Within a year a bridge of the same general shape, though larger and

1967 B-25-12 with faded cherry sunburst finish.

Barry Gibb of the Bee Gees with his B-25-12.

without string pins, appeared; it was glued to the top, and a trapeze tailpiece held the strings. The more expensive B-45-12 fairly quickly switched to a much narrower, rectangular bridge, preceding the B-25-12, which followed in 1966. Around this time the nickel-plated machine heads were dropped for chrome, though some nickel tuners were fitted to B-25-12s into late 1967. By 1969 or 1970 Gibson reverted to a pin bridge, but of a bottom-belly design.

By 1968 few of the B-25-12s came with the standard cherry sunburst; the majority were finished in a dark-edged triple-shaded 'burst. The pickguard of this era was a thick celluloid in a swirl pattern; some were attached to the top with wood screws and featured the Gibson logo. The cherryburst last appeared on this model in 1970, when the veneer peghead overlay in black was dropped.

Gradually, the bracing became much heavier. From the time of this model's introduction, Gibson suggested that the instruments be de-tuned a whole-step; the sound was still good and the body suffered no structural problems. However, because of their string tension, when tuned to standard pitch these 12-strings would self-destruct, especially when something that had loosened up or had broken was left unrepaired. The pin-bridge versions especially would develop significant top twisting, and on the tailpiece models the top would sink. Although the B-25-12s were delicate guitars in need of tender, loving care, because of their smaller surface they generally managed to outlive the B-45-12 model.

By 1971 only a natural-finish top was available, and the back, sides, and neck had become a walnut lacquer. The bracing had also been changed to the "double-X" system.

The final year of production for the B-25-12 was apparently 1971, when 43 were shipped; although another four were sold between 1972 and 1975, these probably were factory orphans. The B-25-12N outlived its cherryburst twin, with the last production batch of 54 leaving the factory in 1975.

HERITAGE 12-STRING: COMPETING IN A CROWDED MARKET

When introduced in 1968 the Heritage-12 entered a crowded market that was to become even more crowded. The folk-music revival was yet a market force to be reckoned with, though after more than a decade of prominence it had begun to wane. Still, Gibson believed that there was room for at least one more 12-string guitar, especially one at the top of the price range.

Why another 12-string model at this time? Gibson's best 12-string, the non-tailpiece B-45-12, was discovered to have difficulty in holding up to player abuse, heavy strings, and full-pitch tuning (the company recommended de-tuning by one full note). Adding a tailpiece had only caused further structural problems by exchanging the stress on the bridge to a downward push from an upward pull. The C. F. Martin Company, for all its glory with standard guitars, never saw real success with its 12-string models, either. Guild was a different story, however, and its heavier-braced 12-string guitars sold consistently well.

For better or worse, the Heritage-12 entered the competition, joining two other Gibson 12-string models, the B-25-12 and the B-45-12, each available with either the cherry sunburst or the natural finish. Apparently feeling that the customer needed even more of a choice, Gibson brought out *three* 12-strings in 1969. Along with the Heritage-12 in 1969 came the Jubilee-12N and the LG-12. In 1970, proving that nothing succeeds like excess, Gibson threw two more models into the competition, the Artist-12 and Blue Ridge-12, resulting in the astonishing total of nine 12-string options from the same company.

Listing for $525, the Heritage-12 was the most expensive Gibson 12-string available in 1969. Its features are the same as the Heritage 6-string model of the day: natural finish only; bookmatched rosewood back and sides; an unbound ebony fingerboard with dot inlays; and a rectangular, non-pin, adjustable bridge of ebony. Among the few differences are a tailpiece with the treble side longer than the bass and a peghead lengthened to accommodate 12 tuning machines.

When Gibson retooled for the major changes, in 1971, the Heritage-12 was dropped from the lineup, as were three competing models: the B-25-12, Artist-12, and LG-12. As the demand for 12-string guitars weakened, so did the selection.

LG-12: GIBSON'S BUDGET BOX

The LG-12 was introduced in 1969 as a less expensive alternative to Gibson's B-25-12, which was itself priced at the mid to lower end of the market. At that time American-made inexpensive guitars were having difficulty competing with the cheaper imports, especially those from Japan, which had begun flooding the domestic marketplace. Ever since the 1920s Gibson had made superior flat-top guitars and sold them at a reasonable price, so the company was accustomed to competing for customers in this segment of the market.

The LG-12 was based on the standard LG body size: 14¼" wide, 19" long, and 4½" deep at the endpin. Because worldwide production of guitars in 1969 was so high that large neck-blank materials were difficult to get, Gibson built the neck as a three-piece mahogany laminate, a design that saved money in materials while adding strength.

The 24¾" scale of the six-string LG models was maintained, but the LG-12 neck is the 12-frets-to-the-body design, with only 18 frets total. Because the soundhole location is the same as on the 6-string versions, the fingerboard had to be shortened for the 12-fret neck.

The solid spruce of the top and mahogany of the sides and back came with only a natural satin finish. The unbound fingerboard was rosewood with dot inlays. The pin bridge was built of rosewood in a pronounced bottom-belly shape and featured an adjustable saddle. Simple binding was used on the body's front, while the back remained unbound. The pickguard accompanying the LG-12 upon its introduction was the long version with a single outward point in the upper bout, like those on the LG-1, LG-2, and LG-3 of the early 1960s. In 1970 a black teardrop guard appeared, as did a non-adjustable bridge. The peghead was standard fare, free of an overlay and with a gold "Gibson" decal.

When this inexpensive 12-string first appeared, it listed for $189.50. By 1973 it had been deleted from the catalogue, though the final two were shipped that year.

BLUE RIDGE 12-STRING: FUNCTION UNADORNED

In 1970 Gibson began producing a 12-string version of the Blue Ridge. The company catalogue of that year emphasizes the instrument's reasonable price, surrounded by some marketing creativity:

> Handsomely styled and popularly priced, the Blue Ridge-12 offers the serious musician the finest in acoustical response and playability. The natural, straight-grained spruce top contributes to the full sustaining power of this exciting guitar.

In most ways the 12-string version imitates its 6-string predecessor: back and sides of laminated, flat-sawn Brazilian rosewood of pronounced figure, with a maple underlayer; white ivoroid binding on top and back; laminated three-piece mahogany neck; 12-frets-to-the-body neck; rosewood fingerboard, bottom-belly bridge, and saddle; and a gold script "Gibson" on a walnut-finish peghead.

The 12-string model's bracing was large and bulky, like the 6-string version's, but with two short extra braces on the bottom half of the "X," one on each side, running parallel to and above both the right and left legs.

Like the Blue Ridge 6-string, the Blue Ridge-12 was an unadorned, simple, functional guitar. Its production probably ceased in 1975, although 12 guitars, probably resting on the factory racks, were shipped over the next three years.

ARTIST-12: QUALITY BUILT IN THE J-200 IMAGE

The Artist-12 was a well-constructed guitar that lasted less than a year. Gibson's catalogue of March 1970 prices this attractive 12-string at $695; however, this model is nowhere to be seen in the following September's catalogue, telling us that the bottom line—sales—led to a brief existence.

It was an elegant and well-made 12-string, built on the fancy J-200 body (maple back and sides) with a five-piece neck of maple that, at 12 frets to the body, resulted in a neck of 17 frets, which necessitated relocating the pin bridge deep into this jumbo's lower bout.

In pearl on the peghead are a large Gibson crown and the company name in block script; balancing on the head are deluxe versions of chrome-plated, individual tuning machines; the bound rosewood fingerboard features the J-200 "cloud" pearl inlays, beneath which are an oval soundhole and an adjustable rosewood bridge; the back's center strip is a marquetry "zipper"; the neck heel is capped with pearloid.

The pickguard is unique. Shaped much like the 1930s flat-top 'guards and following the body's contour, it is elevated and made of curly maple that, like the body, features multiple binding.

Given the quality of its construction and the care put into its design, the Artist-12 deserved a longer life and its day in the sun.

Special Body Styles

Chapter Ten

MARK SERIES: ACOUSTIC GUITAR R & D

Gibson's outstanding research project of the 1970s had as its goal a flat-top of radical new design. This impressive effort culminated in 1975 with the introduction of the Mark Series, which consisted of five highly innovative models ranging in price from approximately $400 to nearly $2,000. Although the results of this major endeavor were mixed, the project recaptured the spirit of anticipation that no doubt had gripped Gibson in decades past when exciting new models, whether acoustic or electric, moved from proposal to showroom to the hands of eager musicians, with fanfare at each step.

The story of the Mark Series is an interesting one and is based on firsthand information given by many Gibson employees who worked at the Kalamazoo plant during the 1960s, 1970s, and 1980s, employees who were involved at all levels: line workers, artisans, supervisors, top-level management, and the designer, Richard Schneider. (Schneider was especially helpful in sending information for the writing of this chapter; volunteering blueprints, photographs, Gibson literature on the Mark Series, marketing materials, original design books, and other information.)

The 1970s was a decade ripe for experimentation with the acoustic flat-top guitar, whether by Gibson or by another major maker. Since the '30s the unelectrified guitar had changed little, and whatever improvements materialized were slow in coming, usually the result of trial and error on the part of builders. Gibson was intent on

Mark 35, the lowest-priced model of the Mark series.

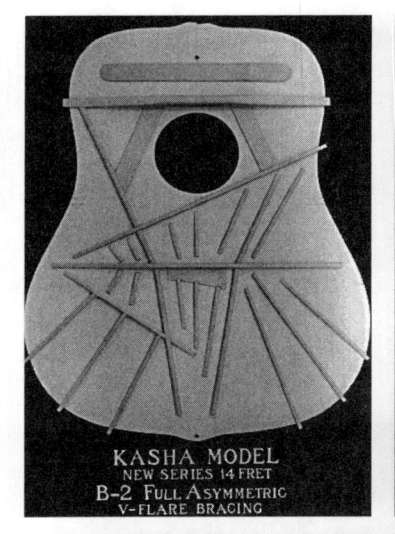

KASHA MODEL
NEW SERIES 14 FRET
B-2 FULL ASYMMETRIC
V-FLARE BRACING

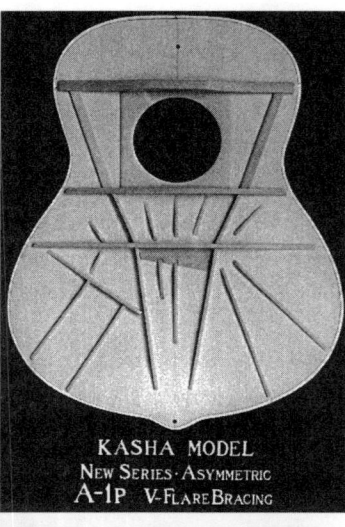

KASHA MODEL
NEW SERIES · ASYMMETRIC
A-1p V-FLARE BRACING

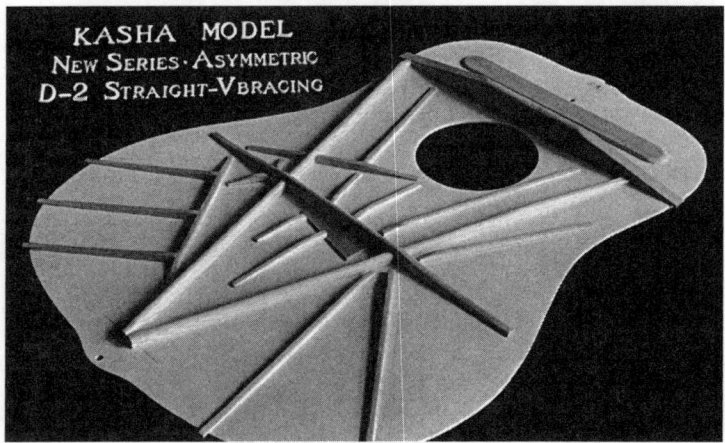

KASHA MODEL
NEW SERIES · ASYMMETRIC
D-2 STRAIGHT-V BRACING

Many experimental Kasha-style bracing patterns were developed for the Mark Series. The A-1p was the closest to the final version; the D-2 was one of the 12-string Mark prototypes.

using scientific advances to create designs that radically improved the flat-top guitar.

An economic imperative also was at work in Kalamazoo. The company had been losing ground to major competitors, especially Guild and Martin, and even to Ovation, an upstart company whose round-backed guitars were scorned by many but whose engineering approach and successful sales made an emphatic point. Even such small builders as Gallagher, Greven, Gurian, Larrivee, and Mossman were making a collective dent in sales.

Gibson's bottom line was suffering from self-inflicted wounds, too. Gibson's manufacturing techniques were dictated by manufacturing costs, speed of construction, and the commitment to avoid excess warranty work—in a word, profit. The resulting guitars were neither competitive nor up to Gibson's reputation for quality, a reputation 75 years in the making. The quick fix of overbuilding a guitar—of making it *too* strong, with an accompanying lack of refinement—in the long run proved counterproductive. Serious guitar players and knowledgeable dealers of the time knew this.

Thus, in 1974 Gibson hired several scientists from around the country to help develop the "ultimate" guitar. Dr. Adrian Houtsma, professor of acoustic physics at M.I.T., Dr. Eugene Watson, professor of acoustics at Pennsylvania State University, and Dr. Michael Kasha, a well-known chemical physicist and director of the Institute of Molecular Biophysics of Florida State University, became consultants on the Mark Series project.

Kasha's research and development of soundboard (top) bracing and bridge design were highly innovative. In collaboration with talented Michigan luthier Richard Schneider, who had worked with him from the beginning, Kasha was gaining attention in the guitar world; his bracing design especially had won the praise of famed classical guitarist Andrés Segovia.

Neither Kasha nor Schneider was new to this business, for both had worked for Gretsch as consultants for a year, before the company dropped their research division. Gibson quickly contacted the two with a contract offer. When they accepted, Gibson prepared to launch the most extensive research project about acoustic guitars ever.

Schneider and Kasha became Gibson's design consultants—Richard on-site, and Kasha visiting a couple times per year, phoning often as well as submitting many reports. Gibson had not had acoustic authorities of this caliber since Lloyd Loar in the 1920s.

Kasha's bracing design, with many tiny braces replacing the traditional larger ones, was scientifically sound but at the time was considered radical. According to his research, this bracing system would offer top stability while yielding more vibration transmission than the traditional "X-brace" system. He had determined that a bridge rocks and "pumps" on a guitar's soundboard. Consequently, a specially designed bridge was developed, one whose bass side was more than triple the width of the treble end. This asymmetrical shape was intended to transmit string vibration to the top with maximum efficiency over the guitar's four-octave range.

The braces were carefully located so as to derive maximum strength and soundboard response; with similar care the vibration bars were placed so as to direct and focus the tone. In his report submitted to Gibson in August 1974, Kasha laid out the criteria to be used in guiding Gibson in their quest: brightness, brilliance, balance, power, and wide dynamic range.

Richard Schneider and his talented assistant/student Abe Wechter were to turn all this high-powered research and theory into practice. (In 1984 Wechter was to play a prominent role in redesigning Gibson's line of flat-tops that would be built in Nashville.) In reality, these two continued to do extensive research and development, not to mention build many prototypes. With their sophisticated research equipment they extensively tested guitars—Gibsons, as well as Guilds, Martins, and Ovations. Watson's "torture chamber" was inflicted upon the Mark guitar, which was put through a whole series of stress and "accelerated aging" tests. These tests helped determine how these newly designed guitars would hold up over extended periods of time, under severe environmental conditions. Meanwhile, Houtsma's essential role was to analyze and evaluate the sound produced by most of the popular stringed instruments.

According to Schneider, some guitars would self-destruct in less than two weeks in the stress chamber, where they were put through extreme temperature and humidity changes while under stress. By means of electronic sensors attached to a guitar at eight stress points, computers analyzed the data and generated valuable information. Consequently, it was learned that the non-sound-producing areas could be strengthened, thus helping to stabilize the instrument. After many models and bracing patterns were frequently tested, Gibson evaluated the merits of its new Mark guitars in comparison to more traditionally braced flat-tops.

The results showed that while all standard acoustic guitars showed permanent distortion of the soundboards, the Mark guitars showed only elastic distortion, meaning that when the vibration caused by sound ceased, the soundboard would revert to its original state. This would mean more longevity for the Mark-style guitar. The new model resulting from the application of such a painstaking study was to be called the Mark—derived from "M" for Michael and "K" for Kasha, with the word *benchmark* acting as a conceptual guide.

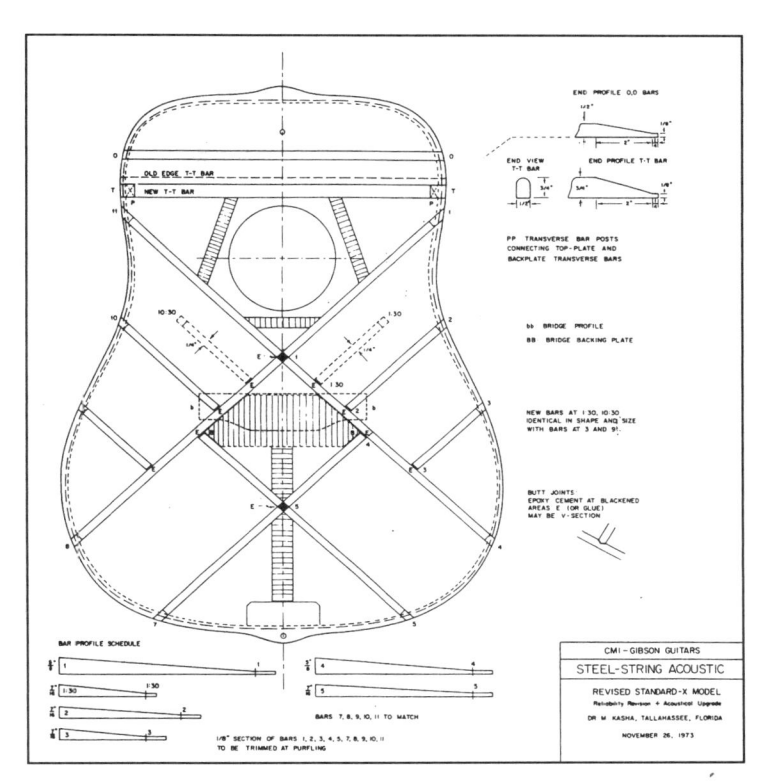

Choosing the name was easier than overcoming numerous problems, however, and this merger of the high-tech and the aesthetic with large-scale mass production was to prove problematic. The personnel side—especially the question of who had control over the decision-making—caused headaches. Although this was a time when most employees and management were willing to support such a huge project, some were threatened by this "modern" approach to guitar design and as a result offered little to what had to be a team effort.

The "double-X" bracing pattern used on tops from 1971 through 1983.

Schneider designed the newly named Mark's body shape for both aesthetics and function. The dimensions of the Mark series, the square-shoulder Gibsons of the day, and the previous slope-shoulder Jumbos are interesting to compare:

	Mark Series	Square-Shoulder	Slope-Shoulder
Upper bout	11 3/4"	11 5/8"	11 5/8"
Waist	10 3/16"	11 1/8"	10 11/16"
Lower bout	16 3/16"	15 15/16"	16 1/8"
Body length	20 5/32"	19 7/8"	20 3/8"
Sides depth	5 3/64"	4 15/16"	4 7/8"

Generally, the Mark Series guitars were more rounded—"curvaceous," as the advertisements stated—than either the square- or round-shoulder Gibsons, though less so than the J-185 or J-200. The Marks were shaped like a large classical guitar. This overgrown classical shape was considered essential to producing the tonal balance and soundboard strength for instruments employing the Kasha bracing.

In order to allow a large volume of guitars to be produced for research, Schneider and his staff would brace the tops and let the factory workers complete the instruments. Relatively quickly it was discovered that if a wide-waist, square-corner guitar were built with the Kasha bracing design, a top with insufficient strength would result. For example, about 100 experimental hybrids were built using J-50 bodies and the Kasha-type bracing, but due to the wide waist of J-50s some tops sank in front of the bridge. These experimental guitars are easily recognized by the bridge design, which is much wider at the bass side than the treble. On the inside of the soundboard, they bear the letters GSKX plus a number. According to Schneider, the "G" stands for Gibson, "S" for Schneider, "K" for Kasha, and "X" for experimental, followed by sequential numbers.

These guitars designed by Richard Schneider have an evenly balanced, steely sound, with rich upper harmonics and strong fundamentals. They do not generate the big and booming low-frequency response associated with a traditionally braced jumbo-shape guitar.

Gibson wanted Schneider to redesign not only the structure of the guitar but also its appearance in each detail. The Mark's headstock was thus a departure from the standard and easily recognizable Gibson fare, with a scooped top radiused downward toward an old-style Gibson logo in pearl; the tall, bottom-flared truss rod cover was also of new design and was edged in white.

Equally unusual was the treatment given the area surrounding the soundhole. Instead of the usual circles of celluloid inlaid into the instrument, the Mark model featured a raised purfling ring protruding perhaps $1/8$" above the surrounding top, creating a distinctly modern appearance and at the same time protecting the soundhole edge. All Mark Series guitars came with a removable pickguard that could be attached or left in the case, depending on player preference. A special adhesive backing permitted the 'guard to be removed and reattached without damage to the finish. Another option offered the player was the adjustable bridge. Three bridge saddles of different heights came with each guitar, allowing the owner to insert whichever height was desired into a slot in the bridge. The saddle slots were first straight through (i.e., visible at each end of the bridge), but some latter ones were closed-ended. Bridge pins were sculpted rosewood with pearl-inlaid dots.

The necks used on Mark guitars were more conventional: three-ply maple measuring $1\,^{11}/_{16}$" at the nut, with a scale of $25\,^{1}/_{2}$". Schneider preferred 12-frets-to-the-body necks, feeling that this design would not only have been more visually appealing but would also have moved the bridge closer to the endpin on the lower bout, resulting in sweeter tonal balance. The 14-fret construction was deemed to be more in demand by the buying public, and marketing considerations won.

The new Nashville plant, which was building only electric guitars at the time, took on the challenge of the Mark Series guitars. Soon it became obvious that the Kalamazoo factory and employees were better suited to producing this new and radical guitar, and so the project headed north, but only after the Marks became the first flat-tops to be built at Gibson/Nashville.

Because of Gibson's marketing considerations and great expectations, construction of the Mark Series guitars began before Schneider was able to

Richard Schneider, Gibson's developer of the Kasha-braced Mark Series, used factory J-50s as experimental guitars as he developed the Mark design.

get them totally prepared for mass production. A little extra time for preparation might have changed the results greatly, and in turn general concepts about steel guitar construction might be different today.

The Mark was clearly a well-designed guitar, and some of the prototypes were outstanding. Gibson's quality control and construction standards of the time left room for improvement, though, and the Mark models suffered. Refinement was lacking; for example, the Mark's very delicate bracing was counteracted by bridges that often were too thick. In spite of the "studio-quality" tone, the Marks didn't generate the sound that most guitarists of the day were looking for. These innovative instruments were in some ways too far ahead of their time; they still have not been given the recognition they deserve.

The Mark Series was introduced in late 1975 and was offered in five models. The following prices are from an early-1976 brochure:

Mark 35	$439
Mark 53	$549
Mark 72	$659
Mark 81	$879
Mark 99	$1,999

Each of the first four models cost $30 less for the sunburst finish, but at nearly $2,000 mid-1970s money, the Mark 99 cost the same, sunburst or natural. Prices were gradually increased until the series was discontinued in 1979 after less than four years of production. This comparison gives perspective to the $1,999 price tag for a Mark 99 in 1976: that same year a J-200 listed for $899.

The least expensive model in the series, the Mark 35 was constructed from book-matched mahogany for its back and sides with book-matched spruce on top, all bound by a single layer of black celluloid, top and back. The bridge and fingerboard were rosewood. Nickel-plated tuners had metal tulip-shaped buttons.

The Mark 53 featured book-matched maple back and sides and was multiple-bound, top and back. Red binding was used to create a striking contrast with the light-colored maple body. Otherwise, most features on the Mark 35 and the Mark 53 were the same.

The plainest of the rosewood models, the Mark 72, used book-matched wood for its back and sides, set off by black/white multiple binding. Its three-piece fingerboard was of ebony/rosewood/ebony construction.

The Mark 81 featured an appropriately fancy trim package: rosewood back and sides, multiple body binding in red, gold-plated tuners, and a rosewood fingerboard with large block inlays of pearl.

About the Mark 99 Gibson's advertisement of the time said it all: "For the perfectionist, Gibson offers the perfect Mark guitar—the Master Luthier model. It's entirely hand made and signed by Gibson's celebrated Master Luthier. With the basic Mark series design criteria plus exclusive hand crafted extras, this guitar virtually has no match." The unnamed master luthier was Richard Schneider. The Mark 99 was advertised as available in either a steel-string or a classical version, but none of the nylon-string models was ever built. Appropriately, this top-of-the-line model featured gold-plated parts and body binding consisting of wood that had been dyed a kingly purple. All of these regal models were built by Schneider with the "pink suspension" bracing system, pink being the color code for tonal rather than structural braces. Only twelve were made, and Schneider cut up two or three because they didn't come up to his standards. That leaves very few out there for collectors to find.

The price of this handmade guitar included the case.

The top-of-the-line Mark 99, with fret dots and bridge pins of silver.

Mark 35-12

In 1977 Gibson produced about a dozen 12-string versions of the Mark 35. According to Schneider, the "D" bracing system ("D" referring to heavier and stronger braces) was designed for the 12-string prototypes. Prior to this, three prototypes had been built, one with lightly constructed straight-V bracing, one with medium bracing, and one with the preferred heavier braces.

Ironically, the most heavily braced one didn't hold up so well as the lighter ones. It was so rigid that it would not flex properly and therefore tended to pull itself apart. All of these 12-strings were prototypes.

THE JUBILEE SERIES: NO TIME FOR CELEBRATION

"Gibson Diamond Jubilee—75 Years of Excellence." The year was 1969, and half of the company advertisement, the first half, was accurate enough: it had indeed been 75 years since Orville Gibson, in his woodworking shop in Kalamazoo, began to revolutionize the stringed-instrument industry in the United States. It was the last word—excellence—that musicians, including legions of Gibson faithful, had begun to take issue with, and for good reason. Gibson, the world's most famous maker of guitars and a nameplate synonymous with quality, had fallen upon hard times, and things were to get worse, much worse, before they got better. Here was the company that not only had survived the Great Depression but had maintained quality control, in fact building many of its best stringed instruments during those dark days—the same company that by 1969 had begun to stray far from Orville's philosophy, standards, and quality. Simply put, the very existence of Gibson was in question.

While it's fitting that a company so steeped in rich tradition as Gibson should publicly celebrate a major anniversary, a grim irony remains that the beginning of Gibson's years of relative mediocrity coincides with the Diamond Jubilee. A second irony is that the guitar Gibson produced for a year to signify their celebration—the Jubilee—more accurately represented the problems beginning in the late '60s than it did their grand and glorious past. The third irony is the most telling: Gibson was unable to get its special models out in 1969—the guitar built to celebrate the 75th anniversary didn't arrive until the company's 76th year.

For the Jubilee line of three models Gibson designed a square-shoulder guitar that was shaped like, but smaller than, the jumbo body and constructed with the recently introduced heavy braces. Other important dimensions for the two 6-string models, the Deluxe and the N: a body 19" long and 4½" deep; a 20-fret neck (14 to the body) built on a 24¾" scale. (These dimensions were identical to Gibson's more rounded, more narrow-waisted LG- and B-Series guitars.) The 12-string N differed only in having 18 frets, 12 to the body.

All had bottom-belly adjustable bridges of rosewood, plain black teardrop pickguards, and spruce tops with a natural finish. The unbound fingerboards were rosewood and featured dot inlays. Typical of that era, the necks were narrow and of three-piece laminated mahogany. A gold "Gibson" traversed a peghead with no overlay.

The advertising for these three was, well, advertising:

> Carefully crafted to a set of demanding specifications, the Jubilee Deluxe is a concert size flat-top that produces a rich, mellow tone . . . A square shouldered flat-top that produces the resonant tone of an instrument twice its size. The Jubilee N is constructed of the finest materials available and will suit the requirements of every serious guitarist. The new square shouldered body design [of the 12N] and the grand concert size provides the guitarist with excellent volume and tonal response.

The Jubilee Deluxe was their most expensive version, at its introduction retailing for $325 and featuring a spruce top on a laminated rosewood back and sides. The Jubilee N differed only in having mahogany back and sides, and of course a lower price tag: $250. The Jubilee 12-N was basically a 12-string version of the Jubilee N; because the neck joined the body at the 12th fret, though, its bridge was moved deep into the lower bout. It listed for $325.

Don't be surprised if you've never seen the Jubilee guitars, for they are rare: because they didn't sell up to company expectations they were produced for only one year.

As a symbol the Jubilee series does less well in celebrating Gibson's 75 years of excellence than it does in representing the frustrations that the company was to endure from the late '60s until two decades later—when the Montana plant started producing guitars that Orville himself would have been proud of.

Montana-Built Flat-Tops

Chapter Eleven

THE MONTANA DIVISION & FACTORY TOUR

In May 1992 we visited the Gibson/Montana facility in Bozeman, spending nearly a week observing the operation firsthand. We had heard from many in the music business that the Montana-built flat-tops were not merely as good as those produced during Gibson's great past but were in many ways superior. By the time we left Bozeman, we were believers.

So that the great importance of Gibson's relocation to Montana is clear, some recent history is in order. All Gibson instruments, whether banjos, mandolins, ukuleles, or flat-top guitars, had been built only in Kalamazoo since the 1890s. The Norlin conglomerate bought Gibson from Chicago Musical Instrument Company in 1969 and built a factory in Nashville in 1974. Both the Michigan and the Tennessee factories were operated simultaneously until 1984, when the Kalamazoo factory was permanently closed.

Gibson's high standards and well-earned reputation for quality had already begun to suffer when Norlin became owners; this decline accelerated because of numerous production problems that arose in the Nashville factory, including excessive humidity, poor factory design, and a shortage of skilled luthiers (most of the former work force chose not to work for Norlin in Nashville). An attempt in 1984 to rectify the many problems was earnest but inadequate: too few flat-tops left the factory and too many were returned.

A Montana-made L-1 reissue.

Gibson/Montana Division President Larry English and a J-180 Artist.

Master luthier Ren Ferguson, a prime mover behind the Gibson flat-top renaissance, making an SJ-200 pickguard.

Businessman Henry Juszkiewicz, long an admirer of Gibson guitars, headed a private group including David Berryman and Gary Zebrowski that bought the company from Norlin in 1985. This purchase marked the beginning of the Gibson renaissance. In 1987 the new Gibson Guitar Corporation bought the Flatiron Mandolin Company in Bozeman and erected a factory there in 1989. Production of flat-top guitars was transferred from Nashville to the new facility that year. During the remarkable period since then, the Gibson mystique and lofty reputation have been restored, and among musicians a reverence for the exceptional flat-tops produced by Gibson has been revivified.

Flat-top production had not come to a complete halt in Nashville as the company made the transition to Montana. Guitars continued to trickle out of the Nashville plant until Bozeman was able to start getting a few guitars out the door. Very few late-1988 or early-1989 flat-tops were made in the Nashville facility, and even in the best of times the plant produced only about five flat-tops per day. When Gibson started production in their new climate-controlled Bozeman factory in 1989, they offered the same models that the Nashville plant had been making, but with many redesigned features. And pre-Norlin standards of quality control instantaneously began to reappear. Those first few guitars to come out of Montana were virtually hand-built by master luthier Ren Ferguson.

The many problems of both the Norlin era and the Nashville factory had been pretty well put to rest by the time of our visit. It was obvious to us that a great pride in workmanship had been established, from the management level that included Ferguson, Division President Larry English, and Product Specialist Robi Johns, through every segment of the work force. Instrument builders we talked to referred to the "Gibson spirit" and to their goal of producing the best guitars possible. It was obvious that many of the workers are avid guitar players who understand not only what a guitar ought to be but also Gibson's high position in the history of instrument making.

During the transition from Norlin/Nashville to Montana, Gibson had remained true to its tradition, allowing considerable experimentation and creativity in the planning of future models. At this time of setting a new direction, the company was training builders, instilling quality control, and managing to build some excellent guitars. Despite the tremendous growth the Montana plant was undergoing, management had been taking the time to listen to musicians, vintage buffs, dealers, and each other. The result: continually improving quality, better tools and methods, better-trained builders, and ultimately better musical instruments.

In this period of dust-settling and roots-planting, Gibson built a smattering of interesting "oddball" guitars and models. There are many reasons for these "irregulars." Perhaps a craftsman would pursue an idea but build only a single instrument or a single batch based on it (for example, the Southern Jumbo 45). Some were special runs, such as some of the koa guitars, or those with mahogany tops, or the "greyburst" J-180s. Others were built with differences between the first and second batches, such as deleting the fingerboard and peghead binding on the J-200 Juniors, while still others were flat-out production errors—a worker would put the wrong fingerboard or bridge on a guitar, or perhaps one model would be given a finish intended for another. A builder's mixup became a player's one-of-a-kind guitar. Quality control is now so tight that this kind of fluke is avoided.

Frustration mixed with excitement during this transition from Tennessee to Montana. Despite the managerial skills of such people as Robi Johns and Bill Gonder and the lutherie talents of Ren Ferguson, John Walker, and other craftsmen, some of Gibson's greatest achievements were not so profitable as hoped. Ultimately, the bottom line is the only line, and while excellent guitars were based on great ideas and were built to the highest of standards, consumer demand had not always been properly evaluated.

Marketing, too, lagged behind the guitar-building expertise at the time, a fact that prevented proper public exposure of new issues as well as of the excellent vintage reissue models. Further, Gibson at first lacked a formal administrative structure and in fact operated for a long period of time without a plant manager.

In 1992 Larry English became Plant Manager and headed a team that included Robi Johns and Ren Ferguson. Together they embarked on a new production and marketing theme. In 1991 and early 1992 Gibson experimented with a wide variety of new and vintage-reissue models. A business decision was made: these new models would be allowed to sink or swim, according to how well they sold. Slow sellers would be dropped from regular production and become special-order guitars only. Unfortunately, some superb models that did not have time to become well known and to catch on fell by the wayside. (They can be special-ordered, though, by those for whom one particular model and no other will do.)

The Gibson renaissance had indeed begun, however, with English, Johns, and Ferguson collaborating, brainstorming, and setting long-term goals in light of what they felt the market would support. A clear system replaced the chaos of previous years. Once they agreed on a new model and English authorized production, Ferguson would go to work developing and testing the prototypes; if these met the team's collective approval, he would then prepare the factory for production. Criticism and advice from workers, musicians, dealers, and collectors no longer fell upon deaf ears.

As a result the Gibson flat-top, which by 1988 was lingering near death, had been resuscitated with unexpected success, the new guitars exhibiting the quality of the best vintage Gibsons ever made. Great guitars were being produced, and Gibson showed a profit, thus assuring future growth and improvement.

In 1992 Gibson categorized their guitars into three groups:

Master luthier John Walker in the Custom Shop.

Gibson Product Specialist Robi Johns and Eldon Whitford examining a Starburst's internal structure.

- Pro Series, consisting of these models: J-30, J-45, J-100, J-200 Jr., J-200 Jr. 12-string, and J-2000
- New Vintage Series: L-00 1936 Reissue, B-45 12-String, Hummingbird, Advanced Jumbo, Dove, and J-200
- Electric Acoustic Series: The Star (cutaway) and J-160E

THE NEW ACOUSTIC MODELS

In 1993 the Gibson acoustic collection was reorganized, this time into five groups, which Gibson called "Series." Because the crew at Montana felt that the models needed to be better understood by the players, they grouped the total offering of 19 production models logically. These five groupings and their models are as follows:

J-200 Series
1. J-200
2. J-100 Xtra
3. J-200 Junior

Historical Series
1. Hummingbird
2. Dove
3. J-160E
4. Gospel

Pro Series
1. J-30
2. J-45
3. J-60
4. J-2000 Custom

L-Series Blues Models
1. L-00 Blues King
2. L-1
3. L-20 Special

Electric Acoustic Series
1. EAS Standard
2. EAS Deluxe
3. Starburst Studio
4. Starburst Standard
5. Starburst Elite

In addition to the regular production guitars listed above, as of 1993 non-production or unique models could be obtained in two ways: the Gibson/Montana Custom Shop would build whatever previous models they had done with whatever special features the customer desired; and each month a non-production model would be featured.

Gibson's Custom Shop deserves some discussion. This small shop overlooking the main floor of the factory is headed by Ren Ferguson and staffed by him, John Walker, and a handful of the best of the regular factory builders, hand-picked and carefully tutored. The guitars they build are the elite of Gibson's flat-top production. Each guitar leaving the shop comes with a signed Custom Shop label affixed to the inside of its body, a Custom Shop logo on the back of the peghead, a signed and certified document, and a Gibson "Ultra Case." Under the leadership of Ren Ferguson, the Custom Shop has quickly established a reputation for the highest-quality work. We can take the word of Emmylou Harris for it:

> When I recently visited the Montana factory to pick up my new SJ-200, I finally got the chance to witness the Custom Shop at work firsthand. Ren Ferguson is an incredible guitar builder. It's amazing how he combines the best of the old-world techniques of guitar building with the new. When I watched him hand-carve the pickguard, I was amazed. There he was, just doing it totally by hand. The custom guitars that he was working on while I was there were simply stunning.

In addition to special-order guitars, Gibson produced a "Montana Special of the Month" in 1993. Each month approximately 31 individual instruments of a non-production model were built, with the year-end total numbering somewhere near 365. Thirty-one selected dealers participated in this special offer of the following instruments:

January: J-200, rosewood back and sides, SJ-200 type bridge, Grover Imperial tuning machines

February: L-1 with curly maple back and sides, Nick Lucas fingerboard inlay, and flowerpot inlay on peghead

March: Advanced Jumbo in natural finish with herringbone binding around the top

April: Dove with pearl top binding and truss rod cover

May: J-60 with curly maple back and sides and tortoise shell style binding

June: 1950s reissue of J-200 with curly eastern maple back and sides, SJ-200 bridge, and Grover Imperial tuners

July: 1962 reissue of J-180 with thick pickguard and pinless bridge

August: Hummingbird in exotic Hawaiian koa mahogany with abalone rosette

September: Robert Johnson L-1 estate edition in black, with pearl signature at 12th fret and pearl truss rod cover

October: Advanced Jumbo with curly maple back and sides enhanced by abalone top inlay

November: J-180 Artist in black with tortoise

shell-style binding on body, neck, and peghead and gold mother-of-pearl inlay

December: J-200 in Hawaiian koa mahogany with abalone binding the top, rosette, fingerboard, headstock inlay, and truss rod cover; Grover Imperial tuning machines

As this book goes to press, on the eve of Gibson's centennial (1894 to 1994), uncertainty about the company's future and its ability to produce exceptional guitars has been put to rest, after some admittedly trying times. The vintage treasures of tomorrow are being built by Gibson/Montana, today.

THE SUPER JUMBOS

The J-200 Reissue: A Once and Future King

The "King of the Flat-Tops" is still the King. More than 55 years after its introduction, the J-200 remains one of Gibson's best-selling flat-tops. While this unique model of unmistakable aesthetics has been always a steady mover on the market, never has it been as popular as it is in the 1990s.

When the craftsmen at Gibson/Montana inherited the J-200 from the short-lived Nashville flat-top operation, they redesigned it, restoring many of the desirable features of the earlier J-200s. The changes had to be gradual as existing supplies of parts were used up. The unseen interior structure, though, was quickly modified, and the "single-X" design with tapered and scalloped top bracing quickly appeared.

Workmanship is cleaner and tighter than on previous J-200s, and premium materials have been carefully chosen, in keeping with this model's pedigree and cost. As a result the J-200 again looks and feels like the 1950s model, in natural finish or the sunburst option.

In 1991 and 1992 Gibson reissued the rosewood SJ-200 as part of its "Limited Editions" series. Because of their expense, relatively few of these replica models were produced. In late 1992 a handful of regular production J-200s were made in rosewood.

In March 1993 Gibson decided to build the J-200 with Eastern American hard maple, rather than the European equivalent that had been used for many years. This exchange of foreign maple for the domestic supply results in a tonal difference greater than that between the Indian and Brazilian varieties of rosewood. Eastern hard maple is much more dense than the European counterpart. Not only is it superior tonally, but its figure takes on a striking beauty when stained and finished. A Lloyd Loar-era F-5 mandolin, a 1930s Nick Lucas guitar, or a 1950s SJ-200: if you're lucky enough to have one of these available, you can both see and hear the beauty of this Eastern maple.

Among the many merits of the J-200 Gibson advertising lists the guitar's "thunderous sound" and its "ultimate visual beauty and tonal quality." No one who has played the "King of the Flat-Tops" could argue with these claims.

SJ-200 Montana: The Rosewood King Returns

It couldn't have taken long for Gibson management to decide that its most distinctive and famous flat-top in history be reissued as part of the "Limited Editions" series in 1991. When the Super Jumbo was introduced in 1937, the acoustic guitar world was forever changed. In its reissue 54 years later, Gibson retained the most desirable features of the original and added the best of modern guitar-building techniques.

J-200.

head "Gibson" was inlaid in pearl in the old-style script. Also carefully duplicated was the binding: the inner edge of the soundhole was bound with a single strip of white celluloid, while multiple binding was used on the body, front and back. Gibson took great care in reproducing the ebony "moustache" bridges—twin pairs of pearl ribbons were retained, as were the two pearl dots covering the bridge bolts. The stair-step tuning machines were gold-plated Grover Imperials. The signature pickguards were all hand-built in the custom shop, with the intricate flower motif engraved manually. Finishes were available in sunburst or natural.

The SJ-200 reissues were made in limited quantities and by 1993 could be purchased only as Custom Shop instruments. One natural-top SJ-200 LE was made for Emmylou Harris that year.

> *"For a while, especially in the '70s, Gibson had their problems, but their new guitars are outstanding. I'm a real vintage-guitar fan, but the new Montana ones are really something. I haven't played one yet that I didn't like. It's good to see Gibson back in the saddle again."*
>
> —Emmylou Harris

J-100/J-100 Xtra: In the J-200 Mold

The J-100 is a survivor. As the SJ-100 it was introduced in 1939, only to be discontinued in 1942. In 1972 it reappeared as the J-100, lasting but briefly. The Nashville plant then reintroduced the model in 1985, with maple back and sides instead of the original mahogany, but few were made. In spite of these numerous transformations and demises, the J-100 arrived in Montana for its latest rebirth.

Gibson advertised its 1989 model this way: "Gibson's J-100 differs only in the ornamentation from the classic J-200. The J-100 is kept simple to put the emphasis on the musician and the music." The result was an attractive but unadorned guitar: sunburst or ebony finish, maple back and sides, rosewood top-belly bridge, simple rosewood neck with pearl dots, teardrop pickguard, multiple-bound body, and enclosed individual tuners.

In constructing this reissue Gibson used the dimensions and internal bracing of their regular model J-200. A more significant difference between the contemporary J-200 and the old SJ-200 involved wood; while the J-200s since WWII have used maple for their backs and sides, the earliest versions featured rosewood, and therefore only rosewood would do for the reissues.

The limited-edition SJ-200s were based on pre-War rosewood versions.

The Montana SJ-200s were careful replicas in the important details. For example, on the peg-

1991 Prototype SJ-100 reissue, with "stair-step" peghead.

1993 J-100 Xtra.

Sales expectations were not reached with the first of the Montana reincarnations, however, perhaps because this version was too simple, too plain. Thus, in 1993 Gibson looked carefully at this model that wasn't living up to expectations, and the changes began. The goal: to make the J-100 more identifiable with the famous and super-elaborate J-200.

Gibson designers then built a couple of prototypes with "moustache" bridges, old-style (1939 to 1942) pickguards, and stair-step pegheads. This new version, dubbed the J-100 Xtra, successfully captured the feeling of the '30s model, which in fact had featured substantial ornamentation, considering that it was advertised as a stripped-down version of the regal J-200. The re-emergence of the J-100 had begun.

The new model represented a return to the powerful personality of the original 1930s SJ-200 model. Mahogany supplanted maple as the wood for the sides and back, giving this huge flat-top the warm, sweet tone that the pre-War SJ-100 mahogany versions were known for. Also, its "moustache" bridge of course identified the J-100 as a member of the same family as the fancy J-200; its pickguard, of the same shape as that on the J-200 but without the engraving and overall fanciness, reiterates the family relation. Although the stair-step peghead design of the prototypes was not retained, Gibson added a vintage-style "Banner" proclaiming "ONLY A GIBSON IS GOOD ENOUGH."

This J-100 Xtra is by far the most interesting revision of the original 1930s SJ-100.

THE NARROW-WAIST JUMBOS

J-180/J-180 Artist:
In the Everly Brothers Tradition

In 1986 Gibson introduced the J-180 acoustic, a Nashville-built, imitative "sequel" to the original Everly Brothers model, whose production run extended from its debut in 1962 until its discontinuation in 1972. In 1991 production of the J-180 was transferred from its Nashville facility to the Montana plant, where the model became part of Gibson's successful "Limited Editions" reissue series.

This Custom Shop J-180/Dove was patterned after a special-order guitar made in the 1960s.

J-185 Montana reissue.

Excepting quality control, a top priority of all the Montana-built guitars, the reissue J-180 differs little from its Nashville predecessor. The "Limited Edition" J-180s, for example, have a slightly wider "X-brace" angle—though at 103 degrees only 3 degrees more—and the braces themselves are scalloped and tapered. All other major features have remained relatively unchanged.

The model has remained a popular stage guitar because of its unique and striking appearance and how it "mikes." The J-180, with its body size and shape, responds beautifully to any kind of electronics; the tone is loud, clear, and rich, but without the boominess that is a characteristic problem with the wide-waist instruments.

The J-180 has also been a popular model for customizing, and stunning examples exist. Visualize this one: a cream-color body contrasting with binding of a tortoise shell pattern; star inlays cut from gold pearl; a truss rod cover of gold plate, harmonizing with tuning machines of similar plating and pearloid keystone buttons; a rosewood peghead veneer; two small pickguards of a thin mock-tortoise shell celluloid. The J-180 has been the '55 Chevy of the Gibson flat-tops.

The customers aren't the only ones taken with this model: Gibson liked the guitar so much that they turned it into a special-run instrument, which they named the J-180 Artist.

The J-185: A Classic Beauty Reissued

The Gibson J-185 is a musical enigma. From its introduction in 1951 to its demise in 1958, the model never sold well, and only about 700 of them were produced. The fans of these guitars—fanatics is the more accurate word—value them above all other models. Instrument builders, including Martin, Guild, and Taylor, to mention just the largest companies, have copied the general body style and dimensions, while Gibson has copied itself by using J-185 features on other models it constructs. As further evidence of its continuing popularity, the J-185 is a favorite body design for numerous small builders of custom instruments. What is it about this model, never wildly popular in its day, that now makes it coveted by so many? Its near-perfect design provides the power of the large, wide-waist guitars but with much more clarity and balance—and in a shape that guitarists find simply beautiful to the eye.

Gibson reintroduced this much-sought-after vintage flat-top in 1990, hoping to capitalize on its mystique. The reissue was carefully and accurately done, including a near-duplicate bracing pattern, and in workmanship and overall quality was superior to the original. One change involved the scale, which had been extended to 25½" in the reissue from the 24¾" of the original.

Despite its many qualities and its faithful following, the J-185 reissue encountered the same marketing problems that faced its namesake 32 years before. The incredible, enduring popularity of the bold J-200 hurt the sales of its more reserved relative once again; and as the more striking J-200 Junior was issued, built in fact on the J-185 body, ironically the J-185 was relegated to limited production. One year after its reissue, this grand model had disappeared from the regular lineup.

Although presently not available as a regular production guitar, the J-185 can still be ordered through the Custom Shop—for those guitarists who will play nothing else.

J-200 Junior: Prince of the Flat-Tops

This recently created model is in many ways not a new guitar so much as a union of two revered models, the J-185 and the "King of the Flat-Tops" J-200. Because over the years Gibson had received so many requests for a smaller-body J-200, they decided to integrate the J-185 body with the ornamentation and trim of the standard J-200; this marriage fruitfully begat the J-200 Junior.

Jeff Bergman, at the time a member of Gibson management, presented a prototype of this model to company co-owner Henry Juszkiewicz, who preferred this guitar's charisma to the more

J-185 custom-order in koa with fire-stripe pickguard and Nick Lucas fingerboard inlays.

J-200 Juniors of the first run were called "J-200 Minis."

1992 J-200 Junior.

reserved aspect of the J-185. Gibson management also liked the idea of producing another model built of curly maple, a superb tone wood readily available in North America. The J-200 Junior was introduced in 1991 and met with quick success.

Gibson advertising gets to the point: "A new favorite of recording artists, the J-200 Junior offers the characteristic features of the legendary Gibson J-200 jumbo in a smaller body size." At quick glance, the smaller size seems to be the only difference, with the Junior slightly smaller: 16" wide at the lower bout, 9½" at the waist, and 11⅜" at the upper bout, built on an overall body length of 20⅛". The Junior differs from its namesake in two related ways: its peghead and fingerboard are unbound, and at a list price of $1,799 (1993 price) it costs about two-thirds as much as the "King" ($2,549). Otherwise, the junior and senior are nearly identical and in fact share finish options—antique natural and vintage sunburst on choice Sitka spruce tops.

Glued beneath the Junior's top is "single-X" bracing located 1" from the soundhole and at an angle of 103 degrees. The braces themselves are scalloped and tapered. Angling off the treble side of the "X" at 61 degrees are the tone bars. The small bridge pad is eastern hard maple. The overall internal structure was well designed by Gibson and makes for a great-sounding guitar, with volume and tone aided by the back, sides, and neck of curly maple; the neck, however, is not solid maple but three pieces, with rosewood sandwiched in the middle.

The signature details of the J-200 are retained in the Junior: the unique pickguard, the fingerboard inlays, and of course the "moustache" bridge, though in a smaller version.

Because the J-200 Junior results from the union of two famous and compatible models, its future seems secure.

1992 Southern Jumbo "Banner" reissue (top left).

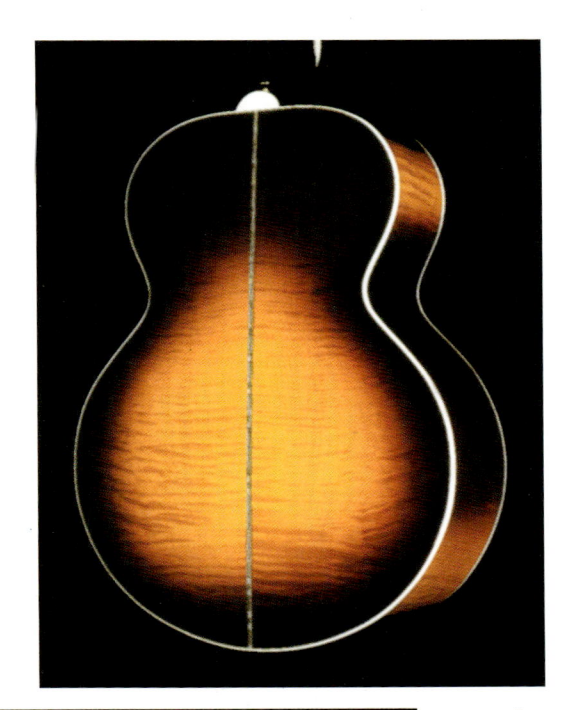

1992 J-200 Junior with flame maple (top right).

Starburst Elite with unusual "bubble" maple used for the top (bottom).

GUITARS FROM THE GIBSON/MONTANA CUSTOM SHOP

Pearl-inlaid Hummingbird (right and opposite page).

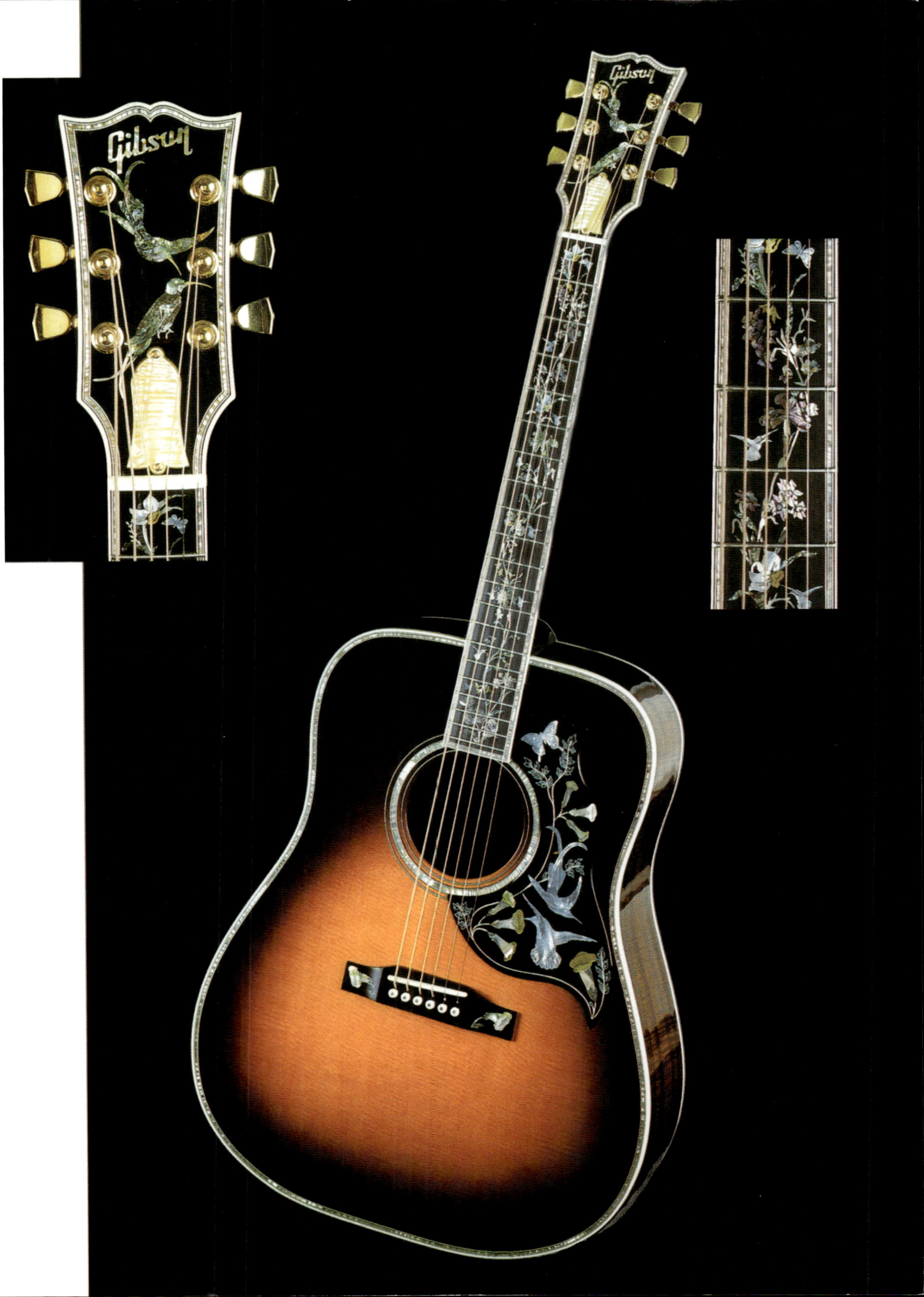
Gibson

J-200 with special gold sparkle trim and gold "lip pearl" (this page and opposite top).

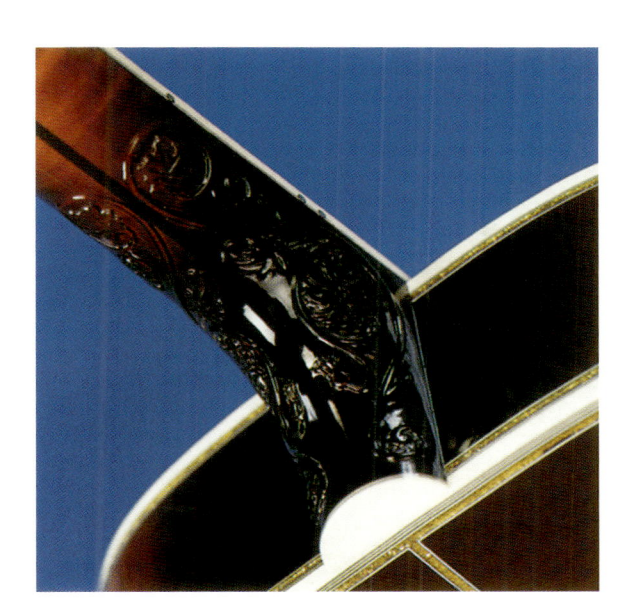

J-2000 built specially for Gibson/Montana Plant Manager Larry English (bottom).

Sunburst J-200.

Two elegant L-1s from the Custom Shop.

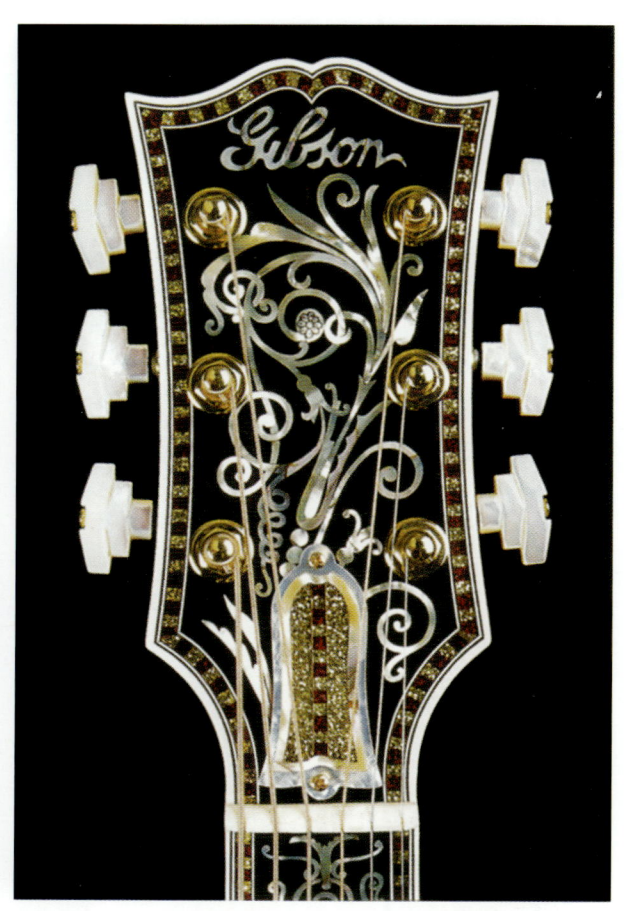

An elaborate Custom J-200 (this page and opposite).

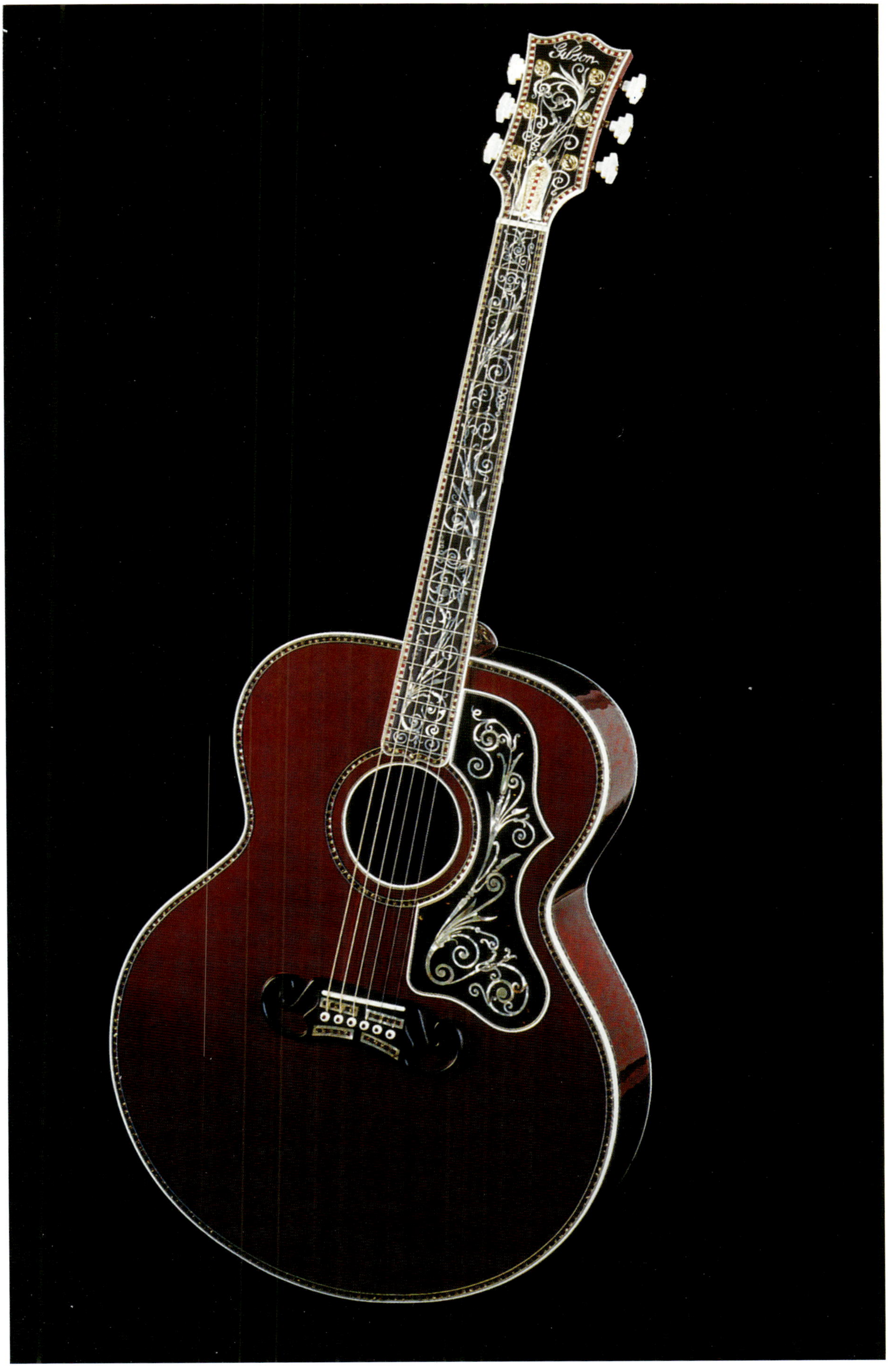
Gibson

Star-studded
J-180.

Gold, white, and tortoise on a J-180 custom.

Custom pearl Dove.

Cherry Sunburst Hummingbird.

This custom-built Advanced Jumbo was constructed with highly flamed hard maple and red spruce.

J-200 in black and pearl.

Custom Advanced Jumbo with Brazilian rosewood, Adirondack red spruce, and abalone.

J-200 Junior 12-String: Short-Lived Luxury

After not producing a 12-string for many years, Gibson brought out two models in 1991, a reissue of the well-known B-45-12 and the new J-200 Junior 12-string.

Differences between the J-200 Junior and the J-200 Junior 12-string are minor. The 12-string version initially had a simple top-belly bridge, but this was soon replaced by one of a "moustache" design, in keeping with the image awakened in guitarists when they hear the name J-200. A 1960s J-200 bridge was used as the model, one with pearl inlay on each wing to simulate the cutout effect from the '50s and earlier. The bridge of the 12-string model has a non-adjustable saddle. An obvious deviation was quickly corrected by Gibson when they added the standard "crown" inlay to all 12-string models after a few were built with only the company name on the peghead.

Two other differences result from the tension accompanying an extra six strings. First, the Junior uses the shorter, 24¾" scale. In addition, for added strength the braces are scalloped but not tapered. Consequently, unlike some of the 12-string Gibson models from the '60s, the Juniors are made to be tuned to full pitch for playing. Because of its body shape and its use of maple rather than mahogany, the J-200 Junior 12 has a more ringing tone than the famous B-45-12 of the 1960s.

A final distinction, the use of gold-plated mini-Schaller tuners, results from the necessity of fitting 12 tuning machines on the peghead, which, even though elongated, would look crowded and cramped when populated with full-size machines.

As Gibson advertising said, and without much dissension possible, "The J-200 Junior 12-string is the most beautiful 12-string available today." Sad to say, because of growth considerations in what was in reality a young factory needing to streamline itself in Montana, all 12-string flat-tops were dropped at the end of 1992, including this model.

The J-2000: 1990s Elegance

Not surprisingly, Gibson master luthier Ren Ferguson accepted when asked to design and build the ultimate master-grade, all-purpose guitar. In his words, "I designed the J-2000 to combine the elegance that is Gibson's tradition with the needs of modern-day guitarists who desire full neck accessibility and demand the finest acoustic guitar money can buy."

A charge to build "the ultimate" creates a delicious dilemma for an instrument maker: what body size and shape, which woods, how much ornamentation? And these questions lead to the company's bottom line: what price? Such a decision is as much a question of what to leave out as what to include. Like many contemporary builders, Ferguson chose the body of a guitar that was introduced in 1951, the much-admired J-185, as the perfect size for all playing styles; and he built the ultra-fancy J-2000 around it.

This new model, introduced in 1991 and renamed the J-2000 Custom in 1993, offers power, clarity, balance, and of course a stunning appearance. Ferguson selected rosewood for the sides and back, Sitka spruce for the top. A slim one-piece mahogany neck and an ebony fingerboard with a 12" radius offer that traditional Gibson feel. A Venetian cutaway allows access to

J-2000, a model intended to approach the ultimate. Rosewood back and sides, ebony fingerboard and bridge, abalone trim, and gold hardware.

the upper registers. The gentle flow of the ebony bridge results from continuous arcs combined in harmony.

As befits an imperial guitar, the trim is intricate, with expensive green abalone outstanding around the body periphery and the soundhole. More of this beautiful abalone is used for the delicate, tasteful inlays in the fingerboard, on the peghead, and on each wing of the bridge; a "Gibson" inlay in the 1930s script is topmost on the peghead and is, of course, green abalone.

The border inlay technique requires "cracking" the abalone as it is inlaid, thus avoiding the flat ends that result when the abalone pieces are filed to fit. This "cracking" makes an invisible transition between the individual pieces.

The J-2000 is available in two finishes, natural or vintage sunburst top. As remarkable as this guitar looks, its tonal qualities keep pace, due in part to scalloped and tapered braces that, like the top, are hand-tuned. The brace pattern employs the "single-X" design in a 103-degree spread. The appearance and total response of this model is exceptional, with playability to match.

In appearance, quality of workmanship, and tonal quality, the J-2000 might well fill the dreams of amateur or professional guitarists who require great versatility in a single instrument; with the piezo pickup and endpin-jack option, the J-2000 does about as much as one guitar can in offering the ultimate to the few.

J-1000 & J-1500: Affordable Members of the J-2000 Family

In 1992 Gibson brought to market two intelligent afterthoughts, the J-1500 and the J-1000, both built as less costly versions of the J-2000, the most expensive flat-top in the company's history. During this period at the Montana factory in Bozeman, many models were designed, built, and then discontinued when the market didn't immediately respond to them. Although this method of market

> The J-2000 Custom was designed and built by master luthier Ren Ferguson.
>
> The J-1500 & the J-1000 were both short-lived models that offered the J-2000 Custom design without the frills.

testing works well for models that take off quickly, many casualties result—quality guitars that for whatever reason didn't generate sufficient sales quickly enough. The J-1000 and J-1500 were casualties, and only a few dozen of these two models were built before their discontinuation.

The J-1500 featured the same body size, shape, and woods as the J-2000. For a guitar that was conceived as a stripped-down version of a more expensive guitar, the J-1500 was very fancy: abalone was used for the "Gibson" script, the fleur-de-lis of the peghead, the soundhole purfling, and the fingerboard inlays that imitate those of a mid-'30s F-7 mandolin.

The J-1000 model was an additional step removed from the J-2000. To bring the list price down even more, Gibson built the J-1000 fingerboard and "moustache" bridge from rosewood rather than ebony, inlaid only "Gibson" on the peghead, and used simple diamond-shaped inlays as fret markers. The J-1000 shares other features with its more elaborate (and expensive) relatives.

Because so few J-1000s and J-1500s were produced, these adorned guitars should prove highly collectible not far off. Ironically, the less expensive J-1000s for some reason exhibited exceptional tone and volume, making them especially attractive to prospective guitar buyers/collectors.

THE SLOPE-SHOULDER JUMBOS

The J-45/J-50: Legends Reissued

From the day it first appeared in 1942, the J-45 and its natural-top cousin, the J-50, have been held in high esteem for their sweet tone and their reasonable cost. In 1991 the Gibson/Montana "Limited Editions" series sensibly included the sunburst J-45 and the natural-finish J-50.

All Montana J-45s exhibit features put in place by master luthier Ren Ferguson, such as scalloped and tapered braces, traditional styling of bridges, and a 98-degree "X-brace" pattern, to name a few. Externally these guitars conform to the old and valued J-45/J-50 features: round-shoulder shape; mahogany back, sides, and neck; Sitka spruce top; rosewood fingerboard and top-belly bridge; 24¾" scale; and the small teardrop pickguard in mock-tortoise celluloid. Internally, the J-45/J-50 has features similar to the other Montana Gibsons, such as tapered and scalloped braces, parabolic arches, and all solid woods. For a while some were made with natural tops and the longer, larger pickguards—these were called J-50s. Also, a few of the "faded" cherry sunburst J-45s were produced.

J-45 reissue.

The new J-45/J-50 captures the special feeling and personality of the originals. A combination of quality and reasonable cost has helped the model continue its successful run.

Advanced Jumbo: The Reputation Returns

In the minds of many who know about such things, the pre-War Advanced Jumbo is probably Gibson's best flat-top ever. Because fewer than 300 of them were made, from 1936 through 1940, these lofty instruments have remained out of the limelight, keeping their reputation unknown except to the few cognoscenti for whom any guitar other than the AJ isn't quite good enough.

The players, collectors, and dealers lucky enough to own original AJs are avid and relentless in singing the praise of the model. These would include North Carolinian Gary Burnette, who in his vintage-instrument shop in Asheville has amassed many choice Gibsons of vintage stature, incredible-sounding AJs among them. When Gibson was selecting the lineup for its "Limited Editions" series, Burnette's expertise was of great help in ensuring that the replicas lived up to the lofty standards embodied in the originals.

The timing was right. Gibson's new factory in Bozeman, Montana, presented a climate ideal for building flat-tops (in contrast to the Nashville facility, where humidity had continually caused problems). They also had acquired the services of master luthier Ren Ferguson. And Gibson had made the commitment to building the best guitars possible, anywhere or anytime.

Burnette's prototype 1935 Advanced Jumbo was lent to Gibson for a complete inspection and a detailed blueprinting. With its remarkable tone, workmanship, and volume, this surely was the right guitar to duplicate. After the homework and the tooling-up, in 1990 Gibson's craftsmen produced the first instruments, and excellent duplicates they were. Burnette in fact has the first two off the line.

What few differences exist between the original Advanced Jumbo and the first of the reissues resulted mostly from the change in availability of materials over a 55-year period: select Sitka spruce tops in the reissue versus Adirondack red spruce in the pre-War versions; back, sides, fingerboard, and bridges of Indian rosewood instead of Brazilian; a fullerplast finish rather than nitrocellulose lacquer; the double dovetail neck joint (in use by Gibson since the mid-'70s) instead of the original's single design; and parabolic top-arching.

The last major difference involved the style in which the braces were scalloped and tuned. The result was the same, however, with Gibson craftsmen tuning the new braces to yield the same tonal response as those of the original, while attempting to produce a little more strength in the tops and backs.

Later that year Gibson reverted to spraying nitrocellulose lacquer. This significantly improved both the appearance and the tone of all Gibsons, including the Advanced Jumbo.

Reissue of 1930s Advanced Jumbo.

Gary Burnette has played a major role in developing numerous Gibson flat-top reissues, especially the Advanced Jumbo. He and his wife, Bonnie, perform bluegrass music on their original AJs.

Meanwhile, back in his shop in Asheville, Burnette began experimenting with the bridges on his two reissues. By replacing the Indian rosewood bridges with identical ones of Brazilian rosewood, he discovered a marked difference in tonal response. He relayed this information to Gibson's Ren Ferguson, who reproduced the experiment with the same results. All Advanced

Advanced Jumbo with natural top.

Montana prototype Advanced Jumbo with Brazilian rosewood and red-spruce top.

Custom Shop Advanced Jumbo top and braces.

Jumbos made after that point came with Brazilian rosewood bridges.

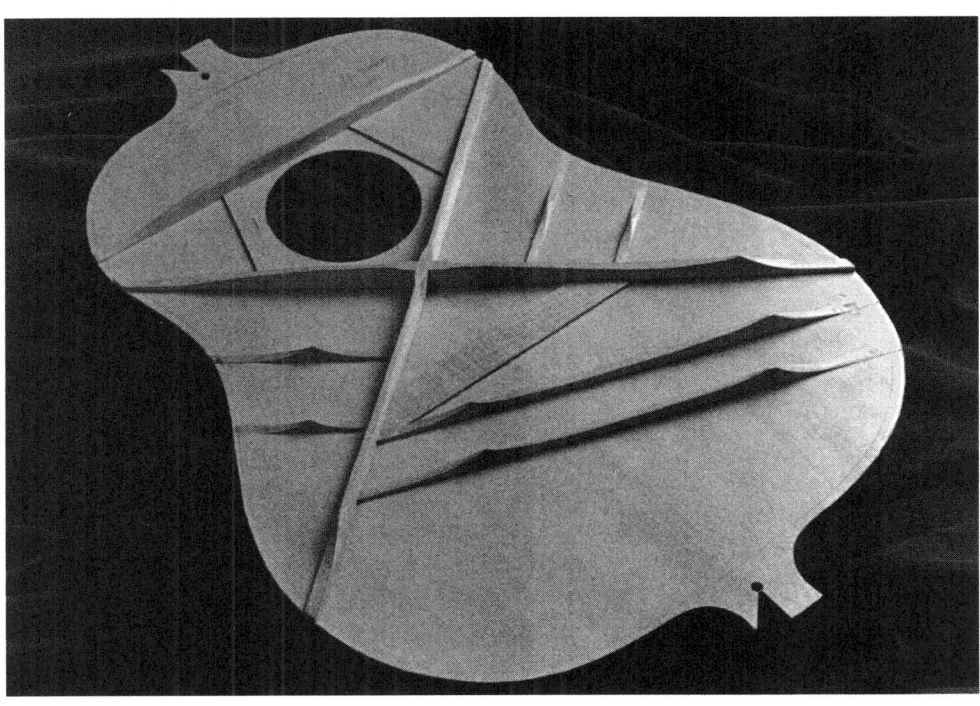

The final change, one that's sure to be appreciated by repairmen 20 years or so down the road, involved the method of attaching the neck to the body. In May 1992 Gibson chose to go with the older-style single-dovetail neck joint instead of the more complicated double-dovetail, and to use the traditional hide glue. Whether this reversion will improve a guitar's tone is debatable; however, there is no question that repair shops in the next century will find it easier to reset necks. Because almost every high-quality flat-top will need its neck reset at some time, it is important that manufacturers build their guitars to simplify this process, so that the integrity of the guitar is in no way compromised. This is the same philosophy that quality violins are made by, allowing tops and backs to be easily removed for repairs.

Custom orders accounted for numerous sales of the Advanced Jumbo. The most common change requested of the Montana Custom Shop was for red-spruce tops (as in the original AJs) instead of Sitka. Also, some had been made with Brazilian rosewood backs and sides rather than Indian, others with curly maple. A few AJs with natural tops instead of the vintage sunburst were constructed in late 1992. Finally, a few buyers preferred abalone over mother-of-pearl for the inlays.

Because of insufficient sales, the Advanced Jumbo reissue ceased regular production in late 1992. It's difficult to explain why such an excellent reissue didn't catch on—perhaps it would have if given another year. Jimmy Martin, Mac Wiseman, Del McCoury, Eddie Adcock, Alison Krauss, Marty Stuart, Sam Bush, Earl Scruggs, and Sonny Osborne: this list of noted bluegrass guitar players who purchased the AJ reissue certainly speaks of the instrument's exceptional tone. Country singer and guitar ace Vince Gill also plays one.

It's true of the Montana reissue just as it was true of the late-'30s original: the Advanced Jumbo is one of the more remarkable guitars in history.

Southern Jumbo "Banner" Reissue

As one of Gibson's most revered models from the past, the pre-War Southern Jumbo "Banner" was a classic, a natural to be part of the reissue series of the early '90s. This was, after all, the guitar of the South, the guitar of Hank Williams and Woody Guthrie. Gibson believed that a model with such a sterling pedigree was a prime candidate to reappear in replica form. And they were right.

Reissue of the 1942 "Banner" Southern Jumbo.

In mid-1942 Gibson brought out both the Southern Jumbo and the J-45, two models intended to fill the void left by two famous jumbo-body guitars that had been recently dropped, the J-35 and the J-55. And fill the void they did, making reputations equal to those of their predecessors.

That Southern Jumbo had new-style braces, a new peghead shape, a gold "ONLY A GIBSON IS GOOD ENOUGH" logo on the peghead, a tastefully shaped bridge (usually bottom-belly), and a small teardrop pickguard fabricated of "flame" celluloid. The 1942 SJ had a mahogany back and sides, except for one choice batch of rosewood. Not surprisingly, Gibson chose these earliest Southern Jumbos for the reissues, which were constructed of mahogany, except for a few of rosewood.

Built on the J-45 molds, these SJ reissues were offered in 1991 and 1992 as part of the "Gibson Limited Editions" series. These quite accurate replicas have the 24¾" scale, tapered and scalloped top bracing, and a rear-belly rosewood bridge, like most of the '42 SJs. The unbound rosewood fingerboards have the twin-parallelogram pearl inlays, one of the signature features of the originals. The Sitka spruce top is bordered by seven-ply celluloid of alternating white and black strips and is finished in a sunburst of Cremona brown. Enclosed individual tuners are used, with white buttons imitating the originals.

When the small factory run of this "Limited Edition" model sold out, these superb replicas of the famous Southern Jumbo became available to the public on a special-order basis only. To some particular players, the rosewood jumbo-size Gibson with the 24¾" scale is the ultimate flat-top—an open, rich, warm sound, with a great feel and look. In July of 1993 a special-issue SJ became available through the non-profit Country Music Hall of Fame & Museum store in Nashville. Under an agreement between the Country Music Foundation and Gibson, only 25 rosewood SJs were to be built and sold, at $2000 each (including a vintage hardshell case). This special-issue model differed from Gibson's previous "Limited Editions" series in small ways only—having a bound fingerboard and Kluson metal-button tuners, for example.

Southern Jumbo "Banner" reissue, with rosewood back and sides.

AJ-35: A Welcome Hybrid

During the summer of 1992 five special-order guitars were made for one of the largest Gibson dealers in the country. These new guitars were going to be custom reissues of J-35s, the famous flat-tops made from 1936 to 1943. However, during the construction process the guitar began to diverge from the exact specifications of the J-35, and the resulting hybrid, part AJ (Advanced Jumbo) and part J-35, was named the AJ-35.

This souped-up J-35 was built with the same forms and used the same bracing as the Advanced Jumbos. The mahogany neck followed the AJ's 25½" scale but with the dot inlays of the shorter-scale J-35; the old-style pearl script was retained. Both the fingerboard and the narrow, rectangular bridge were rosewood. Some instrument tops were finished in natural, others with a vintage sunburst; body binding remained a simple white celluloid.

Gibson's decision to reserve the J-35 designation for a true replica of that revered model proved to be the right one: Gibson/Montana built prototypes of the J-35 reissue in 1993, with expectations of making it a production model. Meanwhile, the AJ-35 hybrid can be purchased as a Custom Shop guitar.

THE SQUARE-SHOULDER JUMBOS

The Montana Hummingbird

Since its introduction in 1960, the Hummingbird has been a famous Gibson trademark acoustic, right up to the present day. Originally designed for country and western players, the Hummingbird also became the standard in folk as well as rock. Today, the Hummingbird is commonly seen in the hands of top rock, folk, and country artists around the world.

Gibson brochure, 1993

Cherry sunburst Hummingird.

Hummingbird reissue with natural-finish top.

Gibson is blessed in having in its line a few models for which the truth and only the truth, varnished or unvarnished, makes for easy advertising copy. The J-200 is perhaps the most prominent of these. The beautiful Hummingbird is another.

This less expensive of Gibson's two "bird" models (the Dove costs 25 percent more) has been in continuous production since 1960. After undergoing gradual transformation, especially in the late '60s and early '70s, the model was reissued as a 1960s-style replica by the Nashville factory in 1984. This reissue gradually improved and by the late '80s had become a good guitar.

It was to become much, much better, though. In fact, the Montana Hummingbirds are in most ways better than the early-'60s instruments.

This reissue follows the original quite faithfully, varying from it in small ways only. Today's cherry sunburst is a near-duplicate of the original's finish. (In 1991 the natural-finish option was dropped, because the great majority of orders specified cherryburst.) The pickguard is now made from a beautiful mock-tortoise material, more realistic than that used on the early 'birds.

In 1984, when the model was first reissued in vintage form, the 24¾" short scale was incorporated; this was changed to the long scale in late 1990, to increase its power. A number of other small differences between the early-'60s Hummingbird and the reissue are worth noting: the Montana guitar's neck is thicker from fingerboard to back; its peghead is slightly longer; its braces are scalloped and tapered; the spread of the main "X" is 98 degrees; and the top is a parabolic arch.

These Gibsons with mahogany bodies and scalloped braces are guitars for all seasons: they are especially warm and sweet for vocal backups, but when the need arises they can be loud and punchy for bluegrass, or clear and cutting for playing lead.

The Montana Hummingbird is built better than even the earliest versions of the model while managing to retain the appeal, beauty, and soul of its predecessor.

The Montana Dove

A more expensive relative of the Hummingbird, the Dove model has been in continuous production since its introduction in 1962. Gibson's advertising shows that their Montana Division didn't hesitate in keeping this famous and ornate model available: ". . . The Gibson Dove has been acclaimed as the most beautiful acoustic ever built in Gibson's long history of original designs. This model is currently considered among the elite dreadnought models of the world."

The Dove has retained the appeal of the original. Its unique decoration includes the special bridge with dove wings of inlaid pearl, flamed maple back and sides, twin-parallelogram fingerboard inlays, and the stunning pickguard that depicts a dove, inlaid in pearl. Like that of the J-200, the neck is maple.

The top braces are scalloped and tapered, but they are set at a more conservative angle than the original Dove's, a correction of potential structural shortcomings that might afflict the square-shoulder, wide-waist Gibsons made in the 1960s. This new bracing system has another purpose—to create "cutting power." The "X-brace" is centered about 1½" behind the soundhole, with the tone bars angling off the treble side of the "X" at 72 degrees.

Because so many Dove owners over the years have preferred a natural-finish top, Gibson now offers the Dove only in a natural-finish top with antique cherry sides and back; other finishes can be ordered through the Custom Shop.

The careful selection of materials, quality of construction, tone, and playability have never been so good. Dove lovers know that this classy guitar is only going to get better as it ages.

J-30: Simple Elegance

The J-30 Montana reissue represents considerable improvement on the original of 1985 and is one of the guitars redesigned by master luthier Ren Ferguson at the new Bozeman site. This model follows all specifications of the more famous Hummingbird, but at approximately two-thirds

Reissue of an early Dove. The original model appeared in 1962.

The J-30: an inexpensive flat-top "with the feel of a Hummingbird."

the cost—$1,299 versus $1,899 for the Hummingbird (1993 list prices). The lack of fancy trim makes for a simple yet elegant guitar. Gibson's 1989 advertising clearly shows the market niche intended for this model:

> Gibson's traditional J-30 and Hummingbird share the same body material specifications. The J-30 is a classic example of value engineering. Designed for the player who wants all the performance of a Gibson classic without the fancy trim. A classic value.

This square-shoulder jumbo with a solid mahogany back and sides, a long (25½") scale, and hand-tuned scalloped bracing is intended to offer quality and tone at not a huge cost.

The J-60: Bluegrass Bound

On the staff of Gibson/Montana is John Lowell, who not only is in charge of ordering materials for the Bozeman factory but who also is an excellent bluegrass guitar player. His expertise in both these areas was put to use in designing the J-60, which, according to the company advertising, "... is designed for the guitarist who demands the maximum volume, projection, and tonal response needed for live solo and ensemble performance." In other words, John conceived of a powerful Gibson entry for the bluegrass market.

The J-60, designed for the bluegrass market.

His regular guitar had been a reissue Advanced Jumbo, a famous model offered by Gibson from 1938 through 1940 whose reputation had taken on mythical proportions in recent years. Despite the Advanced Jumbo's superior bluegrass characteristics, John felt that this model was not "traditional" enough in appearance for many modern bluegrassers. And so he designed and had built the prototype J-60, combining the incredible sound of the Advanced Jumbo in an appearance sure to appeal to modern 'grassers.

Ever since the bluegrass frenzy began in the late '60s and early '70s, pickers had grown to prefer certain makes and models of instruments, even if these instruments were foreign-made lookalikes rather than the real thing. For example, Gibson's 1920s F-5 mandolin, their pre-War flathead Mastertone banjos, and the C. F. Martin Company's D-series (dreadnought) guitars, especially the D-28, came to be considered as proper dress in a bluegrass band. Of course, many other models of bluegrass instruments were excellent in their own right, but the fact remains that the "ultimate," or even a mediocre copy that looks like the ultimate, was the amateur picker's preference. What an instrument looks like therefore greatly affects its sales, and a company's bottom line matters more than a little.

In its striking simplicity, quality of sound, and understated elegance, the J-60 was thought out well. It uses the basic square-shoulder Gibson body, like those of the Hummingbird and Dove, but with rosewood back and sides. The peghead is in the straight-sided 1930s style, as opposed to the inwardly radiused sides that appeared in the 1940s and have remained. In keeping with the less-is-more philosophy, no further adornment affects the peghead, except for a pearl inlay of "Gibson" in the 1930s script. Grover Rotomatic tuners help preserve this instrument's image of regal simplicity.

Upon the solid-mahogany neck is an unbound ebony fingerboard with fret markers on the side only, finished off with a French heel, like most Gibson models of the '30s. The 25½" scale helps to produce the volume expected for bluegrass music.

White celluloid binding borders the rosewood back and the Sitka spruce top that comes with either a natural finish or a vintage sunburst. The ebony bridge is of the bottom-belly design and is similar to those of the early Southern Jumbos. The classic pickguard is of mock-tortoise celluloid in the Gibson teardrop shape. Beneath these features is the exact bracing pattern of the Advanced Jumbo, ensuring that the tonal excellence is retained despite the new exterior.

In some ways, the J-60s are similar to the earliest Heritage guitars, which were introduced in 1965 and in general look like the J-60s; all the differences, however, weigh in favor of the J-60, for it is a much better built guitar with far more bluegrass "bite." Judging from the sound and overall high quality of those first J-60s to be completed, music lovers should expect to see more of them on the bluegrass circuit.

Gospel, Montana-Style

The original Gospel model brought out by Gibson in 1972 was intended to be a big, deep-sounding vocal-backup instrument. The new model's name was well chosen, for as a genre gospel music has given root to a number of other forms, from bluegrass and folk to blues and country. No doubt Gibson hoped that this creation would find such wide appeal among potential guitar buyers.

Henry Juszkiewicz, who became Gibson CEO in 1985, took especial interest in reissuing the Gospel. He wished to keep its good qualities while avoiding the shortcomings of the original, which was built during a time of eroding standards at Gibson (commonly and derogatorily called "the Norlin era," referring to the conglomerate that had bought the company). In 1993 Gibson again offered the Gospel model, 13 years after the original's demise.

The reissue is an attractive guitar far superior to the original. By using a multi-ply, arched back Gibson produced a deep-sounding guitar inexpensively, with the relatively low cost passed to the customer. In addition, the Nashville Division for years has made a similar back for its ES-175 hollowbody electric model, so a ready supply of backs for the Gospel has existed.

An improved reissue meant changes. Most important, the 1970s Gospel used light-colored maple for its back and sides, contrasting this with dark, tortoise-style body binding. Gibson, however, wanting a more responsive guitar than the original, chose mahogany over maple for the reissue. Consequently, the company has maintained a striking appearance in the new Gospel by using multiple white binding that stands out against the dark wood.

The revamped model uses Sitka spruce on top, with hand-tuned, scalloped braces like those on more expensive models. Finish options are sunburst or natural, both in gloss. Rosewood is used for the top-belly bridge and for the unbound fingerboard with pearl dot inlays. The original's 25½" scale is retained for that punchy sound. Instead of the long, single-point pickguard used on the originals, the reissue features a mock-tortoise shell 'guard in a teardrop shape. The peghead retains the decal depicting a dove in flight. Hardware is vintage-style in nickel plating.

Gibson has always built affordable guitars. The Gospel continues this tradition—an American-built guitar that not only competes with foreign-built instruments in price but far surpasses them in quality. This model brings with it a lot of tone and quality for not much money.

Reissue of the Gospel. The original model was built from 1972 to 1980.

> The B-45-12, a 1991 reissue of a popular 12-string that had been introduced 30 years before.

The B-45-12
Montana "Limited Editions" Reissue

When Gibson considered reissuing a 12-string in 1991, they couldn't have needed more than a second or two in choosing the model: it had to be the B-45-12, the most popular 12-string guitar Gibson ever made and one of the finest of its kind in history. As good as the originals were, the Montana version is in many ways an improvement.

Four major changes involving materials and construction should be mentioned at the outset. Unlike its famous predecessor, the Montana model uses only solid mahogany, not a laminate, for back and sides. Also, it uses the superior "single-X" bracing system rather than the "parallel-X" configuration of the earlier ones, and these new braces are scalloped but not tapered, creating greater strength in the top. Next, the Montana's bridge system is in two ways superior, with a solid-maple bridge pad (rather than the original's plywood) beneath the top and a traditional top-belly, non-adjustable bridge above. Finally, the model features a short scale and is meant to be tuned to full pitch, unlike the original that was intended to be detuned by a whole tone and that suffered sometimes terminal damage when cranked up to standard pitch.

Other changes are more matters of trim and aesthetics than construction. The Montana reissue, for example, has been lacquered only in Gibson's "Vintage Cherry" finish—a natural top with cherry back, sides, and neck. The tuning machines, of higher quality than those used on the 1960s version, are gold-plated. The Montana's simple peghead has "Gibson" in gold silkscreen, omitting the elongated, vertically stacked double triangle of the earlier style.

The B-45-12 reissue sold slowly at first, but when it was shown at the NAMM (National Association of Music Merchants) show, the nation's foremost convention for people involved in the music business, interest was stirred and sales increased.

As its 1991 advertising brochure attests, Gibson certainly approached the marketing of this reissue with some vigor and intelligence:

The Gibson B-45-12
In 1961, the B-45-12 was introduced during the rise in popularity of folk music in America. This dreadnought 12-string has the sound that the '60s generation nurtured and later identified with. . . . The B-45-12 bears all of the fine features of the handcrafted Gibson acoustics which include all solid wood construction for the maximum volume and tone and a dovetail joint neck-to-body design for maximum strength and sound transference.

Sadly, this reissue didn't sell in sufficient numbers to keep it in regular production, and it was dropped in early 1993. A fact of life is that 12-string models, no matter how good, are not high-volume sellers.

SMALL-BODY GUITARS

L-1:
Back to the Blues

In 1991 Gibson/Montana began to build a small-body, 12-fret guitar designed with fingerpicking enthusiasts in mind. The result was a quite accurate reproduction of the famous L-1 from the late 1920s, the guitar that the great bluesman Robert Johnson played. The Gibson sales brochure from 1992 says this: "Introduced in 1926, the Gibson L-1 is one of the original American acoustic blues guitars. The style, touch, and sound of the Gibson L-1 helped invent what we now call 'The

American Blues.'" The L-1 reissue preserves the character of the original.

The Sitka spruce top features a dark sunburst finish with a small amber-yellow center. The fingerboard is left unbound and uses simple dot inlays as fret markers. The V-shaped mahogany neck features a French heel and the original straight-sided peghead, on which is inlaid "The Gibson" in pearl.

Mahogany is used for the L-1's back and sides, and ebony for its fingerboard and the pyramid-style bridge. The soundhole purfling rings are close together, in the original style.

Because of the small, narrow-waist body of the L-1, the main "X-brace" is a narrow 90-degree spread. Single side braces branch off from the main "X" asymmetrically, with the bass side positioned lower on the main brace. Two tone bars diverge on the treble side at 65 degrees. Braces are tapered and scalloped.

Gibson advertising identifies the niche they expect the L-1 reissue to fill: ". . . A short scale (24¾") string length . . . gives this guitar its easy to bend string action and brassy blues sound."

The Montana L-00, L-00 Blues King, and L-20 Special

Gibson's L-00 reissue appeared in 1991, advertised as a replica of the well-known 1936 model, which in the heart of the Depression had offered beautiful tone and remarkable quality—for under $30. Although the models built around the L-Series body dimensions (for example, the L-1, L-C, and Nick Lucas) were guitars that played and sounded superbly, they were lightly built, too delicate for the care they received, sometimes resulting in damage over the last half-century.

1991 Ebony L-00, with a scale longer than the original's.

The Montana reissue combines the best of both eras: it sounds every bit as good as its famous forebear but is less fragile. It is not, however, an exact replica of the L-00 and differs in three chief ways: the reissue has the long (25½") scale, while the original used was 24¾"; the fingerboard of the original was unbound; the reissue has a bound back. In this last regard, the Montana reissue imitates a different model from the late '30s and early '40s, the L-0. Why not call the reissue the L-0? Because the L-00 name is better recognized and harks back to the '30s, when this famous model proved a means of musical escape for so many during hard times.

Gibson advertising from 1991 sums up this beautiful reissue:

> The L-00 is a replica of the historic 1936 original. With all solid wood construction in this "parlor size" package, the L-00 delivers a warm, balanced sound suitable for ragtime, blues, and folk. The acoustic guitar builders at Gibson/Montana have meticulously included all the subtle features of this vintage design such as the silkscreen Gibson headstock logo, 1936 style rosewood bridge, and old style tuners.

This model is especially suited to the guitarist who prefers the fingerpicking style. It delivers sweet tone and amazing volume from its small body constructed of Sitka spruce on top and mahogany on the sides and back. The neck shape and old feel from the '30s original have been retained, as have the rosewood fingerboard with dot markers and the rosewood rectangular bridge. The Gibson logo has been faithfully reproduced, with the old script silkscreened in white onto a black peghead. The top, back, and neck are bound in white

Gibson chose a body style from the 1930s to create the L-00 Blues King, the L-20, and the L-1.

celluloid, creating a strong contrast with the vintage ebony finish, which is standard; approximately 20 L-00s were produced with the vintage sunburst on the top, imitating the most popular finish of the 1930s originals.

In 1993 Gibson made some cosmetic changes to the L-00 and renamed it the L-00 Blues King. The fingerboard binding was dropped, in the process reverting to the original design, and two finish options became available: a natural top on antique walnut sides and back, or vintage sunburst. These changes created a more accurate replica of an L-00 while giving the modern buyer some choice in finishes.

Another Montana variation on the L-00 body style, and to some minds the ultimate variation, is embodied in the L-20 Special, an amalgam of a famous parlor-sized body and elegant, tasteful ornamentation. When we toured the Montana factory in May 1992, we recommended that Gibson design a high-quality small guitar—something like a Nick Lucas model, but in the short scale and maybe a 12-frets-to-the-body neck. Coincidentally, the management in Bozeman had been thinking along these same lines, for they too had been players of small-bodied, 12-fret guitars with V-necks and that magical sound and feel that result from these instruments. Plant Manager Larry English played an important role in the basic design, and Ren Ferguson's crew built a prototype that surpassed their expectations. Gibson and Martin both had made these wonderful parlor guitars in decades past, but nothing currently on the market really matched those of our memories.

This shortcoming was remedied at a trade show in January 1993, when Gibson unveiled the impressive L-20 Special that, without modesty, they advertised as "the world's loudest and most tonally balanced small-bodied acoustic steel-string guitar."

As its model Gibson chose the most elaborate of its 1930s L-Series guitars, the deep-bodied Nick Lucas "Special," which in 1932 retailed for $125. The resulting L-20 follows the classic's 24¾" scale and is built with 12 frets to the body. The vintage V-shape neck features a French heel; the ebony fingerboard is widened to allow cleaner playing by fingerstyle guitarists, and its oblong pearl inlays successively decrease in size, top to bottom. Like the fingerboard, the top-belly bridge is ebony. An unusual feature is an optional pickguard kept in the case compartment until the musician wishes to attach it.

Other features support the stature of the L-20, including binding on the fingerboard and peghead, while the body is triple-bound. On the headstock the famous Gibson "flowerpot" is delicately inlaid in pearl under "Gibson" in the contemporary script. The gold-plated hardware fits in with the regal bearing of the L-20 Special. A built-in transducer and a ¼" endpin jack are standard equipment, as a functional reminder that this model is only partly of the past, that it is also of the 1990s. Two finish options are available—antique natural or vintage sunburst.

The Nick Lucas Artist Reissue

On the day it was introduced in 1928 as well as now, the Nick Lucas model (also called the "Gibson Special") was Gibson's most valuable parlor-sized guitar. Then it retailed for $125; now, on the vintage market, it is a much-sought-after model. It therefore came as no surprise that Gibson/Montana decided to reissue one of the most beautiful guitars to come out of the late '20s and '30s.

The Nick Lucas reissue appeared in 1991 as part of the "Gibson Limited Edition" offering. An exquisite curly maple Nick Lucas of 1937 vintage was used for the prototype, rather than the earlier versions with rosewood back and sides. Also, Gibson went with the 14-frets-to-the-body neck instead of the 12- or 13-fret designs of the '20s and early '30s. The Montana reissue deviated from the prototype in one important detail, though, choosing the longer, 25½" scale. Internally, the reissue closely followed the original, with the top and back slightly arched and the top braces scalloped and tapered.

When word of the impending Nick Lucas reissues got around, a few custom orders were immediately placed, resulting in exceptional instruments that stayed as true to the originals as possible, with short-scale necks, Adirondack red spruce tops, and fingerboards and bridges of Brazilian rather than Indian rosewood.

Because of the mystique associated with the Nick Lucas model, because of the excellent replication, and because of the limited production run, these exceptional guitars should become quickly collectible. This most valuable of Gibson parlor-sized guitars is now available through custom order only.

The Nick Lucas Special Edition model, a re-creation of Gibson's famous 1930s flat-top.

ELECTRIC ACOUSTICS

The OP-25: The J-25 Redefined in Montana

When Gibson moved part of its instrument production to Bozeman, Montana, in 1989, certain partially made instruments and components of others went along for the ride. Included in Bozeman's inheritance was a large stack of synthetic backs and sides left over from the J-25 model, a round-shoulder jumbo with a laminated spruce top that had been produced from 1984 through 1986.

These stockpiled remnants were used in constructing the OP-25, an upgraded version of the J-25 that was to combine the old with the new. A mahogany neck of the J-25 style was used, retaining the 24¾" scale and a rosewood fingerboard with dot inlays. On a peghead unadorned except for the company logo were traditional enclosed individual tuners made with pearloid keystone buttons. The bottom-belly rosewood bridge imitated the predecessor's but was glued to a radiused Sitka spruce top instead of the laminate on the J-25. An integral Fishman pickup with a preamp and parametric equalizer allowed an electric option.

The OP-25 came with either a natural top, sunburst, or black finish. The model offered the guitarist a quality electric/acoustic at a low price: when introduced in 1991 it listed at $699, padded gig bag included. In early 1992, after all the synthetic shells from the Nashville era had been used up, production of the OP-25 ceased.

J-160E Montana Reissue

Gibson's "Limited Editions" catalogue (1991) combines the past and the present:

> Made popular in the '60s by groups like the Beatles, the J-160E is still seen in the hands of the legendary artists of the 1990s. Featuring Gibson's soft shoulder body and a single coil pickup at the base of the fretboard, the J-160E is the most unique stage and studio acoustic-electric today.

Plainly stated, Gibson took a classic from the '50s and in one of its Montana reissues made very good great.

Beginning in 1954 and continuing for nearly a quarter-century, Gibson's J-160E sold consistently well, partly because of its association with the Beatles. Through this association and because of its many intrinsic merits, this round-shoulder jumbo has become a popular collectible. Gibson knew it made sense to reissue this classic, which it did in 1991, and with many improvements.

Reissue of the J-160-E, an electric/acoustic made famous by the Beatles.

In order to create a rigid structure so that the P-90 pickup could be used with minimal top noise, Gibson used laminated sides and tops with ladder-type braces on the original model. In contrast, the reissue features solid sides, a solid Sitka spruce top, and scalloped "single-X" bracing. This tremendous improvement can be demonstrated best only by playing an original and a reissue side by side. Additionally, the P-90 pickup, which was good enough for its time, is replaced with a P-100 humbucking unit, which is much quieter and relatively free from unwanted top noise.

All the best of the traditional features have been retained, including the 15-fret neck in the 24¾" scale. This Montana replica is an excellent example of how to reissue a classic with all the feel and appeal of the original, but with the quality and improvements of the 1990s. Gibson's own ad copy hits the mark: "This replica of the 1950s original is hand built with all the added advantages of solid wood construction, hand-tuned bracing, and an ultra-quiet pickup."

The EAS Family of Electric-Acoustic Guitars

When Gibson designed the Star and the Starburst models to be marketed at the high end of the electric/acoustic flat-top scale, they at the same time developed a similar guitar that would sound very good and play very well but would be less expensive to produce, thus giving players an American option at a cost equivalent to imported guitars. This new guitar was called the EAS Classic, its name an acronym for Electric/Acoustic Series. (In its history Gibson had often chosen names in a similar fashion: ES-335 for "Electric Spanish," SG Pro for "Solid Guitar," GS-85 for "Gut String," and ETU for "Electric Tenor Uke," to name but a few.)

Eventually, the EAS family numbered four members: Classic, Classic II, Standard, and Deluxe. The EAS Classic is listed first not because it cost the least, but because it was the first to appear on the market. The body follows Gibson's well-known narrow-waist shape, like those models of the competing Starburst series. The body depth is only 3" at both the neck end and at the endpin, but it gets some extra air chamber space by means of its arched back, in the mode of an electric guitar, though the Gospel and the J-55 square-shoulder, two flat-tops introduced in 1973, had also used pressed, radiused backs to enhance bottom-end response.

EAS Deluxe, a thin-body cutaway.

EAS Standard, a versatile electric/acoustic combination.

The Classic's solid-spruce top uses the "single-X" hand-tuned bracing pattern. The back and sides are maple, while rosewood is used for the short-scale (24¾") fingerboard and the top-belly bridge. The internal electronics have a parametric equalizer; the jack is located through the endpin, the ideal spot on an acoustic.

This Venetian (rounded) cutaway guitar is finished in solid colors—cream, red, and black bound in white. An option offers a vintage cherry sunburst finish with cream binding and trapezoidal inlays, like those of a Les Paul electric.

Gibson designed the EAS Classic II model as a double-cutaway for players wanting greater access to the upper registers and was in fact the flat-top equivalent of Gibson's arch-top ES-335. The Classic II was constructed with arched and laminated maple backs, maple sides, and spruce tops; finishes in solid colors were standard. All other features remained consistent with the EAS series. Only a handful came out of the factory.

Because the EAS Classic sold well, Gibson brought out two companion models in 1993, both variations on the original. As the names attest, one model—the Deluxe—outranked the Classic in degree of elegance and therefore price, while the Standard presented the musician with a less expensive alternative. The Standard differed from the earlier Classic in minor ways only: it was cheaper, its fingerboard inlays were simple pearl dots, and its finish options included antique natural, cherry, and vintage sunburst.

The EAS Deluxe went from dream to design over lunch. Sometime just before soup the Gibson/Montana management team of Larry English, Ren Ferguson, and Robi Johns began talking about guitars—specifically about a fancier EAS model, one whose ornate trim would appeal to the upscale buying public. Shortly after dessert they had the design for the Deluxe sketched out and a prototype planned.

The model is exactly what its name implies: a deluxe version of the EAS Standard. Most striking is the flamed maple top, whose figure is enhanced by the standard vintage cherry sunburst finish. In contrast is the cream color of the body binding, the fingerboard binding, and the streamlined pickguard. On the black peghead overlay are the logo and the Gibson crown, both in pearl; beneath them is a bell-shaped truss rod cover with an engraved "Deluxe." Trapezoids of pearl grace the rosewood fingerboard.

The EAS series has been designed to offer versatile electric/acoustic guitars that produce a rich, sweet electrified tone, while having the playability and quality that Gibson's customers have come to expect. Gibson's advertising copy says it all: "Finally, an electric/acoustic that has a fine acoustic sound as well as the fingerboard access and playing comfort needed for today's live and studio music."

The Star Is Born

For some time the Montana Division of Gibson had known of a market for a modern, hand-built electric/acoustic guitar. True, a couple of plug-in flat-tops had come out of the Bozeman factory, the OP-25 and the J-160E, but each left considerable room for updating. The OP-25, with a spruce top upon a parabolic body of synthetic fiber, was phased out after fewer than 300 instruments were made. Also, the more conventional J-160E, a quality instrument with a noble past, had more in common with the 1950s than the 1990s, though to its credit Gibson had updated this model in its Montana factory. Still, to some it looked dated. Gibson management saw that the time was ripe for a top-end, modern flat-top of high quality.

Then the Star appeared in the West. Designed and built by Gibson master luthier Ren Ferguson, this model was introduced in 1991, following the same size and shape as four other Gibson guitars of the time: the J-185, J-180, J-200 Junior, and J-2000. As company advertising phrased it, "The Star embodies all of the fine features of a world-class handbuilt acoustic guitar with the advantages of a cutaway acoustic electric. . . . The cutaway body offers the comfortable access to the fingerboard needed for acoustic music in the '90s."

This model's name is symbolized by eight mother-of-pearl stars inlaid in the fingerboard and a single larger one on the peghead. Its solid-wood construction includes maple sides and back, with a top of Sitka spruce, bound in white celluloid, enhancing the white edge of the contoured pickguard. The carved rosewood bridge is of the radiused "moustache" design created for the J-2000. The 24¾" scale, in addition to giving the instrument that characteristic Gibson feel, blends well with the hand-tuned, scalloped bracing in producing a punchy yet mellow tone that can be amplified with the acoustic/electric pickup and preamp. Nitrocellulose lacquer finishes are offered in either vintage sunburst or ebony.

The Star lived up to expectations, selling well and filling the targeted void. Gibson accurately predicted that there are enough musicians who want a modern electric/acoustic flat-top that integrates current electronics technology and the highest-quality construction.

The Starburst Models

In 1992, as part of its "Limited Editions" series, the Montana Division of Gibson brought out the Star, a well-constructed electric/acoustic cutaway that delivered the sound and feel of a non-pickup flat-top. No doubt because of the warm welcome given to the Star and to its more elaborate offshoot, the Starburst, Gibson quickly went to work in designing additional electric/acoustic guitars, including three models derived from the successful original. Consequently, at the beginning of 1993, Gibson offered the EAS (Electric/Acoustic Series) Standard, the EAS Deluxe, and the three members of the new Starburst family: Starburst

Gibson's basic Star.

Starburst Elite, with exceptional woods and trim.

Studio, Starburst Standard, and Starburst Elite, each with a pre-amp and transducer (pickup) and a Florentine (sharp-pointed) cutaway.

The Starburst line is the Star in three increasingly more ornate, more elegant, and more expensive embodiments. The least fancy of the three is the Studio. When Gibson dropped the Star in 1993, they replaced it with the Studio, though with even more inlaid stars—three small ones surrounding the large star on the peghead and three more on the right-hand side of the bridge. Distinguishing itself from the two more expensive Starbursts, the Studio has a Sitka spruce top, which comes with either a natural, cherry, or ebony finish; back and sides of solid maple, but with less figure than on the Standard or Elite; multiple binding front and back; nickel-plated hardware; and a pickguard of mottled celluloid, contoured to

Starburst Studio, Starburst Standard, and Starburst Elite, each with an on-board transducer and preamp.

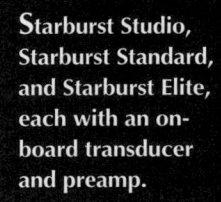

follow the outline of the body's shape, from cutaway to lower bout.

The 1993 Standard is basically the same as the 1992 Starburst and, like the middle-of-the-line Starburst, offers more expensive features than the Studio. The body is maple—a beautiful flame pattern on top, with figured solid maple for its sides and back—and all is multiple-bound and finished in either natural, vintage sunburst, or amber. The Standard's tuners are gold-plated; otherwise, the peghead looks like that of the Studio. The scalloped braces are glued in a 103-degree spread, and the "X-brace" is of mahogany "to maximize the tonal response of its solid maple top," according to Gibson. As is the case with all Montana Gibsons, the neck and body are joined by a hand-fit dovetail. Both the Studio and the Standard feature rosewood fingerboards and bridges.

The Standard is without pickguard—an aesthetic decision that better highlights the beautiful woods and the bright, translucent finish. The most striking contrast with the Studio is in the stars: in distinction with the relatively conservative use of inlaid stars by the Studio, the Standard expands

Jefferson Airplane and Hot Tuna guitarist Jorma Kaukonen with his Starburst.

"The folks in Bozeman have restored my faith in the American way of life."
—Jorma Kaukonen

the mother-of-pearl galaxy to 27 individual inlays on the fingerboard alone.

The Starburst Elite is for the musician who, no matter how incredible a guitar may be, must find that even fancier one: the ultimate. Gibson's Montana Division is of course always happy to oblige. They designed the Elite especially for such hardcore collectors and players who refuse to settle for nothing less than the absolute.

Rare quilted maple is used for the top, while the sides and back are flamed maple. The cutaway body on this elaborately trimmed guitar is triple-bound with backseam marquetry. The galaxy of pearl stars is in the same pattern as on the Standard but the stars are inlaid into a bound peghead, a bound ebony fingerboard, and an ebony bridge. The hardware is gold-plated. As with the Standard, finish options include natural, amber, and vintage sunburst. This most heavenly of electric/acoustic guitars comes in the special Gibson/Montana "Ultra Case."

In the risky business of predicting which models will become the prized vintage instruments of the next century, a collector should do well with one of the Starburst family. Gibson has redefined the universe of electric/acoustic guitars.

Repairing Gibson's Fabulous Flat-Tops

Chapter Twelve

As with all flat-tops, most problems with Gibsons stem from two sources: the top's construction and its reaction to the pull of the strings; the stability of the neck itself and its joining to the body. Being made of wood, Gibson flat-tops are vulnerable to the ravages of time, normal wear and tear, and occasional mistreatment, much like any other fragile piece of art. Maintenance and common sense usually help avoid major problems with a guitar, but nearly all guitar owners at some time have to face the unavoidable repair. It's to educate the guitar owner for this eventuality that the following construction information is given—information from a Gibson perspective.

Some preliminary construction basics are in order. Gibson flat-tops from the '30s to the '60s are not actually flat at all, instead having a gradual curve or slight arch. The top braces were cut to a curve before being glued; then they were attached to the top with radiused gluing cauls to maintain the curve. When rested upon a flat surface a braced Gibson top touches on the outer ends of the "X-braces" and the shoulder braces, but not in the center, because the top has a slight convexity. Even the sides were shaped to receive a top that was curved not only from side to side, but lengthwise, too. Gibson was careful not to press this curve out of the tops while gluing them to the sides. The result was a pre-stressed top needing no breaking-in period. Gibsons started out ready to play and stayed that way.

While the Gibsons from the late '20s until the late '60s exhibited few problems in top bracing (including bridge or bridge pad problems), by the time the '70s arrived, the company had begun gluing tops onto flat surfaces, much like the other manufacturers. And problems with Gibson tops resulted. The following facts about Gibson top bracing, bridge pads, and bridges cover all periods from the late '20s to the present.

Factory employees making "Mona-Steel" strings, Gibson's house brand, circa 1940.

GIBSON BRACING

Gibson braces, both top and back, sometimes come unglued or develop cracks right at the end of the main supporting braces where they meet the sides: in other words, in the large "X-braces," the cross brace(s) in the shoulder area in front of the soundhole, and at the two (sometimes three) tone bars. This is especially true of instruments built from 1930 into the 1960s. There are several common causes of loose ends, cracks, and loose braces on a Gibson flat-top.

- Most of the 1930s braces, except for the two braces at the very back on some Jumbo models, were narrow, tapered, and tall. The brace ends (especially top braces) weren't always tucked or notched into the lining that joins the sides to the top and back. This is especially true of the L-00 tops but not their backs. Untucked (unsupported) brace ends were free to move with the top and occasionally came unglued; this flexibility, however, also accounts for Gibson's unmatched balance of the bass, midrange, and treble tones.
- During the 1930s Gibson experimented with their bracing. Although most was scalloped, tapered "A-bracing" is also found, not all of which is tucked into the lining. Back braces varied: some were short and wide like a Martin's, while others were tall, thin, and tapered, much like the top braces without the scalloping. All Jumbos and some J-35s had three transverse braces ("tone bars") rather than two. Many professionals feel that the scalloped "three-bracers" are some of the greatest-sounding guitars ever made.
- The extremely light construction (thin tops, backs, sides, and braces), coupled with the heavy-gauge strings of the era, often took its toll on the bracing. Fortunately, loose Gibson braces can be reglued cleanly and easily by a professional.
- By 1942 Gibson became sure of their bracing, and it remained consistently narrow, tapered, tall, and scalloped until 1955. Even though they had begun to tuck the brace ends in the early '40s, the ends of the braces were so thin that there was little to tuck. Thus, loose ends remained a problem even through the 1950s. The trade-off to these occasionally wayward braces was flexibility and exceptional tone.
- In 1955 Gibson shortened the height of the top braces, stopped scalloping them, and began using a version of the 1930s "A-bracing," but not quite so tall. The '50s shape, with its long taper towards the ends, looks flatter on top because, being shorter, the top is in a thicker part of the tapered brace. Since the new braces weren't so tall, the tops had a little more give: this slightly increased the chances of pulling up too much, or dipping in front of the bridge toward the soundhole. Generally, though, the guitars of the 1950s were wonderful, and no particular repair problems are associated with the new bracing style. In fact, the woods used in constructing the '50s guitars were better than in the '40s because of the WW II-related shortages. Consequently, you'll see fewer of the cracked braces during this time.

Gibson employees working at benches.

Using clamps to install the lining.

- Although the bracing style used during the '50s remained until 1968, new problems arose around 1960, when Gibson went to the square-shoulder, wider-at-the-waist models like the Dove and Hummingbird. The shorter braces didn't always support the top well, and so glue joint, bridge plate, and buckling problems occurred more frequently.
- In 1968 two construction changes caused problems: the bracing became quite heavy, while the solid maple bridge pads grew enormous. Then the top bracing was changed to a "double-X," in 1971. This second "X"—glued within the main "X"—replaced the slanted tone bars. Because these braces were so heavy and the design so stout, the braces and the bridge pad often came loose—some think from lack of flexibility. The guitars of that

> *Bill Collings, a well known independent guitar maker on Gibson flat-tops:*
>
> *"The funny thing about Gibson is that they were always reasonably priced, but even the inexpensive ones were precisely made.*
>
> *Those '30s and '40s Gibsons were ahead of their time. Of course, they'd just come out of the 1920s, when the craftsman was king. Gibson had the process of guitar building figured out. It was always a planned thing, never a loose thing.*
>
> *Gibson had fun building guitars—look at the Century model from the 1930s. And Gibsons are simply fun to look at.*
>
> *When I look back at my own guitars I've designed and built, like the C-10, I think I give tribute to the L-00. And I've built different models on the same L-00 design from the 1930s."*

period had been so overbuilt to avoid warranty problems that they were too inflexible to handle the natural vibrations; they would sometimes self-destruct. Thus, during the late '60s and '70s any part of a brace might come unglued because of the massive size of the brace itself.

- Also in the early '70s, Gibson began using "RF" gluing technology to speed up the drying time. A radio frequency was directed through the glue joint at a special reactive, quick-curing glue. The result seems to have been glue joints that loosened much more readily than traditional ones. A visible side effect was a "burned" look showing through the tops of many guitars built in this manner. It's not uncommon to see many '70s flat-tops where the entire pattern of the braces is visible from the outside—showing as brown marks against the lighter spruce.
- Braces usually crack from being untucked at the ends, where they move a lot. Also, cracks result from a less-than-perfect piece of wood having been used for the brace, especially during WW II. After the early '60s loose braces led to a top collapsing in front of the bridge and in the shoulder region. And in the '70s, when Gibson's famous quality was under siege, anything was possible.

As Gibson/Montana's Ren Ferguson says, "The wood chosen for braces is important. The wood for the top braces is just as important as the top itself—if not more so. Quarter-sawn braces are the best, although because of their stiffness, some did come unglued as the top flexed. And when flat-sawn wood was used for braces, they often split on the ends or where the "X" crosses. You will not see flat-sawn braces coming from Montana."

- Montana-built flat-tops, which time will probably show to be the best of any era, have returned to the tucked, thin-ended, lightweight, and flexible bracing style begun in the 1940s—the formula for Gibson's wonderful vintage tone. Ferguson says, "The critical [main support] braces—the "X" and "cross-shoulder" brace—are securely tucked, but not necessarily the others (the tone bars and "wing" braces), which add *some* strength while they color and shape the sound."

THE BRIDGE PAD

Other than ordinary repairs necessitated by dryness, excessive moisture, and mistreatment (especially the incorrect installation of strings), Gibson bridges and the supporting bridge pad area inside the guitar had few problems until 1960. It was then that bridge-area troubles unique to Gibson developed, specifically when the square-shoulder Hummingbird was introduced and began to displace the traditional round-shoulder jumbo shape that was a full ⅜" narrower in the waist than its successor. This increase in body size, without a corresponding strengthening of the '50s-style braces, caused a multitude of headaches in the '60s, namely loose bracing and bridge/bridge pad problems. Upon introducing the Hummingbird, Gibson quit using small, solid-maple bridge pads and switched to larger ones of plywood in the hope of strengthening the bridge area. Following is a brief discussion of bridge pads.

- During the '30s, '40s, and '50s Gibson used small maple bridge pads made of select wood that held their shape well. Except for mistreatment when strings were installed (for example, gouging the bridge holes on the underside), the vintage maple plates have held up beautifully over the years. Replacement pads, if ever needed, should be maple shaped to fit a top's curve and avoid flattening its perfect dome.

- In 1960 oversize plywood bridge pads were introduced. Lacking flexibility, they often vibrated loose, so loose that sometimes they can be pried loose with bare fingers. A new pad must be thinner, smaller, and made of solid wood.
- On the less expensive ladder-braced Gibsons (LG-0 and LG-1), the bridge pads were large and made of spruce or mahogany, two woods that because of their softness often get chewed up. Also, without "X-bracing," the tops sometimes develop a distinct kink. The bridge pads can be removed and replaced with smaller ones of hardwood, but the top will never have the graceful dome because it's not "X-braced."
- In 1968 larger, heavier bridge pads replaced the plywood ones, remaining until 1983. These huge, thick, diamond-shaped bridge pads of solid wood harmed the tone of these instruments, especially in combination with the "double-X" bracing pattern. It seems as if Gibson just didn't have any real guitar builders working for them at this time, or at least those in charge weren't asking the craftsmen for advice. Fear of warranty problems seemed to be the chief consideration.
- When problems occur with these '70s bridge pads, repair is difficult because of the pad's inaccessibility. The "double-X" brace is in the way—the diamond-shaped pad completely fills the area between the "X," leaving no edge to get under in order to pry it loose. Sometimes the extra "X-bracing" must be removed just to take out the pad.
- In 1984, as Gibson was restoring the quality construction processes that had disappeared for nearly 15 years, the bridge pads again became thinner, more delicate pieces of solid wood, and the tone returned as well.
- Overall, instruments made in Nashville were decent if they were produced on the right day. Humidity was a huge problem. Flat-tops are built with many pieces of thin wood and have a number of glue joints. If these joints are assembled in a humid environment, they often open up (fall apart) when they dry out. Gibson was relieved when they moved their flat-top operation to Bozeman, Montana.

THE BRIDGE

←

Until the top-belly design arrived around 1950, the vintage Gibson bridge was a simple rectangle. While the smaller LG-style models kept the rectangle shape in the 50s, the J-45, J-50, and Southern Jumbo models all switched to a new style, called a top belly to distinguish it from Martin's traditional bottom-belly design. (Gibson did use a bottom-belly bridge on most SJs during WW II, however.) All Gibson's bridges, both rectangular and bellied, were well designed and nicely made. As a rule Gibson bridge saddles were more precisely located than most others and created consistently good intonation—better than the competition's. Beginning in the late 1950s, though, certain changes were made in the Gibson bridge, and problems followed.

- In 1956 adjustable bridge saddles were introduced. There are no real problems associated with adjustable bridges other than a loss of volume and tone, but it's common for the large anchors holding the height-adjustment screws to vibrate loose. These can be tightened in seconds. Many of these bridges have been converted to solid saddle-style, but a guitar owner should think long and hard about altering these great vintage guitars.
- Sometimes adjustable bridges were raised too high by owners looking for volume (the higher the bridge, the greater the power), thus putting excessive pressure on the top and causing problems.
- In the early '60s the Tune-O-Matic bridge began appearing on certain top-end models such as the Dove and the J-200. This was a good arrangement for owner adjustment, and there are no problems associated with it other than loss of volume and tone (and the occasional loose anchor bushing). These bridges should not be converted.
- In 1962 Gibson began using black plastic bridges on some of the less expensive guitars,

> "Gibsons have been the backbone of popular music in this century.
>
> The first Gibson acoustic I owned was a late-'50s blond J-50 without the adjustable bridge. I regret parting with it, but it always seemed extravagant to own more than one, so I traded a lot during the '60s, much to my regret. Throughout that period I was playing R & B but buying country records. It wasn't until the late '60s or so that I actually got some real use out of an acoustic guitar."
>
> —Albert Lee

affixing them with four screws but no glue. They sounded horrible. Since they weren't glued flat, they warped. Although they were easily replaced, the replacement never lasted long, either. It was a common repair job to replace these with handmade ebony bridges (the color of the plastic) glued to the top. After several years, Gibson scrapped the plastic bridges and went back to rosewood.

Bridge Facts

- Around 1960, when Gibson widened the bridge pad by an inch, they also moved the bridge-pin holes close to the back edge. Less angle at the saddle resulted, which in turn helped to alleviate twisting and tipping of the bridge and/or the saddle. With so little wood on the back side, however, these bridges often warped and split through the bridge-pin holes. Bridge replacement became necessary. Some repair shops install a wider bridge to beef up the holes, but this measure should be considered carefully beforehand. There's another solution, one especially useful if the bridge pad is also loose. A loose bridge pad on guitars of the '60s should be removed. While it's off, the bridge-pin holes can be plugged and redrilled closer to the saddle. A smaller pad of solid maple can then be installed, followed by a vintage bridge copy, with holes closer to the saddle.
- Most Gibson bridges during those early great years (the '30s through the '50s) were bolted on, with the bolt heads covered by decorative pearl dots. Often these bolts are all that hold the bridge on, the glue having given out. This causes particular stress at the two areas where the bolts are fastened. In bridge replacement the bolts can be left out, but of course the pearl dots should remain as before.
- In the '70s a fiber insert was inlaid into the bridge-pin area to avoid the problems with splitting common in bridges of that era. It's no wonder that these bridges split—they were made much too thin so as to compensate for the often underset necks of the '70s.

NECK CONSTRUCTION AND THE NECK JOINT

Obviously Gibson was concerned with good playing action right from the start, given the fact that they patented the adjustable truss rod in the 1920s. Gibson's reputation for building the most playable necks is well-founded. For example, if ten Gibson flat-tops built between 1935 and 1955 were compared to ten built by competing companies, the Gibsons would excel in these neck-related categories: Gibsons don't need neck resets, because their tops held their shape; necks remain straighter and action lower; and intonation is superior, because the saddles are located accurately. A quick look at vintage guitars in a shop will show Gibson's superiority with necks.

Until 1965 or so, when production increased dramatically, Gibson's necks had the most consistently good action of all flat-top guitars, a superiority due in large part to their adjustable truss rod necks. Of course there are the normal humps, kinks, and warps to be expected from any neck and fingerboard made of wood, but further problems are not common, except of course for the unavoidable worn-out frets.

The large jumbo, or "wide oval" frets (.103" wide), were introduced in 1959. Before that, Gibson always used a narrow (.078") wire, much like Martin's. As a rule, Gibson fretwork until the mid-'60s, when production went up, was much better than after that time. And about 1970, quality in the guitar industry as a whole went down because the demand was so high. Both tradition and quality in guitar building were lost by trying to meet the demand, and not just at the Gibson factory.

Around 1971 Gibson started replacing the solid, one-piece mahogany necks used on many models with three-piece laminated maple necks. These lasted until a complete redesign movement began in 1983, the year Gibson began to halt their decline as they prepared for their 90th anniversary.

Neck Sets

Neck resets on the jumbo-body guitars built during the '30s, '40s, and '50s aren't common; and even when a jumbo does need a neck set, it's borderline. The small-body 1930s L-00s almost without exception need neck sets, however.

The backs of L-00, Nick Lucas, and L-Century models often flatten out and lose their arch. Gibson's Ren Ferguson calls this "stretching": the back flattens in both width and length. When the body stretches along its length, the neck pulls up, and the fretboard over the body "sinks" toward the soundhole. The result is high action; a neck set is needed.

This flattening probably results from a combination of things: flat-sawn braces, very thin brace ends that have become too flexible, and untucked brace ends. Also, these 1930s small-body Gibsons had extremely thin backs and sides, .070" at times. For some reason the L-00 shape can't seem to hold an arch as well as the jumbo models.

During the '30s Gibson for unknown reasons sometimes glued the neck dovetail into the block *before* gluing on the top, especially on Advanced Jumbos, Roy Smecks, and other jumbo models. This means that with the top overlapping the dovetail, any attempt at resetting in the normal fashion (steaming the neck/fingerboard out of the joint intact) can be disastrous, for the dovetail pulls the top with it.

Someone planning neck removal might consider the following. First, use a Dremel Moto Tool miniature router and a very small, straight-fluted bit to cut through the 15th fret slot, down through the fretboard and the top. Make this slot 1 ½" long and ¾" to either side of center. Next, when the neck pulls out, the small amount of spruce topwood running lengthwise on both sides of the dovetail will break out easily with the grain, because the difficult cross-grain part has already been cut. Another option is to remove the fretboard in order to see the joint. The first method is preferable.

In the 1960s some sides of mahogany guitars were plywood. With these instruments additional caution in the neck-resetting process is needed, for excessive steam in the neck area could cause de-lamination of the plywood.

In the mid-'70s Gibson designed a new neck joint that used a paddle-shaped tenon at the top of the dovetail. This was to give extra support to the fretboard extension and keep it from dipping into the soundhole or collapsing. This joint is extremely difficult to reset: first, the paddle eliminates easy access to the dovetail area with steam; also, because the paddle is a mortise-and-tenon joint in its own right, a *second* tight-fitting joint has to be loosened. Since the paddle is glued to the underside of the fretboard extension, heating and loosening the fretboard during a reset is difficult.

Also, the paddle dovetail itself is only half the normal length. During a reset the bottom of the heel, which isn't connected to the dovetail and consequently has no strength, may remain glued to the body while the rest of the neck comes loose. These necks can be reset, however, and many guitars built with the paddle dovetail are great instruments—especially those assembled after '84.

The paddle dovetail was discontinued by Gibson/Montana in the spring of 1992. Gibson knew of the strength given by the paddle to the fretboard extension and the entire neck-block area but found the intricate design unnecessary. According to Gibson's Ren Ferguson, "We didn't need it. We don't *have* any problem in that area because our tops are arched and pre-stressed; they don't cave in anywhere. We went back to the traditional dovetail so that future repair people would be able to pull these necks, if they need it, just as easily as pulling a vintage Martin or Gibson. We glue the necks in with animal-hide glue for that reason."

BROKEN PEGHEADS

This has never been a Gibson problem. In 1965 the angle of the peghead to the fingerboard was changed from 17 degrees to a less-severe 14 degrees. To the experienced eye, this accounts for a significantly different look and, mechanically speaking, a decreased string angle at the rear of the nut. A good idea with the 14-degree peghead is to give several more string wraps (wrapping downward) on the tuner string posts to keep good down-pressure at the nut's rear.

The decrease in angle was probably a move to save a little on lumber and perhaps to increase the strength in the peghead area in hopes of avoiding broken pegheads, should an instrument accidentally tip over. Because the truss rod access cavity is machined into the peghead face behind the nut, the peghead would be weakened just enough to render Gibsons more susceptible to broken pegheads during a fall. However, with the shallower angle comes less tension on this area and less likelihood of the peghead popping off during a fall. Statistically, most of the broken Gibson pegheads occur on electric and not acoustic instruments. Flat-tops are less likely to be leaned against the wall or an amp and in general are given better care than most electrics. They are also lighter than those electrics that so often lose their heads.

During the '70s, to give additional strength to the rear of the peghead, a large sculpture of wood called a volute was allowed to remain during the wood-removal process of neck shaping. At times this hunk of wood was huge. Despite the volutes, pegheads continued to break from mistreatment. In addition to being ineffective, the volutes were ugly, uncomfortable, and generally detested by guitarists. As a consequence they gradually shrank, to the point of total disappearance by the time the wholesale redesigning of 1983 took place.

Serial Numbers

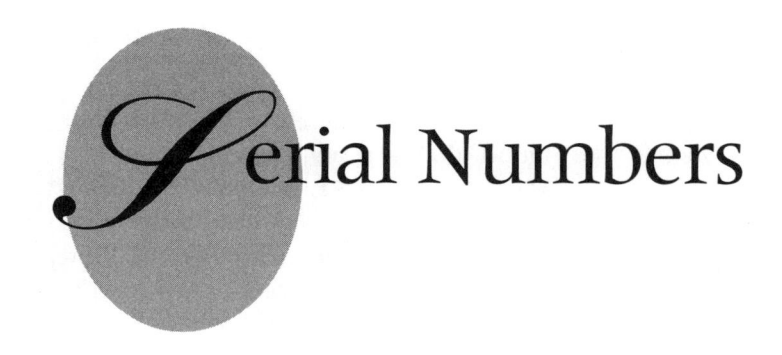

Chapter Thirteen

(HEARTACHES) BY THE NUMBER: GIBSON'S USE OF SERIAL NUMBERS

Complicated, thorough, illogical, accurate, ambiguous, specific, nonexistent: these adjectives describe Gibson's application of serial numbers on their guitars made since 1925. During the period covered by this book, Gibson has used no fewer than eight different numbering "systems" that range from dead-accurate (the current one) to haphazard and chaotic (most of the others). Much of the confusion and misinformation about Gibson flat-tops stems from the company's unsystematic assigning of serial numbers, when they in fact *did* assign serial numbers, and to some degree it's to clarify this muddy water that the present book exists.

Here are a few of the variables that make Gibson-dating so exasperating and often interesting: the company used both serial numbers and factory order numbers (FON) simultaneously; they used one and not the other; they sometimes used neither; they liked some numbers so much that they used the same ones—duplicates, in other words—over and over again, on different models and in different years; and when they did exist, numbers were sometimes written and sometimes rubber-stamped, sometimes in ink and sometimes in near-invisible pencil, and sometimes stamped into the wood itself, though in various locations on the guitars.

The following systems have been compiled from a number of sources, including our own study and experience. Thanks must be given to the following people for their work: Roger Siminoff, A.R. Duchossoir, Julius Bellson, George Gruhn, and Walter Carter. For those who need a more thorough examination of Gibson serial numbers, please consult A.R. Duchossoir's book *Guitar Identification*.

> At times it seems that Gibson has used as many systems of serial numbers as there are guitar models in this photo.

At the bottom line is this sober note: there usually isn't a simple way to date a Gibson by the serial number alone. It's because of this fact that our various chapters are filled with details, specifications, and dates. If we have been successful in writing this book, the reader will finally have a thorough guide that is far more accurate and comprehensive in dating Gibson flat-tops than reliance on serial numbers alone.

Serial Numbers: 1925 to 1947

Year	Approximate Last Number
1925	82700
1926	83600
1927	85400
1928	87300
1929	89750
1930	90200
1931	90450
1932	90700
1933	91400
1934	92300
1935	92800
1936	94100
1937	95200
1938	95750
1939	96050
1940	96600
1941	97400
1942	97700
1943	97850
1944	98250
1945	98650
1946	99300
1947	99999

Factory Order Numbers: 1935 to 1941

A letter was coded into the FON during this period. When two or more letters are found, the first is the more important. In almost all cases, only the high-end guitars from this era received serial numbers; the rest were given FONs.

Year	First Letter
1935	A
1936	B
1937	C
1938	D
1939	E
1940	F
1941	G

Factory Order Numbers: 1942 to 1946

Serial numbers are seldom found on flat-tops from this era, and some instruments do not even have Factory Order Numbers. When present, the FONs contain four digits, stamped in ink on the neck block, indicating the batch number. This is followed by a two-digit number in red pencil, indicating the sequence of that batch of guitars, usually not more than 46 per batch. Apparently, no number with 1 as its first digit was used during this time. Though our compilation of the FONs from this period is continually being updated and supplemented, the following few examples should serve as a guide:

910-3	1942
923-45	1942
2004-1	1942
2224-14	1943
2426-39	1943
2558-46	1944

"A" Serial Numbers: 1947 to 1961

When Gibson reached the number 99999 in 1947, they devised a new numbering system, starting with A 100 in April. Each and every serial number began with the prefix A.

Year	Approximate Last Number
1947	A 1304
1948	A 2665
1949	A 4413
1950	A 6597
1951	A 9419
1952	A 12462
1953	A 16101
1954	A 18667
1955	A 21909
1956	A 24755
1957	A 26819
1958	A 28880
1959	A 32284
1960	A 35645
1961	A 36147

Factory Order Numbers: 1952 to 1961

Starting with the last letter of the alphabet and working back, Gibson used a different letter for each year from 1952 to 1961.

Year	Letter
1952	Z
1953	Y
1954	X
1955	W
1956	V
1957	U
1958	T
1959	S
1960	R
1961	Q

Serial Numbers: 1961 to 1969

In May 1961 Gibson started over again, dropping the A prefix and beginning with the number 100. For the first six years, numbers were duplicates of the those used until 1947. To further confuse the already murky issue, some numbers were used more than once *within this period*. This list may not always be exact, but it will always give an approximate date of construction. The following work was done by A. R. Duchossoir and was then revised for *Gruhn's Guide to Vintage Guitars*.

Years	Serial Number Range
1961	100-42440
1962	42441-61180
1963	61450-64222
1964	64240-70501
1962	71180-96600
1963	96601-99999
1967	000001-099999
1963, 67	100000-106099
1963	106100-106899
1963, 67	109000-109999
1963	110000-111549
1963, 67	111550-115799
1963	115800-118299
1963, 67	118300-120999

Years	Serial Number Range
1963	121000-139999
1963, 67	140000-140100
1963	140101-144304
1964	144305-144380
1963	144381-149864
1964	149865-149891
1963	149892-152989
1964	152990-174222
1964, 65	174223-176643
1964	176644-250335
1965	250336-305983
1965, 67	306000-310999
1965	311000-320149
1967	320150-320699
1965	320700-329179
1965, 67	329180-330199
1965, 67, 68	330200-332240
1965	332241-348092
1966	348093-349100
1965	349121-368638
1966	368640-369890
1967	370000-370999
1966	380000-385309
1967	390000-390998
1965, 66, 67, 68	400001-400999
1966	401000-438922
1965, 66, 68, 69	500000-500999
1965	501009-501600
1968	501601-501702
1965, 68	501703-502706
1968	503010-503109
1965, 68	503405-520955
1968	520056-530056
1966, 68, 69	530061-530850
1968, 69	530851-530993
1969	530994-539999
1966, 69	540000-540795
1969	540796-545009
1966	555000-556909
1969	558012-567400
1966	570099-570755
1969	580000-580999
1966, 67, 68, 69	600000-600999
1969	601000-606090
1966, 67	700000-700799
1968, 69	750000-750999

Years	Serial Number Range
1966, 67, 68, 69	800000-800999
1966, 69	801000-812838
1969	812900-819999
1966, 69	820000-820087
1966	820088-823830
1969	824000-824999
1966, 69	828002-847488
1966, 69	847499-858999
1967	859001-895038
1968	895039-896999
1967, 69	897000-898999
1968	899000-972864

Serial Numbers: 1970 to 1975

Gibson again used the six-digit serial number. The number and "Made in USA" are stamped on the back of the peghead. Because these numbers often duplicate those from the 1963 to 1969 period, it is essential to know other features of the guitars to date them accurately.

Year	Serial Number Range
1973	000000s
1970-75	100000s
1973-75	200000s
1974-75	300000s
1974-75	400000s
1974-75	500000s
1970-72, 1974-75	600000s
1970-72	700000s
1973-75	800000s
1970-72	900000s

During 1973, 1974, and 1975, two different serial-numbering systems were used simultaneously. This is the second one:

Year	Serial Number
1973-75	A plus 6 DIGITS
1974-75	B plus 6 DIGITS
1974-75	C plus 6 DIGITS
1974-75	D plus 6 DIGITS
1974-75	E plus 6 DIGITS
1974-75	F plus 6 DIGITS

Serial Numbers: 1975 to 1977

For these three years Gibson used a simple system—a two-digit prefix followed by a six-digit number.

Year	Prefix
1975	99
1976	00
1977	06

Serial Numbers: 1977 to the Present

Since 1977 Gibson has used an "eternal" eight-digit serial number that indicates the day and year on which the guitar was made, as well as the ranking of the particular instrument on that day:

Meaning	Digits Used
• Year a given instrument was made	1 and 5
• Day and year the instrument was completed	2, 3, and 4
• Rank of the instrument that day	6, 7, and 8

EXAMPLE: The J-200 Junior with serial number 92052010 is interpreted as follows:

1. The first digit is 9 and the fifth digit is 2, indicating that it was made in 1992.
2. The second, third, and fourth digits are 205; thus it was completed on the 205th day of 1992, which was August 24th.
3. The sixth, seventh, and eighth digits are 010 — this guitar was therefore the tenth instrument completed by Gibson that day.*

* The Kalamazoo and Bozeman factories started their "day sequence" (the last three digits of the serial number) with 001, but the Nashville factory began with 500. Thus, if the J-200 Junior had been completed in Nashville on August 24, 1992, the serial number would have been 92052510.

CHRONOLOGY OF GIBSON FLAT-TOP GUITARS, 1926 TO 1989

The accompanying table lists the flat-top models introduced and discontinued, year by year. While this is based on company information, some is by necessity inferential—Gibson over the decades has been notorious for its inadequate, ambiguous, or nonexistent records. These inferences in all cases have been based on solid evidence gathered through lengthy research.

Year	Guitars Introduced	Guitars Discontinued
1926	L-0 L-1	none
1927	none	none
1928	Nick Lucas (Gibson Special)	none
1929	L-2 HG-20 HG-22 HG-24	none
1930	none	none
1931	none	none
1932	L-00 HG-00	HG-20 HG-22 HG-24
1933	Century	L-0
1934	Roy Smeck Stage Deluxe Roy Smeck Radio Grande Jumbo	L-2
1935	none	none
1936	J-35 Advanced Jumbo	Jumbo
1937	HG-0 HG-Century SJ-200	L-1
1938	Jumbo Deluxe	Nick Lucas
1939	SJ-100 J-55	Century HG-Century Roy Smeck Radio Grande Jumbo Deluxe
1940	none	Advanced Jumbo
1941	none	none
1942	J-45 Southern Jumbo LG-2	J-35 J-55 SJ-100 HG-0 Roy Smeck Stage Deluxe
1943	none	SJ-200
1944	none	none
1945	none	L-00 HG-00
1946	LG-3 J-200	none
1947	LG-1 J-50	none
1948	none	none
1949	LG-2 ¾	none
1950	CF-100	none
1951	J-185 CF-100E	none
1952	none	none
1953	none	none
1954	none	none
1955	none	SJN
1956	Country-Western	none
1957	none	none
1958	LG-0	J-185
1959	none	none
1960	SJN Hummingbird	Country-Western CF-100 CF-100E
1961	B-45-12	none
1962	B-25 B-25N B-25 ¾ B-25-12 B-25-12N Country-Western SJN Dove Everly Brothers	LG-2 LG-3 LG-2 ¾ SJN

Year	Guitars Introduced	Guitars Discontinued
1963	FJN F-25 B-45-12N Everly Brothers N Dove N Hummingbird N	none
1964	none	Everly Brothers N
1965	Heritage	none
1966	none	none
1967	B-15	none
1968	Blue Ridge Heritage 12	FJ-N LG-1
1969	Les Paul Jumbo	B-25 ¾
1970	JG-0 JG-12 Artist-12 LG-12 Jubilee Jubilee Deluxe Jubilee-12 Blue Ridge-12	B-25 LG-12 Artist 12
1971	J-40 B-20	F-25 Jubilee Jubilee Deluxe Jubilee-12 B-15 JG-12 Heritage 12
1972	J-250R J-55 (square-shoulder) J-100	Everly Brothers B-25-12
1973	Gospel J-300-12	Les Paul Jumbo LG-12 J-300-12 JG-0
1974	none	J-100 B-20 LG-0
1975	Mark 35 Mark 53 Mark 72 Mark 81 Mark 99	none
1976	none	Blue Ridge 12
1977	Mark 35-12	Mark 35-12 B-25-N B-25-12-N B-25
1978	none	J-250R Country-Western SJN Southern Jumbo
1979	none	Mark 35 Mark 53 Mark 72 Mark 81 Mark 99 Blue Ridge B-45-12 J-160-E
1980	none	Gospel
1981	none	none
1982	none	J-40 Heritage J-50 J-55 (sq.-shoulder)
1983	none	none
1984	J-25	none
1985	J-45 Celebrity J-200 Celebrity J-100 J-35 (square-shoulder) J-30	J-45 Celebrity J-200 Celebrity
1986	J-180	none
1987	none	J-35 (sq.-shoulder) J-25
1988	none	none
1989	none	none

GIBSON MODELS PRODUCED IN BOZEMAN, MONTANA, 1989 to 2008

Model	89	90	91	92	93	94	95	96	97	98	99	00	01	02	03	04	05	06	07	08
SMALL BODY																				
L-1			X	X	X	X	X					X	X	X						
L-1 International Series					X															
L-1 Robert Johnson															X					
L-1 Yamano														X						
L-1 Custom Club					X			X												
L-1 Special of the Month					X															
L-00 Blues King			X	X	X	X	X	X	X	X	X	X	X	X	X	X	X	X	X	X
L-00 Small Body																X	X			
L00 1937 Legend, Lee Roy Parnell																		X	X	X
Nick Lucas	X		X	X	X							X	X	X	X	X	X			
Nick Lucas Elite											X	X	X	X						
Nick Lucas Estate Edition						X														
Nick Lucas Brazilian														X						
Nick Lucas NAMM Special								X												
Nick Lucas Custom								X					X	X						
L-2 Centennial Model						X														
L-2 1929 Reissue											X									
L-2 International Series						X														
Century						X	X													

Serial Numbers

Model	89	90	91	92	93	94	95	96	97	98	99	00	01	02	03	04	05	06	07	08
Century Elvis Costello																				X
L-20						X	X													
L-20 International Series					X															
CF-100 E Centennial						X														
CF-100							X													
LG ¾ Arlo Guthrie															X	X	X	X	X	X
WM-00										X	X	X	X	X	X	X	X	X	X	
Emmylou Harris											X	X	X	X	X	X	X	X	X	X
L-130											X	X	X	X	X	X	X			
L-130 Macasser													X							
L-140											X	X	X	X	X	X				
L-150											X	X	X	X	X					
L-150 Brazilian													X	X						
CJ-165																		X	X	X
CJ-165 Rosewood																		X	X	X
CJ-165 EC																			X	X
CJ-165 EC Rosewood																		X	X	X
Caldera Cutaway														X	X					
Cascade Cutaway														X	X					
Sonoma Cutaway														X	X					
LC-1																X	X	X	X	X
LC-2																X	X	X	X	X
LC-3																X	X			

Model	89	90	91	92	93	94	95	96	97	98	99	00	01	02	03	04	05	06	07	08
LG-2																	X	X		
B-25																	X	X		
Traveling Songwriter																	X	X	X	X
SLOPE SHOULDER JUMBO																				
Jumbo 1934 Centennial						X		X												
Jumbo 1934 Reissue											X									
Roy Smeck						X		X	X			X								
Advanced Jumbo		X	X	X	X	X	X	X	X	X	X	X	X	X	X	X	X	X	X	X
AJ Birdseye								X												
AJ Brazilian													X	X						
AJ Cocobola													X	X						
AJ Dave's Guitar													X							
AJ Fuller Vintage													X							
AJ Luthier's Choice														X						
AJ Luthier's Choice Brazilian															X					
AJ Musician's Friend														X						
AJ Special of the Month-Herringbone					X															
AJ Special of the Month-Maple					X															
J-35						X	X													
J-35 Limited Edition								X												

Serial Numbers

Model	89	90	91	92	93	94	95	96	97	98	99	00	01	02	03	04	05	06	07	08
J-35 Cherry													X							
J-35 Custom														X						
J-35 Fuller Vintage														X						
J-45	X	X	X	X	X	X	X	X	X	X	X	X	X	X	X	X	X	X	X	X
J-45 Brazilian													X	X						
J-45 Bubinga													X	X						
J-45 Custom Vine											X	X	X	X						
J-45 Custom Vine Koa												X	X	X						
J-45 Dave's Guitar													X							
J-45 Donovan														X						
J-45 Fuller Vintage													X	X	X					
J-45 Herringbone													X							
J-45 International Series						X														
J-45 Koa							X	X												
J-45 Macasser														X						
J-45 Montana Special													X							
J-45 1942 Legend Eldon Whitford																		X	X	X
J-45 Quilted Maple													X	X						
J-45 Rosewood								X		X	X	X	X	X	X	X	X	X	X	X
J-45 Rosewood Custom											X	X	X	X	X	X	X	X	X	X
J-45 Rosewood Custom Brazilian														X						
J-45 Special				X																

Model	89	90	91	92	93	94	95	96	97	98	99	00	01	02	03	04	05	06	07	08
J-45 True Vintage																			x	x
J-45 True Vintage Red Spr																			x	x
J-45 Vine													x	x	x					
J-45 Vine Rosewood																x	x	x	x	x
J-45 Vine Yamano													x							
J-45 Yamano					x		x	x	x	x	x	x	x	x	x					
J-50		x	x	x				x	x	x	x	x	x	x	x	x	x	x	x	x
J-50 Yamano												x		x						
J-50 Yamano Special													x							
J-55							x													
J-55 1939 Reissue						x		x			x		x							
J-55 RW Limited Edition								x												
J-160 E	x		x	x	x	x	x		x	x	x	x	x	x	x	x	x	x	x	x
J-160 E John Lennon														x	x					
J-160 E John Lennon Bed In									x	x	x	x	x	x		x	x	x	x	
J-160 E John Lennon Fab 4									x	x	x	x	x	x		x	x	x	x	
J-160 E John Lennon Peace									x	x	x	x	x	x		x	x	x	x	x
J-160 E Lennon Magical Tour										x	x	x	x							
J-160 E P-100								x	x	x										
J-160 E Yamano							x	x	x	x	x	x	x	x	x	x	x	x		
Southern Jumbo			x	x	x	x						x	x	x	x	x	x	x	x	x
SJ Banner Reissue				x	x															

Model	89	90	91	92	93	94	95	96	97	98	99	00	01	02	03	04	05	06	07	08
SJ Buddy Holly							X	X	X	X	X									
SJ Dave's Guitar													X							
SJ Dwight Yoakum														X						
SJ Dwight Yoakum Honky Tonk															X	X	X	X	X	X
SJ Fuller Vintage														X						
SJ Hank Williams Jr.									X	X										
SJ Woody Guthrie								X							X	X	X	X	X	X
SJ-45 Deluxe						X		X		X	X	X	X	X						
SJ-45 Deluxe Yamano												X								
Southern Jumbo 45										X	X	X	X	X	X	X	X	X		X
Working Man 45											X									
Formula 1S								X	X											
OP-25			X	X																
17" JUMBO																				
J-200	X	X	X		X	X	X	X	X	X	X	X	X	X	X	X	X	X		
J-200 Birdseye							X	X												
J-200 Brazilian													X	X	X					
J-200 Celebrity			X																	
J-200 Centennial						X														
J-200 Centennial 1938 Reissue						X														

Gibson's Fabulous Flat-Top Guitars

Model	89	90	91	92	93	94	95	96	97	98	99	00	01	02	03	04	05	06	07	08
J-200 Centennial 1950's' Reissue						X	X			X										
J-200 Commemorative								X												
J-200 Custom Cutaway												X								
J-200 Custom Vine											X	X				X	X	X	X	X
J-200 Deluxe							X	X		X	X									
J-200 Deluxe Rosewood								X		X										
J-200 Dusty Rose																		X	X	X
J-200 Elite											X		X	X	X					
J-200 Elvis King of Rock							X	X	X	X	X	X	X	X			X	X	X	X
J-200 Elvis "the King"								X	X	X	X	X								
J-200 Elvis Signature								X	X	X	X	X	X	X	X					
J-200 Emmylou Harris Rose					X															
J-200 Guitar of the Month					X															
J-200 Highflame Maple						X	X													
J-200 International Series Koa					X															
J-200 International Series Perloid					X															
J-200 International Special						X		X												
J-200 International Special Koa						X														
J-200 Jim Beam														X						
J-200 Koa												X	X	X						
J-200 Limited Edition				X																

Model	89	90	91	92	93	94	95	96	97	98	99	00	01	02	03	04	05	06	07	08
J-200 Luthier's Choice														X						
J-200 Montana Gold								X	X	X	X	X	X	X	X					
J-200 Montana Gold Custom														X		X	X	X	X	X
J-200 Montana Gold Koa													X	X						
J-200 Montana Gold Quilted													X							
J-200 1938 Reissue								X		X										
J-200 1948 Reissue								X												
J-200 Pete Townshend								X								X	X	X	X	X
J-200 Quilted Maple							X						X							
J-200 Ray Whitley Centennial Custom Club						X	X													
J-200 Ron Wood					X						X									
J-200 Rose								X												
J-200 Rosewood			X	X	X	X	X	X	X	X			X	X						
J-200 Rosewood Deluxe					X															
J-200 Rosewood Reissue			X																	
J-200 Smartwood														X						
J-200 Special of the Month					X															
J-200 Special of the Month Koa						X														
J-200 Super 200											X	X	X	X	X					
J-200 Vine												X	X	X	X	X	X	X		
J-200 Western Classic												X	X	X	X	X	X	X	X	X
J-200 Western Classic BF													X	X						

Model	89	90	91	92	93	94	95	96	97	98	99	00	01	02	03	04	05	06	07	08
J-200 Western Classic Brazilian													X	X						
J-200 Yamano							X	X	X	X	X	X	X	X	X	X				
J-200 12				X			X	X							X	X				
J-250 Presentation							X	X												
SJ-100																		X	X	X
SJ-100 1939 Reissue								X	X											
SJ-100 Centennial 1939 Reissue					X															
SJ-100 Xtra																X	X	X	X	X
SJ-150																		X	X	X
SJ-200 EC																X	X	X	X	X
SJ-200 MC																X	X	X	X	X
SJ-200 True Vintage																				X
SJ-250 Monarch							X	X	X			X	X	X	X	X	X	X	X	X
SJ-300												X	X	X	X	X	X	X	X	X
J-100	X	X	X																	
J-100 Xtra					X	X	X	X	X	X	X	X	X	X	X	X	X	X	X	
J-100 Xtra Rosewood								X	X											
J-100 Xtra 12							X	X	X											
J-150											X	X	X	X	X	X	X		X	

16" NARROW WAIST

Model	89	90	91	92	93	94	95	96	97	98	99	00	01	02	03	04	05	06	07	08
J-185		X		X	X	X	X				X	X	X	X	X	X	X	X	X	X

Model	89	90	91	92	93	94	95	96	97	98	99	00	01	02	03	04	05	06	07	08
J-185 Cocobola														X						
J-185 Centennial						X	X													
J-185 International Series											X	X								
J-185 Koa													X							
J-185 Quilted													X	X						
J-185 Quilted Vine														X						
J-185 Reissue 1950s					X															
J-185 1951 Reissue								X												
J-185 True Vintage										X							X			
J-185 12												X	X	X	X	X	X	X		
J-185 12 Vine														X						
J-185 EC Blues King													X		X	X	X	X	X	X
J-185 EC Custom													X	X			X	X	X	X
J-185 EC Cutaway											X	X	X	X	X					
J-185 EC Cutaway Jason's Angel														X						
J-185 EC Cutaway Koa													X	X						
J-185 EC Cutaway Quilted													X	X						
J-185 EC MF																X				
J-185 EC Maple																		X	X	X
J-185 EC Ovangko																			X	
J-185 EC Rosewood																		X	X	X
Dwight Yoakam Y2K															X					

Model	89	90	91	92	93	94	95	96	97	98	99	00	01	02	03	04	05	06	07	08
J-180	X	X	X	X	X	X		X	X	X	X	X	X	X	X	X				
J-180 International Series					X															
J-180 Musician's Friend															X					
J-180 1962 Reissue					X															
J-180 Quilted														X						
J-180 Reissue Pinless Bridge						X														
J-180 Special of the Month					X	X														
J-180 Yamano									X											
Everly Brothers					X		X	X	X		X			X						
Harley Davidson							X	X	X											
Working Man 180										X	X									
J-180 Cutaway									X											
J-180 EC Cutaway											X	X		X	X					
J-180 EC MF																	X	X	X	
J-190													X	X	X					
J-190 EC Spr Fusion																X	X	X		
J-190 Quilted														X						
J-200 Jr.			X	X	X	X		X	X	X	X	X								
J-200 Jr. International					X															
J-200 Jr. Rosewood			X	X																
J-200 Jr. Dwight Yoakum Y2K											X									
J-200 Jr. 12				X																

Serial Numbers

Model	89	90	91	92	93	94	95	96	97	98	99	00	01	02	03	04	05	06	07	08
Star			X	X																
Starburst			X	X									X							
Starburst Elite				X	X	X														
Starburst Flame					X															
Starburst Standard				X	X															
Starburst Studio				X	X	X		X												
Blues King Maestro Electro						X	X	X	X	X	X									
Blues King Maestro Electro Quilted							X	X												
EAS Classic				X																
EAS Deluxe				X	X						X									
EAS Deluxe Standard						X														
EAS Standard					X															
J-1000				X	X	X														
J-1500				X	X	X														
J-2000			X	X	X	X	X	X	X			X		X	X					
J-2000 Brazilian													X	X	X					
L4A																X	X	X	X	X
EC10									X	X	X	X								
EC 20									X	X	X	X								
EC 20 Floret										X	X	X								
EC 30									X	X	X									

Gibson's Fabulous Flat-Top Guitars

Model	89	90	91	92	93	94	95	96	97	98	99	00	01	02	03	04	05	06	07	08
SQUARE SHOULDER																				
Hummingbird	x	x	x	x	x	x	x	x	x	x	x	x	x	x	x	x	x	x	x	x
Hummingbird Artist																	x	x	x	x
Hummingbird Custom												x	x			x		x	x	x
Hummingbird Custom Cocobola													x							
Hummingbird Custom Koa													x	x	x					
Hummingbird Custom Quilted													x							
Hummingbird Firebird													x	x		x	x	x	x	x
Hummingbird International Series					x															
Hummingbird Koa														x						
Hummingbird 1963 Reissue								x			x									
Hummingbird Orpheum													x	x						
Hummingbird Quilted													x	x						
Hummingbird Smartwood														x						
Hummingbird Special					x															
Hummingbird Special of the Month																				
Hummingbird True Vintage																			x	x
Hummingbird Yamano Koa															x					
Hummingbird 12 Koa														x						
Dove	x	x	x	x	x	x	x	x	x	x	x	x	x		x	x		x	x	x
Dove Artist											x	x			x	x				

Serial Numbers

Model	89	90	91	92	93	94	95	96	97	98	99	00	01	02	03	04	05	06	07	08
Dove Artist Cutaway											X	X								
Dove Commemorative						X	X													
Dove Custom Club					X															
Dove Elvis Presley																X	X	X	X	X
Doves in Flight								X	X	X	X	X	X	X		X	X	X	X	
Doves in Flight Brazilian														X						
Doves in Flight Quilted														X						
Dove International Series					X	X		X												
Dove Luthier's Choice														X						
Dove Reissue					X											X				
Dove Special of the Month																				
Formula 1L									X	X	X									
Gospel				X	X	X	X	X	X	X	X	X								
J-30	X	X	X	X	X	X	X	X	X	X	X									
J-30 Cutaway								X												
J-30 Formula 1								X												
J-30 Koa								X			X									
J-30 Rosewood				X	X		X	X												
J-60				X	X	X	X	X	X	X	X	X								
J-60 International							X													
J-60 International Series					X															
J-60 International Special						X														

Model	89	90	91	92	93	94	95	96	97	98	99	00	01	02	03	04	05	06	07	08
J-60 Special of the Month					X															
CL-10									X	X	X	X								
CL-20									X	X	X	X								
CL-30										X	X	X								
CL-30 Deluxe									X											
CL-35									X		X	X								
CL-35 Cutaway										X										
CL-40										X	X	X								
CL-40 Artist									X											
CL-45									X			X								
CL-45 Cutaway										X	X	X								
CL-50									X											
CL-50 Supreme										X	X	X								
CL-60									X	X		X								
WM-10										X										
SJ Sheryl Crow											X	X	X	X	X	X	X	X	X	X
Songbird											X	X	X	X	X					
Songbird Brazilian														X						
Songbird Deluxe											X	X	X	X	X					
Songbird Deluxe Cutaway												X	X	X						
Songbird Deluxe Koa													X	X						
Songbird Deluxe 12													X	X	X					

Model	89	90	91	92	93	94	95	96	97	98	99	00	01	02	03	04	05	06	07	08
Songwriter												X				X	X			X
Songwriter Cutaway																	X	X		
Songwriter Deluxe																X	X	X	X	X
Songwriter Special																			X	X
B-45-12			X	X	X	X														
Master Museum Ren Ferguson																	X	X	X	X

INDEX

Page numbers in *italics* refer to illustrations.

Advanced Jumbo, 3, *9*, 47-50, *47, 48, 49,* 73
Allen, Rex, 76
Anderson, Eric, 77
Arnold, Eddy, 77
Artist, 12, *135,* 136
Ashley, Clarence (Tom), *2, 46*
Atkins, Chet, 2, 91
Autry, Gene, *3,* 76, 77, 78
B-15, 103, 105
B-25-12, 6, *133, 134,* 133-134, 135
B-25/B-25N/B-25N Deluxe (also see LG-2 & LG-3), *95, 98,* 100, 104
B-45-12, 6, *131,* 131-133, 134
Baez, Joan, 103
Banjo, 72
Banjo, Mastertone, 124
"Banner" Peghead, 28, *55,* 64
Banner "Only a Gibson Is Good Enough", 87, 96, 97, 99
Beatles, The, 107
Bee Gees, 134
Bellson, Julius, 2, 74, 86, 91
Berryman, David, 144
Bikel, Theodore, 122
Black, Clint, 77, 107
Blake, Norman, *30, 45, 72,* 73
Blue-Ridge 12 Model, 135
Blue-Ridge Model, *126,* 130
Book Binder, Roy, *36, 53*
Bozeman, Montana, 143
Bracing, Double X, 82, 115, 122, 125, 127, *139*
  Ladder, 101, 108
  Kasha style, *138*
  X-style, *138*
Brand, Oscar, 122
Bridge, "Moustache", 77, 81, 82, 84, 85, 86, 87, 119
  "Special", 100, 102
  "Tune-O-Matic", 81, 90, 109, 119, 120
  Kasha asymmetrical design, *138*
  Pad, 191, 192-193
  Repairs, 193-194
Britt, Elton, 77
Brooks, Garth, 77, 107
Brothers Four, 122
Burnette, Gary, 48, 50
  Gary and Bonnie, *172,* 172
Byrd, Billy, 2
Carlisle, Cliff, 68
Carlson, Steve, 8
Carlton, Gaither, *2, 46*
Carter Family, 122
Cash, Johnny, 77
Century (see also Century, Century of Progress, L-C)
Century of Progress (see also L-Century), 2
CF-100/CF-100E, 101, 106-107
Chicago Musical Instrument Company, 103
Clapton, Eric, 93
CMI, 143
Collie, Mark, 77
Collings, Bill, 192
Corrigan, Ray, 77
Cotten, Elizabeth, 122
Country-Western Model (see also Southern Jumbo), 6
County Music Hall of Fame, 77
Cozzens, Ellsworth T., 68
Crosby, David, 77
Curtis, Ken, *89*
Custom Shop—Gibson Montana, 146
  Advanced Jumbo, *166, 168*
  Dove, *165*
  Hummingbird, *154, 155, 165*
  J-180, *162, 163*
  J-180 Dove, *150*
  J-200, *156, 158, 160, 161, 167*
  J-200 Jr, *153*
  J-2000, *157*
  L-1, *159*
  Photos Of Custom Shop Guitars:
    SJ "Banner", *153*
    Starburst Elite, *153*
Davis, Rev. Gary, *6,* 77, *84*
Dennis, Rex, *89*
Denver, John, 84
Diamond, Neil, 77
Dickens, Little Jimmy, 77, *82*
Diffie, Joe, 107
Dixon Brothers, 68
Dobro, 70
Dove Model, *14, 23*
Dove/Dove N, 113, 116, *118, 119, 120,* 118-121, 122, 126, 128
Dudley, Dave, 77
Dylan, Bob, 77, 103, 122
Eagles, 84
Elderly Instruments, 83, *196*
English, Larry, *144,* 145, 185, 182
Epiphone, 103, 133
  FT-85 Serenader, 133
  FT-Caballero, 103
  Texan, 103
Epiphone Guitars, 6
Erlewine, Dan, 207, *207*
ES-125, 88
ES-150, 88
Everly, Ike, 77, 91, 92
Everly Brothers, 77, 90-93, *90, 91*
  Don, 66, *90,* 91, 92, 93
  Phil, *90,* 91, 93
Everly Brothers Model, 10, 88, 90, 92, 113, 118, 126
F-25, 6, 103-105, *103*
F-5 Mandolin, 124
f-Holes, 70
Ferguson, Ren, 144, *144,* 145, 146, 182, 185
FJ-N, 103, 122-123
FJN, 6
Flatiron Mandolin Co., 144
Flatt, Lester, 124
Folkway Records, 122
Frezzell, Lefty, 77
Fuller, Walter, 81
Garland, Hank, 2
Gibb, Barry, *134*
Gibson, Bozeman Factory, 84, 116, 117, 130
  Kalamazoo Factory, *4,* 70, 73, 74, 77, 82, 88, 91, 101, 119, 129, *190, 191*
  Nashville Factory, *7,* 87, 93, 116, 129, 143
Gibson Flat-Tops, Chronological List of (1926-1993), 200-203
Gill, Vince, 77
Godfrey, Authur, 68
Gonder, Bill, 145
Goodman, Steve, 113
Gospel Model, 127-128
Grammer, Billy, 82
Grand Ole Opry, 107
Green, Douglas B. (also Ranger Doug), 77, *78*
Gresch, 110
Grover Tuners, 81
Grover Tuners, Rotomatics, 82, 120
Gruhn, George, 97
Guild Guitars, 115, 132, 134
  D-25, 128
Guthrie, Woody, *4,* 122
Hammond, John, *121*
Harney, Hacksaw, *80*
Harris, Emmylou, 62, 76, 77, 78, 123, 146, 148
Harrison, George, 107
Hawkins, Hawkshaw, 77
Heritage, 113, *124,* 124-126
Heritage, Heritage 12, 134-135
HG-00, *16,* 71, 74, *74*
HG-20, 69-71, *70*
HG-22, 69-71
HG-24, 69-71
HG-Century, 71, 74
  3/4 size, 74
HG-Series, 2, 69-71
Hiatt, John, 60, *60, 86,* 97, 114
Hill, Bobby, 77
Hillman, Chris, 77
Holly, Buddy, 77
Holt, Tim, 77
Hopkins, Lightnin', *61*
Houston, Cisco, 122
Houtsma, Dr. Adrian, 138
Howard, Clint, *57*
Hummingbird Model, 6, *23*
Hummingbird/Hummingbird N, 79, 90, *111, 113, 114, 116,* 111-117, 118, 119, 121, 122, 127, 129
  Dimensions, 112
  Maple, 111, 113
  Shipping Totals, 113
Ian and Sylvia, *131*
Ives Burl, 103
J-100 (see also Super Jumbo 100, SJ-100), 85-87, *86,* 129
J-160E, *107, 108,* 107-109
J-180, 93
J-180 Artist, 144
J-185, 5, *21*
J-185/J-185N, *87*-90, 91
  Shipping Total, 89
J-200 (see also SJ-200), *14, 21, 22,* 76-84, 85, 86, 87 88, 89, *91, 92, 93,* 109, 111, 112, 113, 116, 117, 119, 126, 127, 128, 129, 132, 136
J-200 Celebrity, 84
J-200 Citation Model, *22*
J-200 Elite, 84
J-25, 67-68, 104, 116
J-250R, 82
J-300 Artist, 83
J-35, 3, *16, 17,* 41-47, *41, 43, 44, 45, 46*
  Dimensions of, 42
  Shipping Totals, 44
J-35 (Jumbo 35), 85
J-35 (Jumbo 35), Square-Shoulder, 122, 128-129
J-40, 127
J-45, *21,* 54-63, *56, 57, 58, 59,* 95-97, 99, 103, 109, 116, 122, 126, 127, 129
J-45, Square-Shoulder, 126-127
J-50, 5, *15,* 54-63, *54, 59, 60, 61, 62,* 99, 122, 126, 127
  as prototype for Mark Series, *140*
J-50, Square-Shoulder, 126, 126
J-55, 85, 127, 128
J-55 (Jumbo 55), *18,* 50-54, *51, 52, 53*
Jackson, John, 54, *54*
James, Skip, *87*
JG-0, 130
JG-12, 130
Johns, Robi, 145, *145,* 185
Johnson, Jack, 57
Johnson, Lonnie, 85
Johnson, Robert, *29,* 85, 95, 180
Jones, Kennedy, 91
Jubilee, 104, 130
Jubilee 12N, 135
Jubilee Series, 142
Jumbo, 71, 72, 83, 111
Jumbo, Square Shouldered, 111-117
Jumbo Deluxe Model, 50, *50*
Jumbo Design (Round-Shoulder), 38-67, *39*
Jumbo Model, 3, *10,* 38-40, *38, 39, 40*
Juszkiewicz, Henry, 2, 144, 179
Kasha Design, 7, 8
Kaukonen, Jorma, 62, *62,* 189
King, B.B., 85
King, Pee Wee, 77
Kingston Trio, 122
Kluson Tuners, 89, 104, 108, 115, 127, 132, 133
Kluson Tuners, "Keystone", 89, 93, 115
Kottke, Leo, 63, 131, 132
L-0, *16, 25, 26, 26,* 69, 74
L-00, *1,* 3, *27, 27, 28,* 74, 95
L-1, *29,* 60
L-1 (Montana reissue), 143
L-2,, 32, *32*
L-48, 88
L-5, 77
L-50, 88

Index

L-Century (see also Century of Progress Model), 13, 33-35, *33, 34,* 73
L-Series, 25-37
   Dimensions, 30
   Identifying, 31, 32
Lamothe, Willy, 77
Lang, Eddie, 72
Lap Steel Guitar, 68
Leadbelly, 131
Lee, Albert, 7, 66, 78, 91, 93
Lennon, John, 107
Les Paul Jumbo, 109-110
Lewis, Furry, 98
LG-0, 6, 90, 96, 97, 98, 101-103, *101, 103,* 105
LG-1, 5, 97, 100-101, *100,* 135
LG-12, 135
LG-2, 3/4 size, 98, *98,* 100, 101
LG-2, 95-99, *96, 97, 98, 99,* 135
LG-3, 5, 97, *99,* 99-100, *100,* 135
LG-Series, 89, 95-105, 106
Lightfoot, Gordon, 131
Limelighters, The, 122
Limited Edition Models, 87
Lipscomb, Mance, *81*
Lockwood, Robert Jr., 24
Louvin, Charlie, 90
Lovin' Spoonfuls, 125
Lowell, John, 178
Lucas Nick, 72
Lucas Nick, "Special Model", 69
Lunsford, Bascom Lamar, 123
Madison Square Garden, 77
Maintenance and repair issues, 190-195
Maintenance and repair issues, Bracing, 191-192
   A-braces
   Cracked braces
   Double-X
   RF glued braces
   Scalloped
   Tucked into kerfing
   Bridge, 193-194
   "Bellied"
   Adjustable & Tune-O-Matic
   Rectangle
   Bridge pad, 191, 192-193
   Neck construction & details, 194-195
   Fretwire
   Neck set to body
   Peghead repairs
   Shape
   Truss rods
Mark 99 Model, *24*
Mark Series, 137-142
   Dimensions for, 139
   Headstock design, pickguard, soundhole ring, bridge details, 140
   J-50 used as prototype for, *140*
   Kasha bracing for, *138*
   Mark 33-12, 142
   Mark 35, *137*
   Mark 53, 141
   Mark 72, 141
   Mark 81, 141
   Mark 99, 141, *141*

Martin Guitar Company, 69, 86, 108, 111, 112, 115, 126, 134
   D-18E, 108
   D-28, 124
   D-28E, 108
McCarty, Ted, 2
McCoy, George and Ethel, *7*
Mellencamp, John, 114
Mona-steel strings, *190*
Montana-built flat-tops, 143-189
   1992 Models:, 145
      Pro Series
      New Vintage Series
      Electric Acoustic Series
   1993 Models: The New Acoustic Series, 146
      J-200 Series
      Historical Series
      Pro Series
      L-Series Blues Models
      Electric Acoustic Series
   Super Jumbos
      J-200 Reissue 147, *147*
      SJ-200 Montana (Rosewood Limited Edition), 147, *148*
      J-100/J-100 Xtra, 148, 149, *149*
      SJ-100 (1991 Reissue), 149, *149*
   Narrow-Waist Jumbos, 149
      J-180/Dove, *150*
      J-180/J-180 Artist, 149
      J-185 Reissue, 150, *150,* 151, *151*
      J-200 Junior, 151, *151,* 152, *152, 153*
      J-200 Junior 12-String, 169
      J-2000, 169, *169,* 170, *170*
      J-1000 & J-1500, 170, *170*
   Slope-Shoulder Jumbos
      J-45/J-50, 171, *171*
      Advanced Jumbo, 171, 172, *172, 173, 173,* 174
      Southern Jumbo "Banner", 154, 174, *174,* 175, *175*
      AJ-35, 175
   Square-Shoulder Jumbos
      Hummingbird, 154, 155, 175, 176, *176*
      Dove, 177, *177*
      J-30, 177, *177*
      J-60, 178, *178*
      Gospel, 179, *179*
      B-45-12, 180, *180*
   Small-Body Guitars, 180-183
      L-1, 180, *182*
      L-00, 181, *182*
      L-00 Blues King, 181, *182*
      L-20 Special, 181, *182*
      Nick Lucas Artist Reissue, 183, *183*
   Electric Acoustics
      OP-25, 183
      J-160-E, 184, *184*
      EAS Acoustics, 184—189
      Deluxe, 185, *185*
      Standard, 185, *185*
      Star, 186, *186*
      Starburst Models, 186-189; Studio, 187, 188, *188;* Standard, 187, 188, *188;* Elite *153,* 187, *187, 188, 189*
Montgomery, Melba, 77
Montoya, Carlos, 104

Moore, Maudie, 119
Moore, Tommy, *57*
Morgan, Lorrie, 107
Mossman Guitars, 132
National Folk Festival, 80
National Guitar, 70
Neck, Volute, 115
Neck construction & details, 194-195
Nelson, Ricky, 77
Nick Lucas Artist, *183*
Nick Lucas Model ("Gibson Special"), 3, *12, 14,* 35-37, *36, 37*
Niles, John Jacob, 123
Nitty Gritty Dirt Band, 86, 87
Norlin, 103
Norlin Industries, 6, 7, 143
Oahu Company, 69
Odetta, 123
"Open-Moustache Bridge", 52
Parsons, Gram, 76, 77
Parsons, Nancy, 76
Paul, Custom model, 93
Paul, Les, 110
Paul, Model, 106
Pedal Steel Guitar, 68
Peghead, "Stairstep", 85, 87
Peter, Paul, and Mary, 103, 123
Pickguard, Firestripe, 96
Pickups, P-90, 108
Poyck, B., 93
Presley, Elvis, 77
Price, "Fiddling" Fred, *57*
Prine, John, 77
Rager, Mose, 91
Redbone, Leon, 106
Reeves, Jim, 77
Repair (see maintenance & repair)
Research, Methods of, viii
RHO Studios, 77
Richards, Keith, 114
Riders in the Sky, 77, 78
Ritter, Tex, 77, 78
Rodgers, Jimmie, 68
Rogers, Roy, 77, 78
Rosewood, Gibson's Use of, 3
Ross, Dr. Isiah, *67*
Ryman Auditorium, 76
Sabicas, 104
Schneider, Richard, 7, 24, 116
Scruggs, Earl, 124
Sebastian, John, *125*
Seeger, Mike, 122
Seeger, Peggy, 122
Seeger, Pete, 122
Seger, Bob, 77
Segovia, 91
Segovia, Andre, 138
Serial Numbers, 196-200
Shaw, Tim, 83, 116
Shines, Johnny, 95
Shultz, Arnold, 91
Silvertone, 109
SJ (see also Southern Jumbo/Southern Jumbo/Country Western), 89, 90, 95-97, 102, 107, 109, 112
SJ (see also Southern Jumbo/Southern Jumbo/Country Western), Square

Shouldered, 121-123, *121, 122, 123,* 126, 130
SJ-100,(see also J-100) 10
SJ-200, (see also J-200), 3, 11, 22
Skunk Stripe Southern Jumbo, 20, 65
Smeck, Roy, 2, *68,* 71-74
Smeck, Radio Grande Model, 68, 71-74
Smeck, Smeck Hawaiian Models, 2, 3
Smeck, Stage Deluxe Model, *15, 71, 72,* 71-74, *73*
Snow, Hank, *90*
Snyder, Hartford, 81, 112
Sons of the Pioneers, 89
Southern Jumbo (see also SJ)
Southern Jumbo Model (see also Country-Western), 19, 63-66, *63, 64, 65, 66, 67*
Sovine, Red, 77
Stairstep Peghead (J-55), *18*
Steel Guitar, 68, 69
Stevens, Cat, 77
Stills, Stephen, 77
Sunburst, 43
Super 400, 77
Tillis, Pam, 77
Travis, Merle, 90, 91
Twitty, Conway, *5*
Tyson, Ian, 131
Ukelele, 68, 72
Van Ronk, Dave, 77, 103
Van Zandt, Townes, 77
Vinopal, David, 207, *207*
Wagoner, Porter, *5,* 77
Wakely, Jimmy, 76, 77, *78*
Walker, John, 145, *145,* 146
Walsh, Joe, 84
Wards, Montgomery, 86
Waters, Muddy, *122*
Watson, Arthel (Doc), *2, 46, 57,* 123
Watson, Dr. Eugene, 138
Watson, Rosa Lee, *2*
Weavers, The, 103, 123
Wechter, Abe, 6, *83,* 116, 138
Wells, Kitty, 91
Werbin, Stan, v, *v*
White, Josh, 103
Whitford, Eldon, *145,* 207, *207*
Whitley, Ray, 76, 77, 78, 81
Whitley, Ray, " "Recording Kings Guitars", 86
Whitman, Slim, 77
Wilburn Brothers, 77
Wilkins, Rev. Robert, *57*
Williams, Hank, 129
Williamson, Sonny Boy, 24
Wolverton, Joe, 78
WW I, 68
WW II, 97, 122
York Brothers, 77
Zebrowski, Gary, 144

Bibliography

A great debt is owed to the following, who already have explored various parts of Gibson flat-top history.

Bellson, Julius. *The Gibson Story*. Kalamazoo, Mich.: Julius Bellson, 1973.

Duchossoir, Andre R. *Gibson Electrics*. Paris: Mediapresse, 1981

———. *Guitar Identification*. Milwaukee: Hal Leonard Publ., 1990.

Gruhn, George, and Walter Carter. *Acoustic Guitars and Other Fretted Instruments*. San Francisco: Miller Freeman Books, 1993.

———. *Gruhn's Guide to Vintage Guitars*. San Francisco: Miller Freeman Books, 1991.

Wheeler, Tom. *American Guitars: An Illustrated History*. New York: HarperCollins, 1992.

Owners' Credits

Thanks to the following collectors for allowing us to show photos of guitars from their collection; the numbers following each name indicate the page numbers on which the photos appear.

Viola Bontrager 101; Gary Burnette 9, 12, 16, 17, 18, 19, 20, 26, 32, 33, 34, 35, 40, 43, 44, 47, 48, 49, 50, 51, 52, 53, 58, 63, 65, 149, 150, 151, 166, 168, 173; Marc Conley 107; Larry English 157; Bryan Galloup 17, 45; Phil Kieronski 116; Phil Noder 23, 100, 114, 126; Donna Paine 100, 124; A.J. Peat 28; Ben Runkle 41; Akira Tsmura 163; David Vinopal 59; Stan Werbin 13, 15, 16, 21, 29, 34, 48, 61, 70, 74, 96; Eldon Whitford 9, 10, 13, 22, 23, 38, 56, 58, 64, 66, 75, 99, 100, 103, 118, 119, 133, 152, 153, 172, 187; Josh Whitford 97; Mac Yasuda 10, 11, 14, 15, 21, 22, 37, 52, 62, 81, 121, 122, 154, 155, 156, 157, 158, 160, 161, 162, 164, 165, 167; Connie Yost 176.

Photo Credits

The main photographer for this book was Tom Erlewine of Tom Erlewine Design, Big Rapids, MI. Thanks also to Ren Ferguson and Gibson/Montana for supplying the majority of the photos that appear in chapter eleven, and to the following photographers and individuals who supplied photos; the numbers following each name indicate the page numbers on which the photos appear.

Gene Autry 3; Nancy Blake 30, 72, 73; Norman Blake 73; Brian Blauser 36, 60, 189; Gary Burnette 59; Don Everly 90, 91, 92; Ren Ferguson 168; Bill Gonder 14, 143, 153, 186; Douglas B. Green 78; Nora Guthrie 4; Jim Hagans 76; Mark Hanauer 94; Keith Jenkins 54; Albert Lee 94; Nitty Gritty Dirt Band 86; Ben Runkle 78; Smithsonian Folkways 46, 57; Hank Snow 90; Porter Wagoner 5; Stan Werbin 71, 196; Mac Yasuda 10, 11, 14, 15, 21, 22, 62, 77, 79, 81, 82, 83, 93, 108, 121, 122

Photos provided by Steve LaVere: pages 4, 190, 191 (photo by Michael A. Gould, copyright 1993 Mimosa Records Productions, Inc.); page 5, 25 (photo by Ivey Gladin, Gladin's Studio, photo archives, Mimosa Records Productions, Inc.); page 7, 57, 80, 98, 121, 122, 125, 134 (photo by Stephen C. LaVere, copyright 1992, 1993 Mimosa Records Productions, Inc.); page 29 (photo by Hooks Bros., courtesy Carrie Thompson, copyright 1989 Mimosa Records Productions, Inc.); page 81 (photo by Nicholas Wilson, photo archives, Mimosa Records Productions, Inc.); pages 85, 95 (photographer unknown, photo archives, Mimosa Records Productions, Inc.); page 89 (photo by Ralph Widman, Hollywood, 1952-3, photo archives, Mimosa Records Productions, Inc.); pages 61, 87, 131 (photograph by Gerrie Blake, copyright 1992, 1993 Mimosa Records Productions, Inc.); page 67 (photo by Tom Pohrt, copyright 1993 Mimosa Records Productions, Inc.).

Page 6: photo by Bob Carlin/courtesy Roy Book Binder; page 24: photo by Dennis Crawford/courtesy Lost Mountain Editions; pages 137, 138, 140, 141: photos by Dennis Crawford/courtesy Richard Schneider; page 93: photo by Barry Grey/courtesy Don Everly; page 53: photo by Dave Peabody/courtesy Roy Book Binder.